THE ANIMAL MIND

James L. Gould
Carol Grant Gould

SCIENTIFIC
AMERICAN
LIBRARY

A division of HPHLP
New York

Frontispiece: Chimpanzees can learn to use an icon-based vocabulary to communicate with humans.

Library of Congress Cataloging-in-Publication Data

Gould, James L., 1945–

    The animal mind / James L. Gould, Carol Grant Gould.

      p.   cm.

    Includes bibliographical references and index.

    ISBN 0-7167-5046-5 (hardcover)

    ISBN 0-7167-6035-5 (paperback)

    1. Animal intelligence.   2. Animal behavior.   I. Gould, Carol

Grant. II. Title.

QL785.G66   1994

591.51—dc20   93-48197

                                                CIP

ISSN 1040-3213

© 1994, 1999 by Scientific American Library

Printed in the United States of America

Scientific American Library
A division of HPHLP
New York

Distributed by W. H. Freeman and Company
41 Madison Avenue, New York, NY 10010
Houndmills, Basingstoke RG21 6XS, England

First paperback printing, 1999

To Jocelyn and Don

PLAC'D ON THIS ISTHMUS OF A MIDDLE STATE,
A BEING DARKLY WISE, AND RUDELY GREAT:
WITH TOO MUCH KNOWLEDGE FOR THE SCEPTIC SIDE,
WITH TOO MUCH WEAKNESS FOR THE STOIC'S PRIDE,
HE HANGS BETWEEN; IN DOUBT TO ACT, OR REST;
IN DOUBT TO DEEM HIMSELF A GOD, OR BEAST;
IN DOUBT HIS MIND OR BODY TO PREFER;
BORN BUT TO DIE, AND REAS'NING BUT TO ERR;
ALIKE IN IGNORANCE, HIS REASON SUCH,
WHETHER HE THINKS TOO LITTLE, OR TOO MUCH;
CHAOS OF THOUGHT AND PASSION, ALL CONFUS'D;
STILL BY HIMSELF ABUS'D, OR DISABUS'D;
CREATED HALF TO RISE, AND HALF TO FALL;
GREAT LORD OF ALL THINGS, YET A PREY TO ALL;
SOLE JUDGE OF TRUTH, IN ENDLESS ERROR HURL'D:
THE GLORY, JEST, AND RIDDLE OF THE WORLD!

Alexander Pope
An Essay on Man, 1733

CONTENTS

The Animal Mind

A CROW, READY TO DIE WITH THIRST, FLEW WITH JOY TO A PITCHER WHICH HE BEHELD AT SOME DISTANCE. WHEN HE CAME, HE FOUND WATER IN IT INDEED, BUT SO NEAR THE BOTTOM, THAT WITH ALL HIS STOOPING AND STRAINING, HE WAS NOT ABLE TO REACH IT. THEN HE ENDEAVORED TO OVERTURN THE PITCHER, THAT SO AT LEAST HE MIGHT BE ABLE TO GET A LITTLE OF IT; BUT HIS STRENGTH WAS NOT SUFFICIENT FOR THIS. AT LAST, SEEING SOME PEBBLES LIE NEAR THE PLACE, HE CAST THEM ONE BY ONE INTO THE PITCHER; AND THUS, BY DEGREES, RAISED THE WATER UP TO THE VERY BRIM, AND SATISFIED HIS THIRST.

Thomas Bewick
Select Fables of Aesop and Others, 1784

Prologue

WHO TAUGHT THE RAVEN IN A DROUGHT TO THROW PEBBLES
INTO A HOLLOW TREE, WHERE SHE ESPIED WATER, THAT THE
WATER MIGHT RISE SO AS SHE COULD COME TO IT?

Francis Bacon
The Advancement of Learning, 1605

In the early 1900s a retired German mathematics professor discovered that his beloved horse, Hans, was a prodigy. Herr von Osten gave Hans lessons in counting and spelling, exposed him to the concept of color and the basics of musical theory, even presented some simple arithmetic. Hans responded to tests of his knowledge by tapping his foot an appropriate number of times in answer to questions.

Entirely uninterested in showing off his pupil for money, von Osten invited only small and select groups that included many highly skeptical students of behavior to observe Hans (widely known by then as Clever Hans). The visitors were encouraged to devise their own tests of Hans's abilities; some examinations were conducted without von Osten's presence, but Hans lost none of his cleverness when his teacher was away. The consensus of the scientific community was that Hans was a genius.

The true nature of Hans's gifts came to light after a long and intensive study by Oskar Pfungst, an experimental psychologist. Pfungst concluded that Hans did not really understand the questions put to him, much less know the answers—the problems could be posed in an unfamiliar language, by whispering them, or even just by thinking them. But if neither questioner nor observers knew the answer, Hans was at a loss to solve even the simplest problem or respond to any of

The fame of Clever Hans inspired myriad attempts to instruct horses. Here, in 1909, a clone named Larif is taught the alphabet.

the questions he had answered correctly on previous occasions. Unless the horse was telepathic, he was picking up unconscious cues from his questioners.

Pfungst ruled out auditory cues fairly quickly and soon concluded that the cues must be visual. Hans's accuracy fell toward twilight and hit zero if the questioner stood behind an opaque screen and no onlookers were present; even von Osten could not coax the correct answers from Hans in these circumstances. The horse, it turned out, was taking his cues from unconscious, almost imperceptible shifts of head and body posture in the members of the audience—movements created by the involuntary relaxation of the tension among the observers when the number of hoof taps reached the correct value. Pfungst himself, even after he understood the process, found it almost impossible not to cue the horse.

Clever Hans was marvelously perceptive—but not in the way most observers had hoped. The idea of some other intelligence—animal or extraterrestrial—has appealed to the human mind for millennia. Many of our earliest stories are about animals endowed with reason and human emotions. Dolphins rescue people, eagles bear them over obstacles, apes and wolves nurture lost or abandoned children. Sometimes the earthly and divine powers are mixed: powerful animal gods appear in the early cultures of every continent.

The concept of animal intelligence continues to hold our imagination today, as evidenced by children's stories from Beatrix Potter to television's Lassie, but an increasing tendency in Western thought toward empirical evaluation has encouraged a more scientific consideration of the animal mind. Darwin wrote in *The Descent of Man* (1871) that the difference in mind between humans and the higher animals "certainly is one of degree and not one of kind. We have seen that the senses and intuitions, the various emotions and faculties, such as love, memory, attention, curiosity, imitation, reason, and so on, of which man boasts, may be found in an incipient, or even sometimes in a well-developed condition in lower animals."

Most people, including scientists, probably continued to agree with Darwin, even after the Clever Hans debacle. But von Osten's student, the Piltdown Man of the behavioral sciences, signalled the end of the spirit of open-minded investigation of the animal mind, and skepticism, even denial, became an entrenched tenet of behavioral faith. This reaction is still apparent in the computer analogies that have become indispensable in describing many examples of animal mentality.

Until very recently it has been anathema in the scientific world to suggest in print that intelligence of some sort, perhaps even self-awareness, might guide the routine and often stereotyped behavior of many animals. And field research into the mechanisms of animal behavior *has* revealed many intricate but innate behavioral programs that, despite their sophistication, have no apparent intellectual component. A question like Bacon's about raven behavior, a behavior recorded by Aesop in the sixth century B.C., now suggests to most researchers not a feather-cloaked hydraulic engineer but an animal responding automatically to an unusual stimulus.

Imagine, then, the reaction when the notably rigorous behavioral scientist Donald Griffin challenged his colleagues to imagine that bees might think and birds engage in conscious deception. In *The Question of Animal Awareness* (1976) he argued that intelligence and an ability to plan are characteristics that would be favored by natural selection as much as any other useful adaptation. Griffin suggested new ways of interpreting behavior that had long been comfortably categorized as innate. Many researchers into animal behavior reacted to these arguments with outraged scorn; most of the rest displayed a polite lack of interest.

Donald R. Griffin studying a beaver lodge in the New Jersey Pine Barrens, November 1993.

But the last two decades have seen a major change in our picture of animal minds. Griffin has kept asking thought-provoking questions about what animals know, taking a new look at older observations and suggesting at least a few ways into the thorny thicket of experimentation. He persists in prodding psychologists and fellow ethologists to reëxamine our basic assumptions about animal cognition, as well as sponsoring and encouraging research on animal thinking.

One of the results of Griffin's persistence has been the confirmation through observation and direct experimentation that ravens *do* use stones as tools and seem to be capable of solving novel problems. This and other work—ranging from observations of herons that use bread crumbs to lure fish within reach to tests indicating that honey bees plan new routes to reach distant food sources—demonstrate that it is becoming increasingly important to ask where the efficiency of natural selection begins to shade into intelligent and independent problem-solving by the individual animal. Today Griffin's questions are no longer quite so heretical, though they are monumentally difficult to answer.

In many ways this book recapitulates the slow but steady breaking down of the walls of resistance put up by a scientific community determined never again to be blinded by the cleverness of Hans. We will begin by formulating some working definitions of thinking and cognition—*working*, because the more we continue to learn, the less apt any facile definition seems. Then we will look at how the remarkable sensory abilities and innate programming of animals can create in our eyes the illusion of thought where none need exist. We will then be able to outline some rough but useful guides for recognizing behavior that goes beyond the innate or automatically learned. Next we will examine a variety of species and types of behavior, in search of the animal mind.

Finally, we will reflect on what our growing knowledge about animal cognition says about the human mind as a remarkable product of natural selection, and how a more complete understanding of what goes on in the minds of animals can, aside from its inherent intellectual interest, show us links between the brain's mysterious processes and our own often inscrutable but always fascinating behavior.

Varieties of
Sensory Experience

n a grassy dune, a hunting fox nears a clutch of eggs that a ground-nesting plover is incubating. The watchful bird spotted the fox almost a minute ago and has been monitoring its movements ever since. She moves quietly away, as far from the nest as she can and as close to the fox as she dares. Then, her body low and crouched, she dashes rustling and squeaking along a route that takes her almost directly away from her eggs.

If we had not seen the plover, we would probably have concluded, as her pursuer apparently does, that the fox has startled a mouse or vole. The fox is now in hot pursuit, but a running plover is faster than any rodent, and soon the fox—no closer to the moving target—is 200 m away from the nest. The plover takes flight along a circuitous route that eventually takes her back to her nest.

During this arresting piece of stage business, what is going on in the minds of the fox and plover? In particular, how much does the bird, which has been observed to have not one but four different nest-protecting techniques that she employs in different situations, understand about the complex and flexible collection of ruses she employs so effectively? Even a misanthrope would grant that most fellow humans are conscious and aware, have thoughts and expectations, learn and make plans. When we look at a bird or an insect, on the other hand, the chance that they have a mental life that is in any way

THESE FALLOW DEER HAVE SENSORY EQUIPMENT—

LARGE SIDE-LOOKING EYES, BROAD EARS THAT

CAN BE AIMED, AND A LONG NOSE PACKED WITH

OLFACTORY RECEPTORS—WELL DESIGNED FOR

DETECTING THE NOCTURNAL PREDATORS THAT

HUNT THEM.

analogous to ours seems remote. Short-lived and oblivious to the grand scale of human existence, they often act in ways that seem arbitrary and robotic. Yet even some insects, as we will see, *do* seem to learn, plan, and act upon expectations. And if even insects can plan and decide, it seems likely that some birds and mammals are at least as clever.

Higher degrees of mental activity are called *cognition*, which is defined, from its Latin root, as the act or process of *knowing*. Cognition can be innate—passive knowledge encoded in an animal's genes and used as instructions for wiring a nervous system to generate particular inborn abilities and specializations. Active cognition—the ongoing process of gathering, analyzing, and using knowledge—can incorporate several stages of mental processing beginning with sensation, which is the detection of stimuli by a sensory receptor organ and the subsequent processing of that sensory information by the brain. Sensation itself does not involve knowledge; it does, however, supply the raw material which, when processed by the nervous system, can become that which an organism knows. It is the processing and analysis of sensory information that engenders knowledge, which can then be stored, recalled, and used in decision-making. To begin, we will look at how an animal's sensory experience is strictly winnowed from the broad range of stimuli available and then systematically emphasized and distorted by the nervous system to create a surprisingly schematic version of reality for the brain to deal with.

DIFFERENT WORLDS

We tend to think of our sensory experience of the world around us as a benchmark against which other species may be measured. Yet the sensory abilities of our species, like those of any other, are simply the consequence of natural selection. The structure and capabilities of our eyes and ears have evolved in response to needs imposed by our environment and our species's unique place—its niche—in the web of life. As a natural consequence, our range of sensory experience is unlikely to match that of other species, whose members are specialized to make their living in ways that necessarily generate different sensory needs. To the extent that an animal's sense organs are blind to a class of cues, its mind will be blind as well.

The German biologist and comparative physiologist Jakob von Uexküll coined the term "Umwelt"—the surrounding world—to

The German scientist Jakob von Uexküll (1864–1944) challenged his colleagues to imagine how the world looked to other animals.

describe the unique, and therefore limiting, sensory world of each animal species, including our own. One of his most memorable illustrations, which suggests the vast gulf between the experiences of different species, is the story of the common tick.

Before she can lay her eggs, a female tick must have a blood meal. Her life is devoted to finding a suitable host and obtaining the nutrient-rich fluid essential to leaving progeny. During her single-minded life cycle, the tick's sensory organs present her with a very select range of stimuli, at once narrow and highly relevant to her needs. Her skin is responsive to light, which leads her up from the darkness of the ground to an elevated position on a plant. There she waits, attentive now only to the odor of butyric acid, a chemical by-product emitted

After climbing toward the light, this female tick will wait motionless for the characteristic mammalian odor of butyric acid. When she detects it, she will drop from the leaf.

by all mammals. The tick has specialized olfactory receptors for this critical substance, and when molecules of butyric acid bind to her receptors, she drops from her perch onto her prey.

Guided now by highly sensitive temperature sensors, she seeks only warmth, oblivious to the other cues that might guide her to food. In her now dark and odorless world, warmth is a sign of blood close under the skin; finding it, she burrows into a soft spot and starts to suck. Usually she strikes blood, but she has no sense of taste, and she will consume any liquid of the correct temperature once she has pierced the skin.

In many species this is the tick's first and last meal; she swells hugely with blood, drops from her host, lays her eggs, and dies. Her entire sensory experience has comprised only light, a single odor, and warmth. Time and space have little or no meaning for the tick; some individuals have been known to wait motionless for as long as 18 years for the one odor that can release them from the spell that holds them captive in this stage of their unvarying cycle of existence.

In von Uexküll's words, "The whole rich world around the tick shrinks and changes into a scanty framework consisting, in essence, of three receptor cues and three effector cues—her Umwelt. But the very poverty of this world guarantees the unfailing certainty of her actions, and security is more important than wealth."

The tick survives by narrowing her sensory windows so as to ignore the irrelevant and distracting. Other creatures, by virtue of the requirements of their niches, have evolved sensory abilities that convey to them a range of stimuli and experience well beyond our own. These abilities—and there is no reason to think we know all of them—have gone largely undetected until this century. We are, unfortunately, blind to our own blindnesses, only haltingly able to imagine what we cannot sense. A telling illustration is the discovery of color-blindness in humans. Though nearly 10 percent of humans (mostly males) are color blind, this defect in the perceptive abilities of tens of millions of individuals was not recognized until 1793. Ironically the discoverer, the English chemist John Dalton, realized that he was himself color blind only after years of working on the colors of chemical compounds.

But even people with intact systems of visual perception are blind to a great deal of the sensory information the world has to offer. Other animals see colors our eyes cannot perceive, sense forces that pass over us leaving no trace, detect sounds too high and too low for us to pick up without instruments, smell chemicals we have no receptors to register.

Imagination, therefore, must often be our initial guide to the un-familiar sensory windows through which animals perceive the world, as well as to nearly every other step of the cognitive process. This is not to say that the study of cognition depends on unconstrained spec-ulation, but rather to acknowledge that our personal experience as human animals is highly limited and rife with potential bias. We must step beyond our own limited experience to make plausible, testable guesses about what is going on in the brains of other animals and then be guided by those results, even when the processes and neural ele-ments revealed are as hard to visualize as the electrons and magnetic fields that we all assume to be real though invisible components of our world.

As nocturnal hunters, cats have sacrificed color acuity for low-light sensitivity. Physiological recordings suggest that in bright light cats probably see the world much as a red-blind human views it: as shown on the right, the reds are experienced as greys; only the range from green to blue is seen in true color. Behavioral tests, however, indicate a slight ability to detect red.

VISUAL PERCEPTION

Vision is our primary window on the world—indeed, it so dominates our lives that blindness is a frequent metaphor for any emotional or intellectual deficit. Because it is so important a factor in our lives as humans, it is perhaps the most accessible aspect of the sensory lives of the nonhuman animal world.

Unlike that of most mammals, our visual experience includes a vivid perception of color: the light waves to which the human eye is

A mouse as seen through an infrared viewer stands out because of the heat it emits. Pit vipers experience something similar, though the image is poorly focused.

A flower photographed in ultraviolet light reveals a dramatic pattern of dark nectar guides that are nearly invisible to humans. Because the ultraviolet sensitivity of honey bees dominates their visual experience, these patterns stand out against a lightly tinted background of yellows, greens, and blues.

sensitive range from red, the longest, through violet, the shortest. In observing motion, we can distinguish a series of discrete steps from a smooth continuous movement if there are fewer than about 20 steps a second, our "flicker-fusion" threshold. Our fovea—the area of the retina most densely packed with sensors—yields a tiny circle in the middle of the visual field (its angular diameter only 2°) in which color is sharpest and we can have up to 20/20 resolution. We have a modest ability to see in dim light, but our "night vision" is blind to red.

The range of colors seen by other animals varies from species to species. Pit vipers, for instance, can see infrared (IR) light, which we can sense only when it is quite intense, and then only as warmth. Pit vipers use this sensory capacity to locate warm-blooded prey at night. Certain beetles that thrive in fire-damaged woods use IR vision to detect trees still harboring heat after a forest fire.

At the other end of the spectrum is ultraviolet (UV) light, a potentially damaging range of wavelengths that can create mutations in the DNA of exposed cells. Most ultraviolet is filtered out in the cornea of our eyes by a yellowish pigment, but nearly all insects can see ultraviolet light; such short-lived creatures hardly need to worry about the chance of developing retinal cancer. The ultraviolet holds important information for many insects: pollinators use the UV-dark marks on flowers, invisible to us, to guide them to the nectar and pollen at the center of the blossom; other insects have UV-absorbing or UV-reflecting patches they use in signalling to one another. Many insects also use patterns of UV light from the sky for navigation, or sense distant water by its enhanced ability to reflect UV.

Many of the shorter-lived vertebrates, particularly birds, lack the corneal screening pigment and thus they too can see into the ultraviolet. Most use the UV in their navigation, and some are probably also benefiting from an improved ability to spot insect prey.

Most animals that use UV light in navigation are responding to a stimulus our species cannot usefully detect without instruments: polarization. The scattering of sunlight by molecules in the atmosphere creates the blue sky we see and a UV sky we are blind to. The scattering also creates a pattern of polarized light—that is, light waves that oscillate in the same direction—that appears as bands arranged symmetrically around the sun. This pattern is strongest in the UV. Many insects and birds, as well as a handful of other creatures, can use a partial view of the sky to infer the position of the sun even when it is hidden by clouds, landmarks, or the horizon. Though we cannot see the polarized light directly, early Vikings used the reflective properties of calcite crystals to discern the patterns in the sky and thus were able to locate the sun during the extended periods of twilight characteristic of far-northern latitudes.

Our relatively low flicker-fusion rate is typical for a diurnal vertebrate species that has evolved to live in well-lighted surroundings. But for vertebrates adapted to lower levels of light, as well as most invertebrates (whose eye design captures light far more efficiently), flicker-fusion rates are higher—about 200/sec in bees. Insects could never enjoy the illusion created by motion pictures, because they would see the distinct periods of darkness between the individual frames as they are projected; they can also see the 100 or 120 times each second that fluorescent lights grow dim, as well as the black bands that sweep across television screens 50 or 60 times each second. Animals with high flicker-fusion rates thus have greater sensitivity to motion, probably a necessity for rapidly moving creatures like many insects.

Our visual resolution is near the high end of the animal scale. Most insects, for example, are legally blind in human terms: 20/2000 vision is about the best, except for dragonflies. Some insects—many army ants, for instance—are completely sightless. Most nocturnal vertebrates have relatively poor vision, usually because their visual processing is designed to emphasize higher absolute sensitivity to light; they are almost always color blind as well. Among diurnal vertebrates, only certain hunting birds (especially falcons) see better than

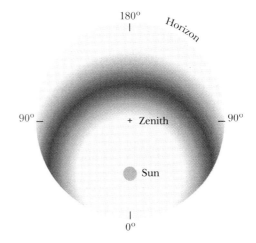

Many navigating insects and birds can detect the symmetrical patterns of polarization in the sky overhead. This view of the sky emphasizes the degree of polarization, which is greatest 90° away from the sun.

Most nocturnal animals have a reflective layer behind the retina that bounces unabsorbed light back through the receptor cells. Photons not captured during this second pass exit the eye in the direction of the light source, creating the illusion of a glowing pupil.

we do, with 20/10 resolution and enlarged foveas that provide a larger area of high-resolution vision. Quite a number of other diurnal hunters greatly surpass us in foveal size; the cheetah's fovea, for instance, extends in a horizontal band that covers much of the visual horizon—just the place to search for prey. Other species, including most birds and some fish, have two foveas. Chickadees, robins, and plovers, for instance, have one fovea specialized for looking straight ahead at food and another for looking to the side for predators.

Night vision, as we might expect, is much better in most nocturnal creatures than in our species. A reflective layer behind the retina bounces unabsorbed light back through the receptor cells for another chance at being captured; it is this reflective layer that creates the illusion that the eyes of cats, foxes, and raccoons glow in the dark. The sensitivity of nocturnally specialized eyes is sufficient to allow deer and owls to see about as well by starlight as we do at twilight.

Our experience of the world—the aspects of the available sensory stimuli that we are equipped to detect—clearly differs from that of other animals. The ways that information, once detected, is handled in the neural processing units of the brain affect each species' experience of the world.

PROCESSING VISUAL INFORMATION

Mammals typically have at least a hundred times as many receptors as there are neural cables (axons) to carry information from the eye to the brain; therefore once light has been gathered and focused on photoreceptors, the retina must begin summarizing the output. In part this reduction involves simply combining the output of many receptors to achieve greater sensitivity; it is particularly common in the areas of the retina that deal with a creature's peripheral vision, as well as among the highly sensitive rod cells that permit night vision.

But beyond any pooling of receptor responses, every axon running from the retina to the brain carries signals that represent a specific abstraction of reality. Nearly all the axons emerging from the retina report not absolute values but the *ratio* of light (white or of a specific color) at some point in the visual field to the light surrounding that point. The major result is that contrast is emphasized: boundaries between areas of the visual field that are of differing brightness or color are exaggerated, and therefore it is easier to distinguish objects and detect subtle changes in texture.

The contrast-enhancement strategy of the retina leads to a number of visual illusions, one of the most revealing of which is encountered whenever we watch television. Televison screens (and computer monitors) are generally some shade of grey, ranging from nearly white through medium grey to charcoal; a few are brown. The image we see when the set is on is created by electrons, aimed by magnetic coils, that are accelerated from the back of the picture tube and strike phosphors on the front of the tube; the irradiated phosphors emit the light that we actually see. It follows that no part of an image can ever be darker than the screen is when the set is off, and yet we typically see parts of the image as pure black. These apparently black areas are an illusion created by the retina, which, as we have seen, is in the business of exaggerating contrasts rather than reporting accurate measures of color and illumination.

In the brain, information about color, shape, and motion begins to be segregated and processed separately, in parallel pathways. Each

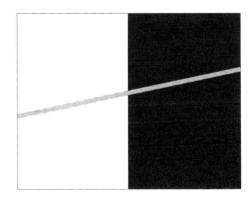

In this visual illusion the grey bar crossing over the background appears to most observers to be darker against the white and lighter against the black. The illusion is caused by inborn circuitry that heightens contrast at the expense of accurate reporting of brightness.

After extensively modifying the information coming from the eyes, the visual system in the brain begins interpreting it for us, creating experiences that may be illusions. In this example not only does the brain fantasize two triangles, but it even imagines that the "closer" one is slightly whiter than the other.

of these pathways involves layer after layer of increasingly abstract filtering. The shape pathway, for instance, combines the output of the spot detectors to sort for lines of every possible orientation. Each cell has a particular preferred direction, and in many animals there is a strong bias toward cells specialized for nearly vertical and almost horizontal lines; this curious bias enables us to notice with surprising precision when a picture on a wall is not hanging quite straight.

After the systematic exaggeration of features, the pathways are recombined to create the conscious illusion of a seamless and straightforwardly honest visual experience. The blind spots in our visual world (present because there are small areas in each retina that lack receptors in order to make room for the bundle of axons that carries information to the brain) go unnoticed because the brain fills in the missing area, extrapolating from the information in surrounding regions. Though the left and right halves of our visual field are processed in different lobes of the brain, there is no hint of a dividing line in what we see. Missing contours are supplied, hidden edges imagined, and a variety of other tricks performed that produce the grist for most of the more complex visual illusions that enliven psychology texts.

The distinction between the information in the light that enters an animal's eyes and the animal's eventual conscious visual experience is enormous, and it differs greatly between species. The unconscious processing that intervenes between the cornea and the mind's eye controls our perception of reality in ways that have served our species well over the course of evolution, but we should expect the picture of the world experienced by creatures with very different niches to be attuned to a different set of features—ones, perhaps, to which we are essentially blind.

AUDITION AND OLFACTION

Hearing is our second widest "window" on the world. Humans can detect sounds ranging over a continuum from 20 to 20,000 Hz, although the upper limit drops with age. Most insects can also hear, though their ears are quite different. Many invertebrate ears are simply body projections that are moved by sound waves; hairs on the antennae of male mosquitoes, for instance, resonate like tuning forks at just the frequency produced by the humming wings of a flying female.

Even insects that, like the locust, are equipped with membranes like our eardrum for detecting sounds, have only a narrow range of responsiveness; like real drums, the membranes are tuned to resonate only to certain tones. Most insects are thus selectively deaf. In an experiment in the late 1800s the French naturalist J. H. Fabre set off a gun next to a singing locust; the insect did not react. Fabre concluded that locusts are deaf and sing as an antipredator ploy, but in fact their membrane-based ears hear their species' stridulation frequency quite well.

A number of invertebrates hear through their feet. Roaches, for instance, are about 100,000 times more sensitive to surface vibrations than we are, an adaptation that helps them to flee in the face of approaching danger. Scorpions, water striders, and spiders, by contrast, use what they hear with their feet to locate prey.

The auditory experience of birds and mammals is much more like our own, though a variety of nocturnal hunters (including owls and wolves) are able to hear quieter noises than we can. A large number of animals can also hear frequencies above 20,000 Hz, a range we refer to as ultrasonic. Ultrasonic sensitivity may serve them well since a variety of prey species, including most rodents, have ultrasonic calls which have only recently been discovered (by humans). It may be that the running plover produces ultrasonic sounds to help capture the attention of hunting foxes.

The champions of ultrasonic hearing are the echolocating bats: some species can hear sounds as high as 100,000 Hz, which they project from the mouth or nose. From the time delay, strength, and modulation of the echoes of these sounds, bats can judge the location of obstacles and the position, direction of movement, and often the species of flying prey. In response, a number of nocturnal insects, including crickets and many moths, have evolved ears sensitive to high frequencies that pick up the signals of hunting bats and trigger avoidance manoeuvers. A fairly simple test for ultrasonic hearing in moths is to rattle some keys: accompanying the jangle we hear is a high-frequency swish that causes bat-avoiding moths to drop to the ground.

While we are excluded from the many ultrasonic messages that fill the air, we may be missing much less as a result of our deafness to infrasound, vibrations below our lower limit of 20 Hz. To date only elephants are known to communicate at subsonic frequencies, though whales are probably also able to. But there are other species that hear

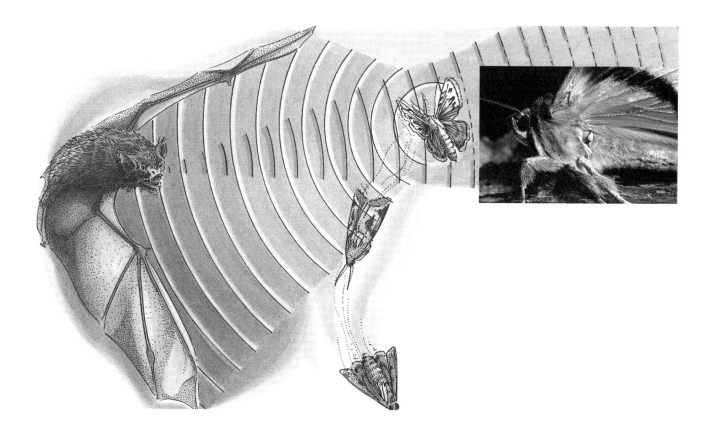

Donald Griffin discovered that bats detect insect prey at night by the echoes of their own high-pitched cries. Some moths and most crickets can hear these echolocation signals, and take evasive action when a bat gets too near. The ears responsible for this ability have evolved independently several times. In the photograph, the ear, visible midway along the moth, has an eardrumlike membrane that vibrates when sound strikes it.

infrasound—most notably homing pigeons, which some researchers have suggested might use the low thunder of waves on distant shores or wind passing over faraway mountains to take navigational bearings. Low frequencies travel much farther than high frequencies: whereas the 100,000 Hz cries of bats are absorbed by the air before they have travelled more than a few centimeters, the United States Weather Service regularly uses infrasonic "hearing aids" to track thunderstorms acoustically up to 3000 kilometers away.

The limitations on human experience are even more obvious when we look at another sensory modality we share with other species. Although our olfactory range makes that of the lowly tick with her single-minded concentration on butyric acid look impoverished, compared to most mammals we have a poorly developed sense of smell.

Other species are far more sensitive to odors and are thus able to detect friend, foe, or a potential meal upwind long before we notice anything. Moreover, most mammals are more discriminating: a well-trained human—a perfumer, for example—can identify at best a few thousand smells, while dogs can apparently distinguish any number of individual humans by scent alone. Bloodhounds perform this feat with no more odor than what passes through the soles of a person's shoes. Whereas the first thing we usually do with a novel object is to look at it carefully, most mammals sniff things to form an initial impression. The olfactory Umwelt we experience is certainly "infirm and erring" compared with theirs.

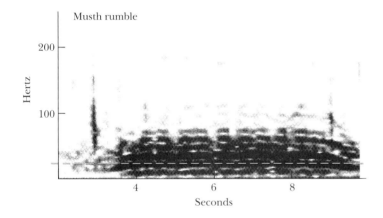

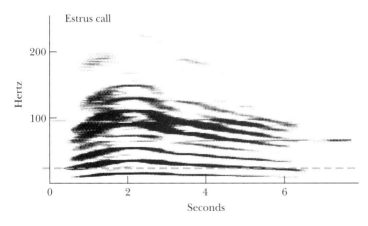

Much of the threat call made by male elephants in their sexually aggressive phase, known as musth, is below the range of human hearing; only the subsonic sounds carry long distances. Most of the estrus call of females ready to mate, on the other hand, is clearly audible to humans. These sonograms, made by bioacoustician Katy Payne, display frequency against time; the darkness of the plots indicates sound intensity. The dashed blue line shows the approximate lower level of human hearing.

Bloodhounds have been bred for the ability to detect and identify faint odors. This one is a member of a rescue unit in Albany, New York.

BEYOND HUMAN PERCEPTION

We have a truncated range of experience of visual and auditory cues, and are unaware of most of the odors that surround us. Moreover, there are other stimuli, critical to some species, that are wholly foreign to us. A variety of insects, fish, amphibians, reptiles, birds, and mammals (including dolphins), for instance, use the earth's magnetic field as a compass. There are even magnetically sensitive bacteria.

The magnetic sense must have evolved independently several times because it is based in different animals on at least four different detection strategies. What the species that possess magnetic sensitivity have in common is the need for a nonvisual compass, either for navigating in their home ranges or for migrating over long distances.

Some species, including homing pigeons and (almost certainly) whales, seem to use tiny variations in the earth's field strength to judge not only direction but also their own location on the planet; the gradual increase in magnetic intensity from equator to pole must play a major role in this map sense. And honey bees apparently use daily fluctuations in the earth's field strength to calibrate their internal clocks.

Another sensory window entirely shut to our species is electric-field sensitivity. A number of freshwater and marine species can detect electric fields that seep through the skin of other animals; sharks and the remarkable platypus, for example, routinely locate their prey in this way. Other electrically sensitive fish produce their own fields and monitor them for distortions, which are produced by obstacles and potential prey. These fish can pulse or otherwise modulate their fields to send messages to other electric fish.

We have found a number of other special senses in animals, and it would be rash not to assume that there are still others yet to be discovered. The point to take away, however, is that even at this first stage of cognition, the reception and processing of stimuli from the environment, human sensitivity (and thus the value of introspection and analogy in judging the mental activity of other animals) is both restricted and biased. As a result of our sensory limitations, certain thoughts and ideas are difficult or impossible to formulate. The rich tapestry of smells that forms the landscape of a dog's world, for instance, is an enigma to us, as much as what a bee really *sees* through that strangely faceted eye.

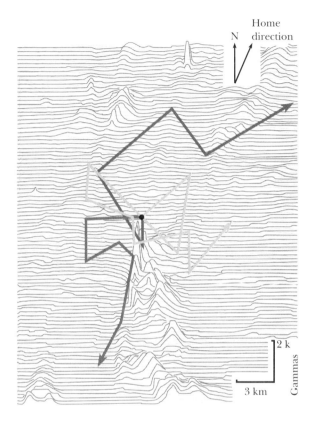

Home direction

N

2 k

Gammas

3 km

Homing pigeons can sense the magnetic topography of their surroundings and use it to help determine their location relative to home. Pigeons released at magnetic anomalies are disoriented until they have flown out of the disturbed area. Shown here in light blue is the physical topography near Iron Mine Hill, Rhode Island, that is visible to both humans and pigeons; in dark green is the topography of a magnetic anomaly detectable by pigeons. The dark blue, yellow, and red arrows show the tracks of three pigeons released at this site. At magnetically normal sites a pigeon will trace one or two 50-m circles (hardly visible at this scale) and then fly directly toward home.

If animals have mental experiences that are in any way like ours, they too must be colored by the sensory specializations and limitations imposed on them by their evolutionary history. When we examine the evidence in other animals for such higher levels of cognition as thinking and planning, we will need to remember the variousness of these species-specific versions of the world. The logic of behavioral decision-making depends critically on the view of the world available to the mind at work.

 # Innate Behavior

ising from her nest at the edge of a pond, an incubating goose methodically turns her eggs. Several times each day she or her spouse rotates each egg, an action that keeps the developing embryo from becoming stuck to the inside of the shell. While the goose pushes and prods the eggs with her beak, one rolls out of the nest unnoticed. Her nest-tending complete, she settles down to continue her month of incubation.

Suddenly her attention is riveted by the sight of the errant egg. She extends her neck and peers, as if to confirm her initial assessment of the emergency. She rises at once, puts her bill carefully on the far side of the egg, and rolls it gracefully and gently back between her legs into the nest. She settles back on the nest, preens herself, and visibly relaxes.

To all appearances the goose has recognized a serious problem and solved it in a straightforward way. And yet, as we will discover, what we have just witnessed is probably as mindless as the operation of an automobile windshield washer and wiper. The bird has not responded to her egg as an object, a package of her genes destined to immortalize her at least into the next generation, but rather to a schematic set of innate cues that her brain is neurally equipped to

CHICKS PROVIDING THE STIMULI THAT TRIGGER

FEEDING BY PARENT BIRDS.

look for. Her reaction probably occurred without anything like what we would call thought; her apparent understanding is only a beguiling illusion.

Cognition begins with the perception of external stimuli, which differs enormously species to species. Raw sensory information in some instances is altered extensively before it ever reaches the brain: for example, spot detectors in the retina register only certain combinations of stimuli, and thus completely rework the information provided them by the photoreceptors.

But the differing pictures of reality perceived by geese and humans do not explain our very different perception of eggs, which are to us unremarkable oval solids but for geese are powerful visual icons. After performing its conjuring tricks of sensory enhancement, the brain imposes another revision of the information at its disposal as it moves layer by layer and region by region through the visual area of the cortex. This second wave of processing, which makes an egg so special to geese, is even more species specific than sensation, and underlies much of the mental experience and behavior of animals. It is particularly important in guiding innate behavior—that is, behavior based on inborn neural circuits. These circuits are responsible for data-processing, decision-making, and orchestrating responses in the absence of previous experience. The "knowledge" encoded by this genetically specified wiring is commonly called instinct.

An understanding of the workings of innate behavior is an essential foundation for an informed exploration of the animal mind and its levels of consciousness or comprehension. We now know that much of the more flexible behavior that appears later in an animal's life is built upon inborn patterns of analysis and response, and so at least some of what is taken to suggest cleverness and insight in animals turns out to be, in the light of what is known about innate mechanisms, just highly adaptive contingency plans prewired into the brain. To be sure, the presence of innate behavior does not exclude the possibility that an animal may understand something about the situation it is facing; indeed, some degree of thought could be very useful if an organism has several innate responses to choose among. Being able to distinguish between the pragmatic programming success of natural selection and genuinely intelligent behavior on the part of an animal, whether in creating or choosing a response, is essential to understanding the animal mind. As we will see, however, this distinction is often difficult or impossible to make.

SIGNALS AND RESPONSES

One of a continuing series of surprises in the study of animal behavior was the discovery that many behaviors that seem to imply comprehension are fully triggered by only fragmentary components or attributes of a natural stimulus. Such fragments, presented in isolation, elicit the same response from the animal as would the object as a whole. Consider, for instance, the way ground-nesting birds like our goose recognize their eggs. We might suppose they know what their own eggs look like—that they have some innate picture of these important objects, or at least that they learn what they look like during the weeks of incubation. Yet if eggs of another species different in size, color, and markings are substituted, geese (and birds of most other species) appear not to notice. It's not that they pay no attention to the contents of the nest: they will promptly remove a variety of other objects—pencils, cockle shells, bottle caps, pieces of paper, and so on.

Although the goose we described earlier displayed painstaking care in recovering her egg, in fact she would have displayed the same

The highly schematic stimuli used by most birds to recognize their eggs is exploited by some nest parasites. Here a cowbird has added her own, visually quite distinct eggs to the nest of a wood thrush. Most host parents will rear the cowbird chicks as though they were their own offspring.

Among his many other achievements, Niko Tinbergen (1907–1989) popularized ethology by producing several excellent natural history films.

Most birds will incubate nearly any rounded object. In this case the "egg" is a grapefruit.

care for a number of other objects. The motley range of items that she and other ground-nesting birds will roll in tells us just how schematic their idea of eggness must be. The list, as worked out by the Nobel-prize–winning ethologists Konrad Lorenz and Niko Tinbergen in the 1930s, includes light bulbs, batteries, beer bottles, soda cans, oranges and grapefruits, and baseballs—in short, almost anything with rounded edges, regardless of color, markings, or (up to a point) size. Occasionally even a wooden cube was accepted.

From an evolutionary perspective, it makes sense that birds should not be too discriminating: where potential offspring are concerned, better safe than sorry. Besides, most of the detritus that gulls and geese collect in this way are either relatively recent artifacts of human manufacture or natural objects unlikely to be found near a nest. There has been no time for selection to work to perfect egg recognition in the face of human littering behavior.

The initial assumption that roundedness is all there is to egg recognition has, however, turned out to be wrong. Ground-nesting birds *do* know more about their eggs than that; they are slower to recover most (but not all) unnatural objects than real eggs, and may ignore them altogether if the nest is full of normal eggs. The precise criteria by which gulls judge the probability that an object is an egg have been worked out by Tinbergen and his students. They offered pairs of objects to a nesting bird and recorded which was recovered first. From such studies it is clear that the incubating parent weighs—independently—not only roundedness but also size, color, and degree of speckling.

Thus the actual stimulus that triggers the bird's egg-recovery response is not the physical egg considered as a whole, but rather some aggregate of its independent attributes. Each of these independent features of an egg is called a sign stimulus. Each stimulus category is judged separately by the brain, and the set is then summed to determine whether the bird should respond, and if so to what degree. Each is an abstract parameter in some sort of multidimensional "egg space" within the bird's mind. If we assign the stimulus potency value of 1.0 to a normal egg, by tabulating preferences we find that batteries score about 0.7.

More interesting, however, is the observation that 1.0 is not the top score: artificial eggs that are larger, greener, and more speckled

Most of Tinbergen's experiments with model eggs are summarized in this matrix. A normal egg is shown in the center; models of the same size are connected by lines. The "ideal" egg would be a large green ovoid with speckles; in fact larger speckles (not shown here) are better than natural-size markings.

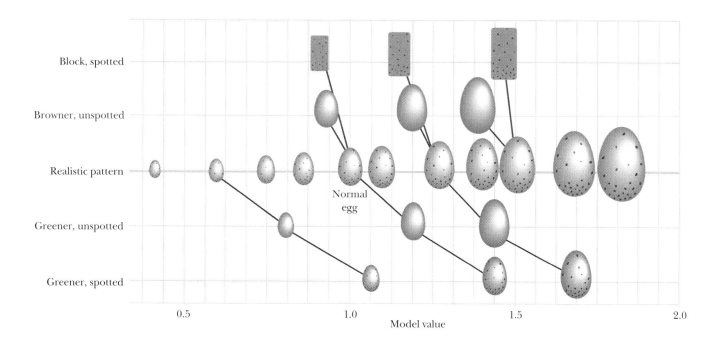

than normal can score well above 2. Tinbergen and Lorenz coined the term "supernormal stimuli" to describe unnaturally attractive cues. Clearly then the innate criteria used by gulls and geese are sufficient to identify eggs by the sign stimuli they display, but the circuitry is not optimized for the actual characteristics of their natural eggs.

Gulls and humans obviously experience eggs in a way that is fundamentally different. To us, eggs, regardless of color or speckles, are just one more class of object; for gulls, they radiate a set of cues that have a powerful fascination, that rivet the birds' attention and elicit a response unlike anything that would occur to a member of our species. To gulls, eggs embody stimuli that set them powerfully apart in kind rather than degree from the other natural objects in their world.

THE ROLE OF RELEASERS

Sign stimuli, hidden from us but inescapably obvious to the animals that depend on them, are often called releasers—they trigger, or release, behavioral responses without requiring knowledge or understanding on the part of the animal in order to perform the action. Most innate behavior is initiated by such stimuli. For example, as soon as they hatch gull chicks must beg for food from their parents. The inborn etiquette requires the chicks to peck at their parents' beaks, which chicks identify by several independent cues whose combined potency determines the strength with which they will peck. Meticulous experiments by Tinbergen, ourselves, and others have shown that the sign stimuli include verticality (the angle of the downward-pointing bill), narrowness, horizontal movement (the parent instinctively moves its bill from side to side when it is ready to feed its brood), and color (a red spot in the case of herring gulls). Just as with eggs, it is possible to create a supernormal set of stimuli; in this case it is a narrow dowel with several red bands, held vertically and moving back and forth, which the chicks prefer over their parents.

It seems highly likely that sign stimuli correspond to the features—spots, lines, edges, and simple shapes—that are automatically abstracted by the brain as it processes visual information. For instance, birds, like mammals, have many cells in the visual system that are keyed to respond to vertical bars moving horizontally, and other cells that identify red spots moving in the same way; each of these feature detectors in the nervous system responds best to a particular rate of

Newly hatched herring-gull chicks peck most vigorously at horizontally moving narrow vertical objects with red spots or bands. Though the lifelike model is as effective as an actual parent, the narrower multibanded model is even more stimulating.

apparent motion of the stimulus, and so do the chicks. Shape detectors uniquely attuned to the convex edges of eggs are known as well.

Or consider European toads, whose prey-capture circuitry has been charted in almost complete detail by the German neurobiologist Jörg-Peter Ewert. These amphibians attack and eat moving worms and crickets in the wild. In the lab a hungry toad will strike at any bar-shaped model moving, as do worms and crickets, along its long axis; during this behavior, electrodes reveal that the neurons in the toad's

Toads respond preferentially to elongated stimuli moving lengthwise. After orienting to the target, members of this European species strike with the tongue, then (whether or not anything has been captured) close their eyes, swallow, and wipe their mouths.

brain that function as moving-line detectors are firing. The relationship between the response of feature detectors, designed to pick out the sign stimuli unwittingly provided by prey animals, to the prey-capture behavior of the toad is perfectly correlated: the gradations of neural response observed as the model's height-to-length ratio is systematically altered (falling as the increasing ratio nears 1.0 and the model approaches a square) is mirrored by the animal's decreasing interest in the stimulus. The conclusion we draw from these observations is that the species-specific nature of releasers arises not so much from any special processing in the brain as from the particular set of

The ideal stimulus for eliciting prey-capture behavior in toads is 4 to 16 times longer than it is wide and moving lengthwise; the same targets moving sideways can cause the toad to cower or flee.

Shape and motion of stimulus

Responses per minute

40

30

20

10

0

0.0625   0.125   0.25   0.5   1.0   2.0   4.0   8.0

Height-to-length ratio of stimulus

automatically abstracted cues that are selected and summed and then used to trigger a particular response.

Auditory sign stimuli are also common. Swamp sparrows, for example, recognize their species' song by a particular acoustic feature and a certain chirp rate; this pair of criteria, acting in parallel, exclude all other likely sounds from the sparrow's consideration. Female crickets listen for a specific ratio of interchirp intervals as a key to identifying males of their species. When the normal song is taped and then run backward or scrambled in a way that makes it sound completely different to our ears but still preserves the chirp intervals, the female will find it just as attractive. But if one of the intervals is altered, even in a way virtually imperceptible to us, she will reject the call. The bases of these distinctions are acoustic feature detectors in the auditory processing pathway that are set up to respond to only one cue.

Even further from our range of experience are pheromones, like the butyric acid that attracts ticks, which act as chemical sign stimuli. The redolent air draws male moths to female moths, beetles to other beetles, flies to flies. The specificity of these chemicals, often virtually odorless to our noses, becomes apparent if we examine the catch of ordinary garden insect traps: gypsy moth traps, baited with the female moth's unique pheromone, contain only male gypsy moths; Japanese beetle traps contain mostly Japanese beetles. (To draw females as well, most traps have a powerfully scented floral lure that also attracts bees, wasps, and butterflies, most of which escape; the

Males of many species of butterflies and some moths (including the Caribbean moth pictured here) release pheromones from brushlike hair-pencils (left) that are everted from the tip of the abdomen during courtship. A receptive female will land and allow the male to mate.

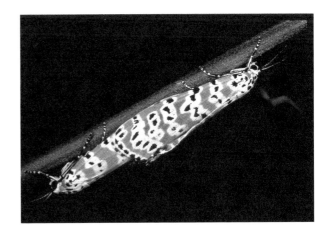

flies we find are attracted by the smell of the dead beetles that accumulate in the trap.)

Some species respond to large repertoires of chemical sign stimuli, perceived not by active discrimination but by the simple presence or absence of specialized receptors to which the pheromone molecules bind. Honey bees can post dozens of pheromonal messages: one odor releases attack, another elicits alarm, another serves to attract fellow foragers; others identify the queen and cause nurse bees to groom and feed her. Specific pheromones are emitted by developing larvae, by queens on mating flights, and by all bees when they die. These odors have little or no meaning to other species. To our unresponsive senses the attack pheromone (when there is enough for us to detect at all) smells vaguely like bananas, the attraction odor has a citrus note, the alarm odor is reminiscent of paint thinner, and the potent queen pheromones are utterly odorless.

For animals that live long enough to benefit from learning, releasers are still useful as efficient ways to guide early activity before there is any opportunity for behavior to be modified by experience. A gull chick that had to work out by trial and error what it should peck at—its feet, blades of grass, its parents' wings, or many of the other objects that crowd its world and compete for attention—would starve before it perfected its behavior. Throughout the life of an animal, whenever the stimulus it needs for successful behavior is highly predictable—such as the pheromone emitted by members of the opposite sex—releasers are a reliable solution. Releasers can serve as expedient neural shortcuts that bypass higher-level mental processing, and generate the right results.

BEHAVIORAL RESPONSES

The reactions elicited by sign stimuli are sometimes covert, not manifesting themselves until later. Covert reactions include some forms of learning, the alteration of an animal's sensitivity to another cue (a phenomenon called priming), or a physiological change that prepares the organism to perform a specific function, such as egg laying or migration. Overt responses, however, are far more common, and much easier to study. The gull chick's pecking is a response to the releasers provided by a parent's bill; its parent's subsequent regurgitation of food is a response to the releaser provided by the chick's pecking. Parent birds will allow their offspring to starve if the young fail to produce the correct stimuli.

Early ethologists called many of these species-specific behavioral responses "fixed-action patterns," a label that emphasized the innate and stereotyped nature of the actions. In the face of withering criticism from psychologists through the 1950s, attention has shifted more to the *flexibility* of innate behavioral responses (which was noted but not emphasized in early studies). Fixed-action patterns are now more commonly called "motor programs," a designation that simply means that the behavior is generated by a specific set of neurons. The egg-rolling response of geese illustrates this balance between rigidity and flexibility.

Even without knowing intimately what their own eggs look like, the behavior of nesting geese ensures that errant eggs will be recovered before they become fatally chilled: the birds will roll any object with the right sign stimuli into the nest. At first sight this looked like

The egg-rolling response of geese, seen here in Tinbergen's photographs both from the side (a–d) and the front (e, f), begins as the goose fixes her gaze on the egg, rises, touches it, and finally rolls the egg into the nest. Although the elements of the response visible from the side are stereotyped, observing the behavior from the front reveals that the goose makes sideways movements of her head to keep the egg rolling straight over the uneven surface.

The courtship display of male mallards is a stereotyped and innate motor program that helps identify the signaler's sex, species, and motivational state.

a thoughtful solution to a serious problem, but like many behaviors the cleverness is largely or entirely an illusion created by efficient programming. Once the goose has stood up and extended its neck, the egg can be removed in plain sight and set aside, and the goose will go through the entire recovery process nonetheless, gently rolling a nonexistent egg back into its nest. The egg stimuli were necessary to trigger this long and elaborate response; once the response is triggered, the egg is no longer necessary. The only change is that the side-to-side motion of the head that would keep an actual egg rolling straight on an uneven surface disappears; without feedback from the egg as it touches the bird's bill, the flexible component of the behavior vanishes.

This simple experiment reveals that egg-rolling is a behavioral unit, controlled entirely by a neural circuit laid down long before nesting begins. Once triggered, the response proceeds to completion whether or not there is any egg to roll. In a similar way, the prey-capture routine of the European toad is a unit. After the toad initiates an attack, its target can be removed, but nevertheless the toad launches and then retracts its tongue, closes its eyes and swallows what it has not caught, and then wipes its mouth with a forelimb. As with most other cases of innate behavior, the predictability of the appropriate behavioral action is sufficient to make the prewiring of a specific response more efficient than the time-consuming and error-prone alternative of learning. And, as we saw with visual, auditory, and olfactory courtship signals, species-specific sexual interactions tend to be highly predictable; thus it is no surprise that many of the motor programs associated with courtship and copulation are innate.

DRIVES

But animals are not always courting, or begging food, or rolling eggs even in the presence of the appropriate stimuli. Sensitivity to releasers is modulated, both in the short term and over longer intervals. Geese roll eggs only from about a week before they begin incubating until about a week after the young hatch; the same priming cues that initiate courtship (changes in hormone levels, which themselves are primed by the celestial sign stimulus of increasing daylength in the spring) appear to modulate the drive to roll eggs, because at other times of year geese show no interest in recovering eggs.

The strength of a drive to perform a specific behavior can fluctuate over time. In the short run, for example, nesting geese do not recover eggs when they are away from the nest to feed, or when some more important stimulus presents itself—a predator, for example. Short-term motivational control is essential if an animal is to organize its priorities and avoid investing its time foolishly. The repertoire of activities available to a nesting bird is far larger than most people imagine: self-grooming (a good spare-time activity), sleep, and nest repair are three possible behavioral choices.

Natural selection has resulted in circuitry that modulates both immediate and long-term behavioral proclivities. Such inborn control

Breeding behavior in most temperate-zone birds is triggered by changing day length (as registered by the pineal gland) and, to a lesser extent, rising temperature. Hormones released by the pineal begin a cascade of hormonal secretions that, one by one, activate a series of behavioral centers in the brain.

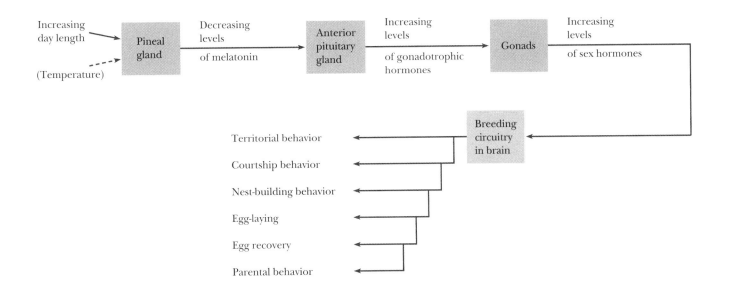

In most cases innate behavior appears at a characteristic age with or without opportunity for learning. This "maturation" of behavior is evident in humans as well: infants bound in a carrying cradle nevertheless begin walking at about the same time as their unfettered peers.

systems suppress unnecessary or inappropriate behavior and generate decisions when competing stimuli are of equal value (so that animals do not usually dither).

One of the consequences of the operation of a drive is that it creates the illusion of learning when an innate behavior appears later in life. Such behavior appears spontaneously even when an animal has been isolated from any opportunity to learn it. Birds are often said to "learn" to fly after they fledge, but in fact the motor programs are innate (as are similar ones in humans, despite the pleasure we take in "teaching" a baby to walk). Flight movements do appear before flying begins, but the increasing drive to flap the wings is actually working to incite fledglings to develop their flight muscles. While the subtleties of graceful landing must be learned by experience, birds no more learn to fly than fish learn to swim.

IMPRINTING

Most birds have no need to recognize their eggs with much precision: any ovoid object in or near the nest is almost certainly one of a pair's eggs. But for the chicks that hatch from these eggs the situation can be very different. In species like geese and ducks (and even antelope), in which the young must follow their parents among flocks (or herds) of similar creatures almost from birth, it is essential that the young be able to recognize their protectors individually as quickly as possible. We tend to think of learning as at least somewhat intellectual, requiring judgment and active mental engagement on the part of the student. But the sequence by which goslings memorize the voice and appearance of each parent is more like calibration than learning.

Goslings are enabled to recognize their parents through a phenomenon Lorenz called parental imprinting. In sexual imprinting, a similar process, they also memorize the diagnostic characteristics of their species, acting on this information months or years later when they choose mates. In both kinds of imprinting there is a critical (or sensitive) period during which the phenomenon is most likely to occur, and there is little or no reversal—that is, once in place, imprinting usually cannot be undone or even forgotten. The inability of imprinted animals to forget or change their preference after more experience leads many psychologists to conclude that imprinting does not qualify as true learning.

Konrad Lorenz with three ducks that have imprinted on him.

Parental imprinting has been studied most extensively in mallard ducks. Generally all the members of a clutch of mallard eggs hatch at about the same time, even though they have usually been laid over the course of three or four days. To ensure this synchrony, the parents wait to incubate their eggs until all the eggs are laid; and the chicks communicate vocally among themselves in the last few days before hatching. About 10 to 18 hours after hatching the female leaves the nest, her young following. Within minutes the ducklings recognize their mother as an individual, staying with her even in the presence of other birds of the same species.

Researchers who experiment with the imprinting process in an effort to disentangle its component parts discover that much of the behavior seen in the lab corresponds to Lorenz's initial reports of imprinting. Chicks imprint best about 16 hours after hatching; birds that do not imprint by 30 hours almost never imprint; and once chicks have become imprinted early in the sensitive period on a real or lifelike stimulus, exposing them to other models almost never has any effect. The early part of this timetable corresponds to the period of limited social experience near the nest soon after hatching, when the only adults close by are the parents. The latter part matches the time when the young begin to encounter other animals on the pond.

When imprinting studies go awry

This form of imprinting works because the parents provide a set of sign stimuli that trigger following behavior in young chicks. These include a species-specific "exodus" call they produce as they move away from the chicks, a distinctive waddling motion, and one or more visual stimuli. Chicks *can* be imprinted on unnatural stimuli that merely move—a red ball, for instance—but only later in their critical period; it is as though their requirements for the "correct" imprinting stimuli decline as time begins to run out, or rather as their drive to attach themselves to some object—*any* object—rises. In addition, a chick that has followed a red ball early in its critical period will switch to a more realistic model if it is offered before this window closes, but the opposite never occurs: once they have seen the real thing, chicks will not switch their affections to anything less real. Imprinting, then, is like other innate behaviors in that the vigor of the response, as well as the latency between a stimulus and the behavior it triggers, depends on the summed strength of the sign stimuli presented.

Parental imprinting in ducks, though triggered mostly by visual cues, focuses in the end primarily on auditory stimuli. Thus when a chick that has been imprinted on a realistic model producing the exodus call is offered a choice between an identical but mute model and a box that generates the call, it will follow the box. This preference makes some sense because in the wild the many other parent birds on a lake or pond look much alike, but each has a distinct voice. Nevertheless, chicks do recognize the appearance of the model they have imprinted on and therefore in the wild they can identify a parent even when it is not calling. Thus, imprinting is usually cue specific and relies on a hierarchy of remembered stimuli.

In some species, sexual imprinting determines the features to look for in a potential mate when the time comes. It generally occurs later than parental imprinting, but still in an early stage of development. It has a longer critical period, and can involve a wider variety of stimuli: it can be specific to one parent, or only one sex of young may imprint, or the imprinting may be directed at nestmates rather than parents. When birds of these species begin to seek mates, usually the following year, memory guides their choices. In one particularly striking laboratory experiment by Klaus Immelman in the 1970s, a male zebra finch was reared by a related species, a female Bengalese finch. Afterwards the zebra finch was kept only with other zebra finches and mated each year with a female of his own species, though only late in the season. After eight years the male was placed in a cage with a zebra and a Bengalese female; he immediately began courting the Bengalese. In at least this case, the permanence of sexual imprinting seems clear, as well as the conflict during the previous years between the increasing drive to mate as the season wore on and the absence of a potential mate offering the full range of remembered "ideal" behavioral and morphological characteristics.

It is the reliability of the basic cues—that is, the sign stimuli—associated with the parents, combined with the chicks' limited social exposure just after hatching, that makes imprinting a useful way to memorize very rapidly the distinctive characteristics of a specific adult or pair of adults. Those aspects of the parents' voice that are unique, and therefore unpredictable, are thus the most useful cues for the young to imprint on, since they allow the young to recognize their parents as individuals. Many ethologists refer to imprinting as a learning program, a use of computer jargon that emphasizes the highly orchestrated nature of the process. Indeed, one prevalent school of thought considers most learning to be as automatic as imprinting. In the next chapter we will consider whether most instances of learning differ from imprinting in kind or merely in degree.

THE PROBLEM OF COMPLEX BEHAVIOR

Analogy can be a useful tool in formulating testable hypotheses about animal cognition, but, as with Clever Hans, it can be misleading. Often it is much more difficult to imagine the alternative—that a complex and apparently clever piece of behavior could be preprogrammed and will develop in isolation. And yet, outside of humans, much of the really intricate behavior of animals—courtship displays and nest-building, for example—is innate. The secret to its misleading complexity lies in the programming strategies that control behavior.

Let us look at one of the clearest examples of how complex behavior is organized, from a study of nest building by an Australian species of digger wasp. This species excavates a tunnel about 8 cm long and 8 mm in diameter which it lines with mud. Before beginning to rear any offspring, however, the wasp constructs an elaborate funnel that projects above the ground; this funnel serves to prevent a specific parasite (another species of wasp) from entering the nest and laying its eggs on the prey the wasp provides for its own young. The funnel consists of a stem, neck, flange, and bell. The wasp could have some sort of mental picture of the structure it seeks to build, and figure out a way to satisfy that goal; as we will see, however, the wasp

Konrad Lorenz's sketch of Clever Hans.

A completed funnel nest includes a mud-lined tunnel (constructed first), the funnel (consisting of stem, neck, flange, and bell), and sealed brood chambers (built last). Each chamber is stocked with caterpillars for the wasp larva to eat. The larva in the first chamber to be stocked has already pupated, while the one in the last chamber has yet to emerge from its egg. Once the tunnel has been completely filled with brood cells the owner will destroy the funnel and seal the entrance.

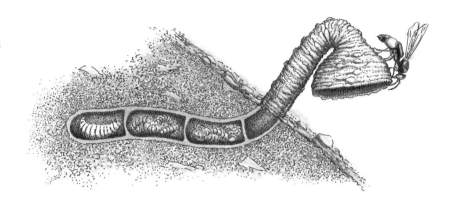

appears to have no overall conception of the finished product; instead, she seems to follow slavishly a set of innate instructions.

The wasp begins the project by collecting mud, which she holds with her front legs, setting it in place, smoothing and spreading it with her mandibles. She leaves the outside of the funnel rough but polishes the inside slick. The first step is the construction of the 3-cm stem, which projects perpendicularly from the soil. If, as often happens, the nest is built on a slope, the stem is not vertical in absolute terms but perpendicular to the surface. Once the wasp has begun stem construction, however, she pays no more attention to the soil slope: the nest can be rotated, or the stem broken off and reattached at a completely different angle, and the wasp will continue to build along the same axis as the existing part of the stem.

If this were a computer program, stem-building would be called a subroutine. The wasp enters the subroutine when the tunnel is complete, repeating the same steps over and over again: collecting mud, extending the stem along the same axis, collecting more mud, extending the stem, and so on. At some point, however, the wasp must exit this routine and begin the neck. Most stems are about 3 cm long, so the exit contingency might be "build 3 cm of stem," which in turn might correspond to some fixed number of mud-collection trips. In fact, the criterion is "build until I measure 3 cm of stem." The distinction is that the wasp uses her own body as a measuring unit and returns to the main program when the criterion is satisfied. As a result, smaller wasps inevitably build shorter stems.

When a hole is drilled in the neck of a funnel the owner does not repair it; instead the hole is treated like the opening of the tunnel and a completely new funnel built atop it.

A telling demonstration of the wasp's lack of information (or, perhaps, interest) about the stem is that if the base of the stem is buried repeatedly, so that the exposed portion never extends a full 3 cm above the soil, the wasp simply continues to build. Once the criterion is met, however, and the first steps taken toward the construction of the neck, burying the stem has no effect: the wasp has entered the next subroutine, and there is no provision for returning to an earlier stage.

The neck is a curved section of funnel with the same diameter as the stem; it is built in the same basic way, but the criterion for exiting this part of the program is the achievement of a 20° angle from the horizontal. Thus a neck built on a vertical stem curves through 160° while one added to a stem extending from a vertical bank sweeps through just 70°. Again, altering the stem angle during construction can prolong building, and may even force the wasp to construct a 360° neck; she does not measure the necessary effort in advance but, like a computer, measures the status of the project after each pass through the subroutine. And again, once the criterion has been met, there is no going back: a start on the flange leaves the wasp oblivious to further alterations in the neck angle. There is no attempt—that is, there is no provision in the program—to move back a step to restore the 20° angle that had seemed so important just a few minutes earlier.

The flange opens uniformly to a diameter of about 2 cm and then is enlarged asymmetrically toward the stem. Finally, the wasp adds a cylindrical bell to a depth of about 2 cm. When the structure is complete the interior is too smooth to allow a parasite purchase when it

The funnel-building wasp extends the stem until it is about 3 cm from the ground and then begins the curving neck. If the stem is buried before the wasp has begun the neck, she continues lengthening it, but once she has started the neck, experimental manipulations of the stem are ignored. A wasp that understood the purpose of the funnel or what it should look like when completed presumably ought to destroy the neck and extend the stem, or abandon the project.

tries to land, and too large for it to reach the neck with its front legs while holding on to the bottom of the bell with its back legs. The wasp itself, on the other hand, can just manage the stretch—indeed, this is how she judges when to stop extending the bell.

Her defenses against that particular predator complete, the wasp begins hunting caterpillars, which she leaves paralyzed in the tunnel. When she has collected enough she lays an egg, seals off the section of tunnel with mud, and stocks a new chamber in the tunnel. When the tunnel is filled with developing larvae, each with its own provisions, she closes the tunnel and destroys the funnel.

The wasp's technique, then, is to break down a complex task into a series of simpler tasks, each of which requires a cycle of repetitive behavior until some innately specified subgoal is achieved. Successful completion of each subroutine carries the wasp into the next step until her overall task is complete. There is almost no provision for going back; the sole exception is an apparent contingency for dealing with complete loss of the funnel, in which case the wasp rebuilds. This contingency can be triggered in another way: if a hole is drilled through the neck before the bell is finished, the wasp, apparently at a loss how to repair this trivial damage, simply builds a complete new funnel atop the hole in the neck.

It may have been the development of the computer, with its necessary emphasis on the uncreative and repetitious nature of the steps that underlie its amazing achievements, that alerted scientists to the incremental and repetitious nature of much that goes on in the brain.

Now, conversely, the animal mind is being studied for what it can contribute to the concept of artificial intelligence. What makes the wasp's behavior more like that of a computer than an architect is the lack of any comprehension of the *goal*. Instead, the insect focuses on a series of immediate *tasks*. This distinction between "local" tasks, which could be accomplished by innate programming alone, and "global" goals, which may require a more complete perspective and understanding of the need a behavior serves, will be crucial to our analyses of more complex behavior.

A close look at the impressive feats of building by many other species, ranging from spiders to birds, reveals that the same pattern of individual tasks organized into subroutines underlies each web and nest. In the case of birds the material used, whether lichens and spiderwebs or grass and mud, is usually specific to the species and innately recognized. Though the general pattern of building is preordained, there is usually some evidence of improvement with practice. Nevertheless, even the impressive nest of the weaverbird with its nest cup, waterproof roof, and long entrance tunnel that keeps out nest predators (especially snakes), must be constructed entirely on the basis of innate instructions organized as steps, because hand-reared birds build the same sort of nests as their wild-reared peers, and human experimenters can accelerate or prolong each phase by manipulating the cues used by the birds.

Perhaps it should not be so surprising that much of the most complex behavior seen in nature should be innate: after all, it would be very hard if not impossible to learn anything so intricate. Learning in animals tends to focus on far simpler tasks, like the motor pattern involved in mimicking a parent bird's song. It might be a serious mistake to restrict our search for the animal mind to the most complex behavioral accomplishments if it leads us to overlook the apparently simpler but less predictable problems that confront animals. If natural selection has not favored an automatic response to deal with a particular situation because it is rare or new, an animal would be forced to depend on its intellectual wherewithal, if any, to devise a solution to a novel difficulty facing it. Since some animals do seem able to take control of even the innate subroutines of their building programs when necessary, and sometimes deal with unusual contingencies in a relatively sensible way, we can study those instances for indications of intelligence and comprehension.

These complex weaverbird nests are in various stages of construction. Many are ready for the addition of an entrance tube, which is not built until a female accepts a male's nest; most of the rest have incomplete tubes.

 **The Nature of
Learning**

 young chickadee pounds energetically with his beak at a sunflower seed, but to no avail. Between intervals of scanning the sky for predators, he shifts the seed and tries a new angle of attack. He knows that there is a highly desirable kernel inside: an hour earlier, attracted to a sunflower head by the sight of another bird already feeding, his exploratory probing turned up a cracked seed with an exposed kernel. Ever alert to a new source of food, he immediately made an initial association between the appearance of the seed and the kernel inside; a second broken seed cemented this correlation in his mind.

At length the seed he has been hammering at gives way and he gains his reward. He selects another seed and this time begins the attack from the direction that gained him access before. Adjusting his grip and his pecks to a narrower range of angles, he breaks into the shell a bit sooner. His speed will improve slowly as he perfects his technique; by the end of the day the chickadee will have added sunflower–seed–harvesting to his large and growing repertoire of learned foraging behaviors.

When knowledge is not innate—and no bird is born programmed to open every imaginable kind of seed—cognition in animals must

MANY ANIMALS MUST LEARN NEW WAYS

TO SOLVE OLD PROBLEMS.

inevitably involve learning. How does learning work in animals—is it rote, or creative—and what can the process of animal learning tell us about the ways their minds work?

LEARNING BY ASSOCIATION

The two steps in the chickadee's understanding of sunflower seeds correspond to the two basic forms of learning identified earlier this century, now known as classical and operant conditioning. The process of classical conditioning was first described by the Russian physiologist Ivan Pavlov around 1905. In studying the mechanisms of digestion, Pavlov measured the amount of saliva produced in the mouths of dogs during feeding. He was surprised to discover that after they became accustomed to his procedure, the dogs began to salivate *before* the food was presented. A cue in the laboratory—the sound of the food being spooned into a dish—foreshadowed feeding, and the dogs had learned this association.

Pavlov called the food that released the innate act of salivation an unconditioned (unlearned) stimulus (US), and the spontaneous

Ivan Pavlov (1849–1936) discovered classical conditioning while studying digestion. The device on the side of the dog's face monitors saliva secretion; as the dog learns to associate a stimulus with food, saliva is secreted in anticipation of the actual presentation of food.

salivation that ensues an unconditioned response (UR); in the vocabulary of ethology these are, of course, sign stimuli and motor programs. The normal course of events, therefore, is: US → UR.

Pavlov discovered that when a bell or buzzer was regularly sounded just before the US was presented, this conditioning, or training, stimulus (CS) would eventually trigger the response itself. In training, therefore, the sequence is: CS + US → UR. After several such pairings of conditioning and unconditioned stimuli, the result of the learning becomes evident: CS → UR. The animal has learned that the conditioning stimulus is as good a predictor as the unconditioned one, and therefore it alone can produce the response. (Because the UR may change slightly to accommodate the nature and timing of the CS, the altered UR is often called a conditioned response, or CR.)

Pavlov believed that any cue the animal could sense could be used as a conditioning stimulus for any response. "It is obvious," he wrote, "that the reflex activity of any effector system can be chosen for the purposes of investigation, since any signalling stimuli can be hooked up to any of the reflexes." He also found that presenting a CS *after* the appearance of the US yielded little or no learning, and that allowing too much time to elapse between the CS and the US was also less effective. He concluded that the value of this learning sequence, which we now call classical conditioning, is to allow an animal to respond sooner to a stimulus. For instance, our chickadee (like most birds) is innately frightened of animals with paired forward-looking eyes; he will learn to associate the appearance of cats with this instinctive fear, and thus will be able to recognize and fly away from anything catlike before it gets close enough for him to see its eyes.

The concept of the conditioned response fell on fertile ground in the United States. In 1913 J. B. Watson published *Psychology as the Psychologist Views It*, the charter for a new school of psychology that he called Behaviorism. In reaction to the profoundly embarrassing Clever Hans incident, he insisted that psychologists should confine themselves to studying carefully defined stimuli and the overt responses they elicit, formulating rules to predict what animals will do when presented with experimentally controlled cues. Behaviorists were to avoid any speculation about what might be going on in the nervous systems of animals between stimulus and response.

The phenomenon of classical conditioning led Watson to go beyond even Pavlov's claim of its powers and assert that *all* behavior is

J. B. Watson (1878–1958) began his career studying unlearned behavior, including the powerful grasping reflex in newborn humans and nesting responses in terns.

learned, even the automatic physiological processes of the body: "There are then for us no instincts—we no longer need the term in psychology. Everything we have been in the habit of calling an 'instinct' today is largely the result of training . . . . [T]hink of each unlearned act as becoming conditioned shortly after birth—even our respiration and circulation." Behaviorism dominated experimental psychology for over 50 years, through the 1960s, and its extreme aversion to investigating mental processing is still widespread, even among scientists who reject the Behavioristic notion that learning underlies all activity.

Studies of classical conditioning since Pavlov's work have emphasized the question of predictability in this form of learning. Researchers have found, for example, that learning will occur so long as the CS is often associated with the US but does not often occur without it—that is, if the CS has a high probability of predicting the imminent arrival of the US and little chance of triggering a false alarm. In short, the animals must be measuring the reliability of cues in a behaviorally sensible way. Moreover, once one CS has been learned, the addition of a second cue has little effect: animals tend to ignore it since the first one works perfectly well. This phenomenon, known as blocking, does not mean that animals cannot remember more than one cue at a time: if the two cues are present together from the outset, they are both learned.

The central role of predictability is especially evident in the phenomenon of conditioned inhibition. In this form of classical conditioning, animals learn to suppress any spontaneous unconditioned responses in the presence of a CS that has been presented without the US; in these experiments, for instance, a flash of light could mean that no food is forthcoming. If this negative stimulus is sufficiently prominent and common, especially near the usual feeding time or in the test apparatus where feeding occurs, the animals learn that the conditioning stimulus is reliably associated with the *absence* of the unconditioned stimulus. Conditioned inhibition played an important but unrecognized role in learning experiments for decades. Researchers found that many animals learn a CS best when they are trained with two alternative conditioning stimuli, one (the CS$^+$) that is associated with the US and another (the CS$^-$) that is not. Thus, when a rat in a classical conditioning test is trained simply to associate the presentation of a square black shape with food and then tested with other simple black forms, it will often respond to rectangles, quadrilaterals,

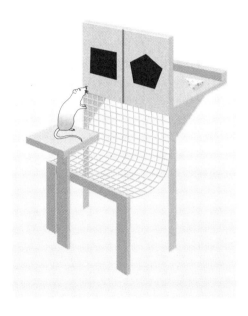

The rat's task in this jumping-stand experiment is to leap toward the unlatched door and thus obtain food; a mistake causes the rat to bump its nose and fall into the net. To master this task the rat must learn which pattern marks the safe door. (The food is probably irrelevant: during training the stand is electrified, and thus the rat first learns that jumping prevents the shock; next it learns to avoid bumping its nose by choosing the correct pattern.) The more difficult it is for the rat to distinguish the two patterns, the more it learns about them.

triangles, and pentagons. But if the square CS^+ is alternated with a CS^- rectangle that has very nearly the same dimensions as the square, the rat will learn the distinguishing features of the CS^+ so well that all other shapes will be ignored. Without a contrast in training stimuli, then, animals that have the ability to make fine discriminations simply don't, instead learning only enough about some limited part of the CS^+ to allow recognition. But when the learning task is made more challenging from the outset, animals pay much closer attention to the CS^+ and make many fewer "silly" errors with novel conditioning stimuli.

Ethologists regularly observe classical conditioning in the wild, particularly with regard to food learning. To many ethologists, the most important role of classical conditioning is one of improved recognition rather than quicker response, though the learning may also produce that effect. A crude sign stimulus—the sight of an object moving away, for instance—is replaced by a detailed picture of the object: a visual and auditory profile of a particular parent bird that includes all the associated conditioning stimuli the chick can memorize. A detailed image allows the individual or object—in most cases parent, predator, prey, or food—to be spotted more reliably, even when farther away or partially hidden.

Many animals, from invertebrates to primates, can learn both positive and negative associations. The knowledge they obtain from this interaction with their environment clearly forms an important part of their cognitive repertoire. A deeper question is whether the animals are merely learning machines, genetically programmed to isolate predictive correlations automatically, or whether they are taking a more active mental role in selecting and solving the cognitive puzzles researchers call conditioning.

LEARNING BY TRIAL AND ERROR

While classical conditioning can be described as "learning to recognize," operant conditioning is "learning to respond." All learned responses were thought by Watson to be chains of unconditioned responses: an animal learned to use its own performance of one UR (or some cue the behavior produced) as the CS for triggering another UR. Thus a complex behavioral motor program like maze-running was, in Watson's words, a "reflex chain": $UR_1 \rightarrow UR_2 \rightarrow UR_3 \rightarrow$

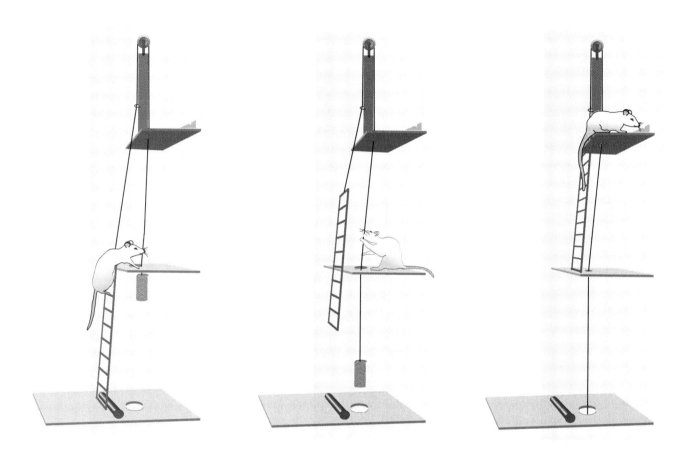

Through shaping, this rat has been trained to climb the ladder, hoist it up one level, and then climb to the food.

$UR_4 \rightarrow UR_5 \rightarrow UR_6 \rightarrow UR_7 \rightarrow UR_8 \rightarrow UR_9 \rightarrow UR_{10}$, and so on; in learning the maze, actions such as running forward, turning left, and turning right would serve as unconditioned responses.

The alternative explanation for learning a successful response is trial-and-error learning, or operant conditioning. The assumption underlying operant conditioning—the theory that made B. F. Skinner's name a household word—is that the response is a novel behavior, not a reflex chain, and that the animal acquires the behavior through a kind of self-conditioning called shaping. To be shaped, the creature must have some sort of goal it is seeking to achieve. The birds Pliny described were encouraged to learn by being fed when they produced reasonable copies of the training sounds. Today animals in the lab are starved to 80 percent of their normal body weight and thus are highly motivated to find ways to harvest food; other experiments rely on the universal desire of animals to avoid punishment.

Under laboratory conditions, shaping occurs as any partial performance of the desired behavior is rewarded by the experimenter. If the object is to train a rat to press a lever bar in a "Skinner box," the researcher might provide a piece of food near the lever whenever the rat looks in the general direction of the bar. The rat, for its part, seems to experiment through trial and error to determine which of the many things it had been doing when the food appeared—turning, looking, scratching, sniffing, or perhaps nothing at all—correlated with the reward; soon the rat has suppressed scratching and sniffing and is looking at the lever.

Now the researcher raises the threshold, requiring the rat to touch the bar. The hungry rat initiates increasingly frantic experimentation in the vicinity of the lever when the previous behavioral formula fails it. Eventually, the rat bumps the lever and food appears. The rat quickly works out that touching the bar is the key. Then the experimenter requires that the lever be pressed: eventually the rat figures that out as well and is soon pressing the lever bar fifty or more

B. F. Skinner with some of his experimental subjects.

A rat in a Skinner box. When an appropriate cue is present, the hungry rat must touch the bar just below the food hopper to receive a reward.

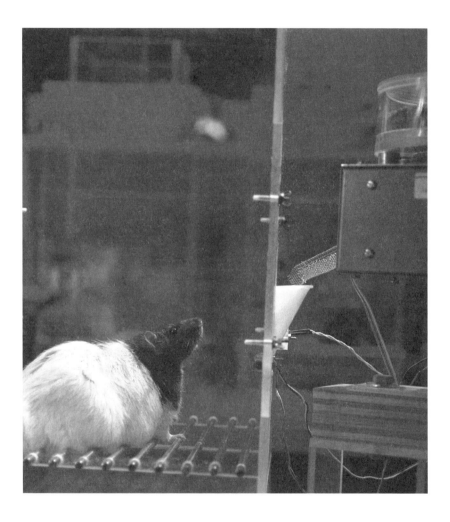

times a minute. Psychologists once maintained that any animal could be conditioned to perform any behavior of which it was physically capable. As Skinner put it, "All behavior is constructed by a continual process of differential reinforcement from undifferentiated behavior, just as the sculptor shapes his figure from a lump of clay." We will see presently that this picture of the power of trial-and-error learning, which shaped educational and social policies for decades, has proved overly optimistic.

Trial-and-error learning occurs in nature all the time, mostly in connection with harvesting food. Seed-eating birds like our chickadee will experiment, clumsily at first, with unfamiliar seeds in an effort to solve the problem of removing the shell or husk. During the process of self-shaping, the bird in the wild, like the rat in the lab, experiments in a variety of ways, performing with higher frequency any behaviors that take it closer to the goal and discarding elements that seem irrelevant. Eventually a streamlined seed-husking behavior emerges that, like shoe-tying or bicycle-riding in humans, is a learned motor program. The animal benefits not only from increased efficiency in eating but also from having its attention freed for other tasks, like looking for more seeds or watching for predators.

Operant learning is clearly an important component in an animal's cognitive repertoire. Moreover, the repetition of attempts in the trial-and-error process suggests that the learning may be less intellectually passive than the correlation-extraction process of classical conditioning: the creature seems to comprehend the nature of the task and conjure up alternative guesses about what might work. But although the germ of insight and creativity may be a factor in some operant conditioning, there is often less to trial-and-error learning than meets the eye.

BIASES IN CLASSICAL CONDITIONING

Though the natural behavior of animals, and whatever evidence it provides for mental activity, is best observed in the wild, convincing tests are often possible only in the controlled conditions of the laboratory. The pattern of learning biases that has turned up in laboratory research provides the primary caveat in the attempt to link animal learning and thinking.

It is important to remember that the species that can thrive and perform in the lab environment are not a simple cross section of the world's fauna: rats, mice, and pigeons are relatively flexible species that have adapted over generations of scavenging a living in changing urban environments to live in proximity to humans. It is perhaps not too surprising, then, that learning plays a relatively large role in the success of these generalist species. A highly instinct-dependent specialist species like the koala, with its sole diet of eucalyptus leaves, would probably have difficulty adjusting to the artificial environment of the lab.

The learning-dependent feeding strategy of rats and pigeons, however, makes these species entirely appropriate candidates for the

Rats live successfully in association with our species because of their nocturnal habits, generalist diet, and readiness to learn.

psychologists' efforts to understand general-process learning, the kind of plastic learning we see in ourselves. If there are basic learning rules (as there seem to be), they should be more conveniently discovered in lab animals than in humans. At the same time, the narrow focus on learning in two or three generalist species could blind us to any wider range of learning "styles" in animals. The inherent learning biases of rats and pigeons that are coming to light are strong evidence that much of what is critical in understanding animal cognition has been systematically overlooked.

The first widely recognized instance of a learning bias, discovered by John Garcia in the 1960s, involved food-avoidance conditioning, in which animals learn to shun food that has made them ill. The anomaly researchers noticed was that although hours could pass between a rat's ingestion of the toxic CS and the US, the consequent illness, learning still took place; in normal classical conditioning, the maximum CS–US interval is a few seconds at most. But in the context of food-avoidance learning, the longer association interval makes sense: poisons often take some time to act. (The exact delay in the onset of illness—the unconditioned stimulus that triggered the avoidance learning—was controlled in Garcia's later work by using a nontoxic CS for learning and then exposing the animals to X rays rather than poisoning the food to induce nausea.)

More significant than the anomaly in time course, however, was the observation that the rats learned food-avoidance only when the conditioning stimuli were either odor or taste; visual cues and sounds were ineffective. We know rats are *able* to sense sound and light, because they can be conditioned to them in other contexts. But as indicators of food quality, or even of the presence of food, these cues were virtually ignored. Shortly after Garcia's study was published, other groups of researchers reported that pigeons and other seed-eating birds could associate visual cues with food, but not odors or sounds. Another surprise was the finding that sound *is* effective in the same birds as a conditioning stimulus for the predator-avoidance response (in the laboratory, the "predator" is shock; the avoidance behavior is escape).

The common thread running through these biases in classical conditioning is that they correlate with the probabilistic contingencies of the prehuman environment in which rats and pigeons evolved. Rats are primarily nocturnal scavengers, rarely relying on visual or auditory cues to recognize food. The seeds pigeons eat, however, rarely have odors and never make sounds. An animal that ignores the extraneous sounds it may hear when it first encounters a novel food and focuses instead on the cues likely to be of some use—odor for rats, visual cues for pigeons—is an individual that will learn faster and more reliably. If this learning bias is genetically based, natural selection will favor such innate guidance of learning when there is a measure of predictability in the situation.

Another sign that classical conditioning involves less of an animal's rational faculties than we might have supposed becomes apparent when we look at blocking more closely. Recall that if a conditioning stimulus with two cues is used, both are learned: $CS_1 + CS_2 + US \rightarrow UR$; later the first conditioning stimulus produces the unconditioned response on its own, as does the second. On the other hand, when a single stimulus is conditioned first ($CS_1 + US \rightarrow UR$; then $CS_1 \rightarrow UR$), and a second cue is added later ($CS_1 + CS_2 \rightarrow UR$), the second is not learned: $CS_2 \rightarrow$ No Response. This makes no logical sense because CS_2 has full predictive value.

It turns out that when the strength of the UR can be precisely measured (the number of drops of saliva in the case of Pavlov's dog, for instance), we can see that the releasing power of either CS_1 or

When an animal is taught to respond to a single CS cue like light or a tone with the US, its performance rises steadily and then reaches a plateau. But when a second CS is added later (in this case, light, after the animal has already started to associate a tone with the US), normal learning of the new CS is blocked.

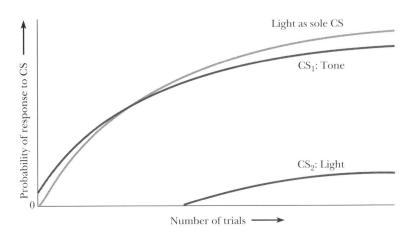

CS$_2$ in the joint-training scenario (CS$_1$ + CS$_2$ + US) is only about half the power of the two together. The algebra of classical conditioning can be described as CS$_{total}$ → 1.0 UR; in the case of joint conditioning, CS$_1$ → 0.5 UR and CS$_2$ → 0.5 UR, whereas if either stimulus had been the only cue, it would have had full (1.0) releasing value.

The real evidence that there is a mindless algebra at work here is provided by the results when an animal is conditioned to two cues separately: CS$_1$ + US → UR; later CS$_1$ → 1.0 UR; next CS$_2$ + US → UR; then CS$_2$ → 1.0 UR. Finally, we try the blocking in a different way by adding a new cue, CS$_3$: CS$_1$ + CS$_2$ + CS$_3$ → 1.0 UR. If the calculator of conditioning is so completely in control that the animal is unable to recognize a clear absurdity, it follows that if CS$_1$ → 1.0 UR and CS$_2$ → 1.0 UR *and* CS$_1$ + CS$_2$ + CS$_3$ → 1.0 UR, then CS$_3$, a perfectly good and highly predictive cue from our perspective, *must* have a value of −1.0 UR: 1.0 + 1.0 + (−1.0) = 1.0. Though hard to credit without demonstration, when this idea is put to the test by offering CS$_1$ *or* CS$_2$ with CS$_3$, the behavior is blocked: CS$_1$ + CS$_3$ → No Response (0.0 UR); 1.0 + (−1.0) = 0.0.

Of course it is not enough to look at only two species before generalizing about learning; it may be that context-specific cue biases and counterintuitive conditioning algebra are somehow artifacts of labs or lab animals. We will look in a moment for signs of analogous biases in less well controlled naturalistic situations. But for the present, however, if we worry that classical conditioning may turn out to require less cleverness than it had seemed—that animals come supplied with a kind of genetic crib sheet to focus their search for correlations, as well as a hard-wired internal calculator to work out the strength of positive and negative associations—it could be that the more active process of operant conditioning is a better place to search for a role of higher-level cognition, perhaps even thinking, in the process of learning.

BIASES IN TRIAL-AND-ERROR LEARNING

One of the first hints that even operant conditioning might have guiding biases came in the 1950s from attempts by Skinner's students Keller and Marian Breland to train a variety of nonlaboratory animals, including chickens, pigs, and raccoons, to perform in commercial displays. Shaping of behavior appeared to proceed normally, until suddenly the animal would introduce a spontaneous and undesirable behavior that, though unrewarded, not only persisted but actually came to dominate the creature's activity. When some pigs were shaped through food rewards to take coins and place them in a piggybank, all went well for a time—but eventually each pig would begin to "volunteer" behavior, dropping the coin and rooting around before putting it in the bank. The irrelevant behavior, which delayed the reward, became more and more common until the pigs became obsessed with rooting. Making the pigs hungrier only made matters worse: they spent all their time rooting around the coins, refusing to put any in the bank.

Close observation of this and other failures led the Brelands to the discovery that the "misbehavior" was invariably an innate behavior associated with the feeding repertoire of the species. When the process of conditioning, already linked in the animal's mind with food, strayed too close to this innate pathway, the behavior shifted more and more into instinctive channels, something like a river that breaches a levee and then scours the opening ever wider. As the Brelands put it in their amusing account of their failures, "[T]he Watsonian . . . may have some premonition that he will encounter his bête noir in extending the range of species and situations studied. We can assure him that his apprehensions are well grounded. In our attempt to extend a behavioristically oriented approach to the engineering control of animal behavior by operant conditioning techniques, we have fought a running battle with the seditious notion of instinct. . . . After 14 years of continuous conditioning and observation of thousands of animals, it is our reluctant conclusion that the behavior of any species cannot be adequately understood, predicted, or controlled without knowledge of its instinctive patterns, evolutionary history, and ecological niche."

Even casual observation cast doubt on the idea that the tasks typically used in lab situations—lever-pressing by rats and the pecking of

Through shaping, the dog in this scene from the silent movie *The Callahans and the Murphys* has been conditioned to cover its ears when the actress Sally O'Neil begins playing.

Pigeons pecking a key to obtain food strike with the kind of wide grasping peck used for seizing grain, complete with partial eye closure; when the reward is water the birds use a narrow drinking peck, followed by swallowing.

pigeons—are the novel and arbitrary behaviors operant theory labels them. This impression is strengthened by the discovery that pigeons that have been operantly conditioned to peck are employing unreinforced specializations: pecks at keys that are rewarded with food have a biting flourish typical of feeding, while pecks at keys that are rewarded with fluid are made with the tongue extended as for drinking. In short, there are spontaneous, innate components to the responses.

Lab animals volunteer a variety of other unrewarded behaviors. If pigeons in a cage are shown an illuminated key just before food is delivered nearby, they quickly pick up the classical association; the further, unexpected result is that they then begin to peck the key when the light behind it goes on, even though no pecking is required. This spontaneous appearance of pecking—evidence perhaps of an innate avian work ethic—is so strong that if the researcher alters the wiring of the apparatus so that pecking an illuminated key *blocks* the delivery of food, the pigeon will literally starve to death pecking the key that *prevents* feeding. It seems clear that pigeons associate pecking with feeding, and treat the keys in their experimental containers as extensions of the food, or perhaps as the shells that must be broken open to liberate the meal inside.

More telling still are the biases in motor-program learning. Rats are readily taught to press a lever for a food reward, but if pressing the lever is the behavior to be shaped so that the rat can avoid a shock, the same manoeuver becomes exceedingly difficult to condition; on the other hand, rats are easily taught to jump to avoid shock, but jumping to obtain food is almost impossible to teach. Pigeons show a similar set of behavioral prejudices: they will peck to get food but not to avoid shock; they will learn to hop on a treadle to avoid shock but not to obtain food.

Just as we saw with biases in classical conditioning, these predispositions match the realities of nature: rats generally feed by manipulating food with their forepaws, while they escape through gross motor movements like hopping and leaping, which primarily depend on the powerful rear limbs. Pigeons normally feed with the beak rather than with the feet, but escape from danger by running or (if necessary) flying.

The biases make sense, and individuals with predispositions to experiment in a specific context with the correct body parts, even at the expense of slighting less plausible but possibly useful behaviors—like striking food with the tail—are likely to solve the problem sooner and more reliably, and thus be favored by natural selection. In short, operant biases are adaptive when the situation has a certain minimum degree of predictability, and the evolution of such motor prejudices should not, in retrospect, be surprising.

INNATELY GUIDED LEARNING

The pattern of helpful innate biases in learning is not restricted to laboratory animals; in fact, it is far more evident in creatures studied in the wild. To the extent that predictability is a useful index, we would expect generalist species to show the fewest and weakest learning biases. On the other hand, species that depend on a single food-gathering behavior should typically demonstrate little or no learning: where the behavioral routine is unvaried and there is nothing to be learned, wasting time acquiring useless information would put an individual at a competitive disadvantage. It is in the middle range of moderate generalists, for whom the world is more or less predictably unpredictable, that the maximum degree of learning predisposition ought to be (and generally is) observed.

One such case is seen in the way birds learn to recognize an enemy. Nesting birds routinely mob predators such as owls, crows, and

cats. Mobbing behavior includes a series of short scolding "chats" (with easily localized wide-band frequencies) combined with physical group attacks on the trespassing predator. The sight of myriad small birds in spring attacking a flying crow several times their size is familiar to many of us.

How do birds come to know which predators to mob and which to ignore? They are not born with a mental field guide to dangerous species: birds on islands show no fear of newly introduced species, as Darwin saw when he discovered that the finches on the uninhabited

Bird-catchers exploited the automatic mobbing of owls by nesting songbirds to capture birds for later sale. The tethered trained owl attracted the birds, which, when they tired from their mobbing, alighted on the perches nearby. A sticky substance on the perches entangled the birds' feet, causing many to tumble to the ground.

Curio's experiment used a rotating box to show different stimuli to two cages of birds. The bird on the right was taught to mob a stuffed nectar guide by hearing another bird producing the mobbing call in response to a stuffed owl. Later it taught the bird on the left to mob nectar guides.

islands of the Galápagos group were virtually tame, while finches elsewhere show a wise fear of humans. Nor do birds have the leisure to learn by direct personal experience, losing one brood to crows, the next to an owl, and so on until the full scope of the danger is evident.

Instead, young birds learn to recognize their local cast of predators by a simple adaptation of classical conditioning. Laboratory tests devised by Eberhard Curio in 1978 showed that the older generation teaches the younger birds via the mobbing call. The experiments that elucidated this process used a rotating box in one compartment of which was a stuffed owl (recognized by the birds as a predator) while another held a model of a nectar-feeding species native to another continent and never before seen by the birds used in the test. The owl was shown to one cage of birds, the nectar-feeder to a second cage. When the birds exposed to the owl began to utter the mobbing cry at the owl on their side of the rotating box, the birds in the second cage, unaware of the owl the others were seeing, joined in and attempted to mob the nectar-feeder *they* saw.

If the nectar-feeding bird is withdrawn and presented again later, the "learners," none of whom has ever suffered at the hands of that species, will mob it instantly and pass the aversion to other birds. So mindless is this programmed mechanism for conveying cultural prejudices that the experimenter was able to substitute a bottle of laundry detergent, which was duly added to the select enemies list and became an object of official hatred. In the enemy-learning program, the sound of the mobbing call is the US, which specifies the context; the object being mobbed is the CS, and both mobbing and memorization of the appearance of the object being fended off are the unconditioned responses.

In a sense, then, this kind of programmed learning is more like calibration than anything we might call flexible or plastic learning. This pattern is particularly evident in honey bees, which, because of their commercial importance and experimental convenience, have been studied far more than any other insect. Honey bees make their living by collecting nectar and pollen from flowers. They maximize their harvesting efficiency by specializing on one species at a time, learning to recognize the blossom and extract the food with a minimum of uncertainty and delay.

Once a forager bee has found a blossom that provides food (the US), she begins to learn enough to recognize it. But the learning (the UR) is highly specialized and seems to violate several rules of classical conditioning. For instance, different naturalistic conditioning stimuli, though present simultaneously, are learned at different rates: bees learn odor quickly, shape slowly, and color at an intermediate rate. These differences in rate correlate with the reliability of each cue in nature. Odor is highly species specific, while flower color among even uncultivated species can vary somewhat from plant to plant (or even from blossom to blossom on a single plant), and the perceived shape varies enormously with the bee's angle of approach.

Even for a single class of cue, there are biases: complex shapes are learned faster than simple ones, a memory of violet is acquired more rapidly than green, and floral odors are picked up faster than nonfloral scents. Despite these biases, any color, odor, or shape is, in the end, learned equally well after enough visits.

Recognizing the enemy, as drawn by Konrad Lorenz.

Honey bees learn the odor of a flower much faster than its shape. The color is learned at an intermediate rate.

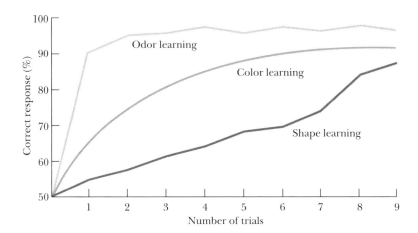

Foragers also use trial-and-error learning: they discover the optimal harvesting procedure for the kind of blossom on which they are specializing by experimenting with different approaches. But unlike most animals, they can remember the "operant" only during the part of the day it was learned and used. Indeed, all the information about a flower is time linked. This makes good sense for bees, since flowers of a given species all produce nectar at about the same time each day, a trick that concentrates foraging on a particular species into a narrow time window and thus increases the probability of cross-pollination even by very forgetful insects like butterflies.

Bees accommodate this strategy by remembering all the details of one food source at one time of day, specializing on it as long as the species blooms, then learning about and specializing on other species that bloom at other times of day. Their memory is organized like an appointment book, with each floral rendezvous entered on a separate line.

The flower-learning program of bees seems well tuned to the realities of the floral market they must exploit. Bees have sensible relative learning rates calibrated to the reliability of the cues involved, and they store the information in a highly useful way. None of this need be worked out by trial and error. Moreover, in the context of flower learning bees are blind to stimuli they readily perceive and learn in other situations where they are relevant. For instance, they are exquisitely sensitive to polarized light, but refuse to learn it as a floral CS even if it is the only stimulus available; in nature, of course, flowers do not provide polarization cues.

Clearly, a forager programmed in this way will forage more efficiently than one that had to slowly work out the same optimal strategy on its own. The situation is predictably unpredictable: flowers come in a variety of shapes and colors, offer a range of odors, and provide nectar at differing times of day. Odor, however, is a uniformly good guide, nectar is produced in a twenty-four–hour cycle, and polarized light is never useful in identifying flowers. Thus a learning program can capitalize on these regularities and guide a bee to "calibrate" itself to individual species of flowers by, in effect, entering data into lines on a preprinted questionnaire.

LATENT LEARNING

Classical and operant conditioning do not offer evidence for higher mental processes in animals: the ability to learn per se is not enough

Latent learning was first demonstrated when a rat was observed to formulate its behavior based on previous but unrelated experiences: exploration of a two-arm maze on one day and being shocked in another room the next. When on the third day the rat was returned to the maze and released, it put the two experiences together to plan a safe route.

Day 1   Day 2   Day 3

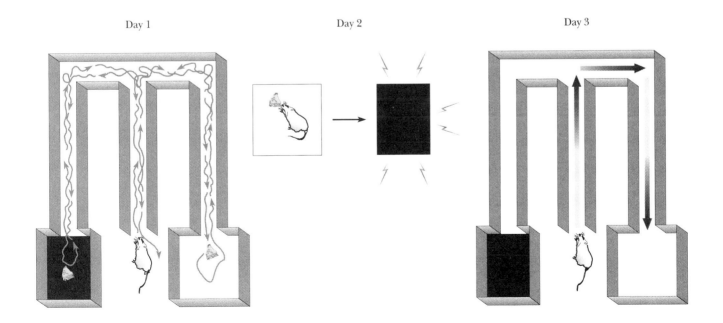

E. C. Tolman (1886–1959) was the first researcher to prove that rats can plan novel behavior.

to infer any sort of comprehension, even in the most elaborately trained dressage horses, talking parrots, performing dolphins, and sheep-herding dogs. But though the discovery of biases and anomalies has undercut the initial assessment of the mental capacity of many animals, one anomaly in operant conditioning does just the opposite: it demonstrates that even lab animals can exceed the expectations of those who study them.

The accepted wisdom of operant learning maintained that animals learn novel behavior by goal-directed trial and error. Consider, however, the following observation, first reported in 1948. A researcher allows a rat to explore a two-arm maze, each end of which terminates in an enclosed box with a small amount of food. The box at the right end, not visible until the last turn in that arm of the maze has been negotiated, is wide and painted white inside; the box at the left end, similarly out of view until the rat is near it, is narrow and painted black inside. (All things being equal, rats prefer to be in a narrow, dark space.) The experience with the maze offers no differential rewards: both ends are equally rewarding.

On the next day the same rat is taken into another room and placed into a wide, white box with a small amount of food; when the animal has consumed its meal, it is placed into a narrow, black box and shocked. The animal is then taken back to its cage. This experience requires no learning and conditions no operant; nevertheless, it is possible that the rat may have formed some slight classical association between the box (a potential CS) and the food, though such one-trial learning is exceedingly rare.

On the following day, the same rat is taken back to the maze and released. If the rat learned anything during its previous exploration of the apparatus it might be that the left arm leads to the innately preferred conditions of narrowness and blackness. What actually happens, however, is that the rat navigates directly to the wide, white box at the right end of the maze.

A variety of well-controlled tests along similar lines have revealed a phenomenon often called latent learning: the rat has taken independent experiences, separated in time and space as well as by context, and integrated two or more items of apparently irrelevant information to create what seems to be an expectation that there will be food at the right-hand end of the maze. This behavior, which is not predicted (and cannot be explained) by either classical or operant theory, suggests that at least some animals may be able to plan behavior in advance.

The discoverer of the phenomenon, E. C. Tolman, was widely ridiculed at the time, and his many experiments were studiously ignored for two decades. Tolman called the mental processing that must underlie this supposed ability a "cognitive map," a term that is now very much in vogue in psychology. It is the apparent ability of certain animals to plan that offers the most tantalizing hint so far that at least some creatures have mental abilities beyond those of a self-calibrating computer program.

 # Insight or Instinct?

NATURE NEVER DECEIVES US;

IT IS WE WHO DECEIVE OURSELVES.

Jean-Jacques Rousseau
Émile, 1762

uman intuition and introspection can be treacherous guides to assessing the cognitive components of animal behavior. Our increased understanding of the neural and genetic bases of behavior reveals that what looks clever can be entirely innate. Behavior that seems inexplicable may be relying on cues invisible to our species, or processing that we lack, or stimulus selectivity wholly different from our own. What apparently is learned may instead be the emergence of a latent but instinctive behavior; what certainly is learned may have been acquired automatically through the use of an innate neural checklist and be governed by an algebra of conditioning that can lead to absurd behavior under experimental conditions.

While innate processing, instinctive behavior, internally orchestrated motivation and drive, and innately guided learning are all essential and important elements of an animal's cognitive repertoire, they are not likely to be part of that more esoteric realm of mental activity that we associate with thinking, judgment, and decision-making. But what is thought, and how are we to recognize its operation in other creatures within that most private of organs, the brain? What behavioral criteria can permit us to distinguish between the true thought that we are wont to believe goes into our own aesthetic, moral, and practical decision-making on the one hand, and thc intricate programming that can create the illusion of thought in at least certain

HOODED MONKEYS SOLVE THE NOVEL PROBLEM OF

EXTRACTING YOGURT FROM A NARROW PLASTIC

TUBE BY MAKING SPOONS FROM BAMBOO SHOOTS.

other animals? Or could it be, as advocates of artificial intelligence suspect, that *all* thought, including ours, is just the consequence of clever programming?

WHAT CRITERIA ARE USEFUL?

"Thought," according to dictionaries, implies the mental formation of an idea, insight, or intention, or the mental activity involved in weighing, considering, pondering, reflecting, remembering, imagining, planning, creating, anticipating, and reasoning—in short, nearly the entire gamut of conscious human mental activity. The issue we face is how we can reasonably infer in an animal the presence of any of the mental processes generally associated with thinking and, by extension, the presence of some degree of consciousness.

Common to all the aspects of thought listed above is the implication of a substantial degree of flexibility and creativity, an ability to slip the bonds of instinct and generate novel solutions to problems. For experimenters or observers seeking to design a test or interpret an episode recorded in the field, a full appreciation of both the power of innate programming and a species' natural history is essential. An ideal experiment would present an animal with a problem it is so unlikely to have faced in nature that a prewired solution will not have evolved. Alternatively, the experiment would offer a relatively commonplace problem for which, in the particular conditions of the trial, the routine solution will not work. In either case, the creature must then draw upon whatever other intellectual resources it may possess, such as the ability to associate two separate memories.

Our goal in this chapter is to examine a few well-known cases of behavior that appear to fit one or more of the accepted definitions of thinking. Most of these examples involve what Lorenz called "natural experiments"—accidental concatenations of events that reveal something previously unknown about the animals involved. Historically, field observations have provided the richest source of inspiration for well-controlled tests, and the modern effort to study the animal mind is recent enough still to depend heavily on chance observations. We will look closely at each of these examples, some of which turn out to be red herrings, to see what the possible pitfalls and ambiguities of interpretation can be. Armed with this cautionary knowledge, we will devote most of the rest of the book to a systematic look at the workings of the animal mind in a series of behavioral contexts.

THE FALLACY OF FLEXIBILITY

Alfalfa is a popular forage crop in North America, where for 200 years it was pollinated by the native bumble bees living in the hedgerows or forest edges that bordered each field. Modern farming methods, however, have cleared the wooded land and plowed the hedgerows under to create vast fields of single crops. Their habitat destroyed, the bumble bees have been replaced with honey bees, which can be moved from field to endless field on flatbed trucks. Alfalfa blossoms, however, have spring-loaded anthers designed to flick pollen up onto the underside of nectar-seeking bees. Although well designed for the larger bumble bee, the anther delivers a jarring blow to the more delicate (and now far more numerous) honey bee foragers; in some cases the anther can even trap the honey bee briefly. Some honey bees simply avoid alfalfa after one or two unpleasant encounters, but if there

Honey bees in many agricultural areas fight an ongoing battle with alfalfa blossoms. Since most foragers learn to avoid alfalfa or rob it from the side, another species must be brought in to pollinate this important crop.

is nothing else to forage for miles in every direction, others learn to recognize tripped from untripped blossoms and avoid the ones that can fight back. Still others cheat the system by forcing their tongues in from the side to remove the nectar in safety. Are the foragers acting with insight or from instinct?

Alone, adaptability in a behavior is not a reliable guide to judging whether the action is an instinctive response or a creation of the animal's own mind: most innate motor programs include provisions for modifications to deal with less predictable contingencies of the routine situations they are designed to handle. But these foragers, like certain other animals, seem able to take their behavior into their own hands, employing an unusual strategy to deal with a common problem. If there is an innate species-specific solution for harvesting blossoms, the existence of one or more alternatives to the stereotyped conventional strategy of flying directly into the blossom could provide evidence for insight, planning, or some other sort of creative thinking on the part of the behavioral iconoclasts.

The problem with this criterion is that the behavioral alternatives observed in some species are themselves innate. Bees, for instance, will chew through the side of any flower whose nectar is too deep for their tongues to reach. The logic behind the choice of one such behavior over another is called frequency-dependent selection, biological jargon for the commonplace real-world observation that the payoff for doing something often depends on how many opportunities exist for that approach relative to another or, when there is direct competition for resources, how many others are doing the same thing rather than something else. In our lives we see this tradeoff in the job market, where salaries tend to be higher for occupations in which there are more vacancies than applicants.

The asymmetry in payoffs for different skills affects recruitment into the specialties involved. When the time course of recruitment and training is long, alternating cycles of excess and shortfall (whether of jobs or behavior) can be generated; when the latency period is short, as in the choice of which supermarket checkout line to join, the distribution of individuals opting for the various alternatives tends to even out fairly promptly. Honey bee foragers, for instance, respond relatively quickly to the ratio of tripped to untripped blossoms: a preponderance of untripped flowers, for instance, favors bees that opt for robbing alfalfa.

Examples of innate alternative techniques abound in nature. Until recently, for instance, researchers assumed that all male crickets sing; how otherwise could they hope to find mates? But singing is not without its costs: it is energetically expensive, and it attracts predators and parasites—especially parasitic flies that home in and drop larvae on singing males; the larvae burrow into the male and feed on his tissues, eventually killing him.

As an alternative to this high-risk approach, some males behave as "satellites": they wait mutely near a singing male and attempt to intercept and court incoming females. These males have a lower success rate, but the overall long-term payoff for high-cost/high-reward singers and low-cost/low-reward satellites is equal, because the silent types live longer. The proper numerical balance between singers and satellites that leads to equal payoffs is achieved because individual males are able to measure the relevant variables (number of males already singing, their own ability to produce a competitive call—one that is sufficiently loud and is repeated sufficiently often—and so on) and act accordingly. These orthopteran cost/benefit analyses are reviewed periodically by the crickets involved: if a singing male is removed, there is a good chance a nearby satellite will begin calling.

Hangingfly males have similar options, in their case three of them. Males capture flies and then release a pheromone to attract females. An arriving female evaluates the prey while the male attempts to begin copulating with her. Once she is satisfied that the prey is worth consuming, she allows the male to begin transferring sperm. When she finishes consuming the gift, she departs: thus the amount of sperm transferred—and so the number of eggs a male will father—is proportional to the size of the meal he provides.

Flies are notoriously hard to catch, and a male hangingfly must feed himself as well as any potential mates. Some males play it straight, consuming some prey and offering other captured flies as courtship meals. Ethologists were surprised to discover, however, that other males attempt to pass off prey they have already sucked dry as satisfactory nuptial gifts; this is one reason females are so coy.

Another strategy available to males is female impersonation. The impersonator approaches a male that is offering a gift, pretends to examine the present while the conventional male fumbles around trying to match his abdominal claspers to the corresponding (but, given the object of his attentions is another male, missing) morphological appurtenances found on a female; then the impersonator attempts to wrest the prey from the courting male. The decision whether to cheat or adopt the conventional strategy depends on the cost in time and effort of catching a meal and the relative size of the male. Naturally,

Mute satellite males surround a large calling bullfrog and attempt to intercept females attracted by his costly acoustic display.

the chance of successful theft is greatly increased if the impersonator is substantially larger than his intended victim.

Bluegill sunfish males have four size-dependent strategies for mating. "Conventional" males build nests and court females in an attempt to collect several clutches of eggs, and then guard and care for the eggs. Large "pirates" temporarily take over a nest that already has some fertilized eggs, mate with additional females, and then return the nest to the original owner, who will then care for the pirate's eggs along with his own. The female impersonators in this species are small and can insinuate themselves between a courting pair and shed sperm when the two conventional fish begin releasing their eggs and sperm into the nest. Tiny "sneakers" dart into nests and quickly unload sperm while the courting pair is depositing their gametes. Of course, the distinction between large, average, small, and tiny depends on the local size distribution of males: a pirate in a pond of young bluegills might, in another body of water dominated by large older males, be best off using the impersonator strategy.

These examples make the point that animals can be—and in fact often are—programmed to play the odds, employing one of several possible strategies as appropriate to maximize their harvesting efficiency or reproductive output in the particular set of circumstances in which they find themselves. Since flexibility can be genetic, only a thorough knowledge of a species' natural history can allow us to judge whether a "novel" solution to a problem is truly novel or is a rarely used (or rarely observed) backup strategy. Even in the cases we have mentioned, however, it could be that one or more of the species actually do consider their innate alternatives and make wise decisions between them. However, there is no a priori reason to assume that conscious choice is necessarily involved, and no obvious way to distinguish thinking from programming in these particular cases. In later chapters we will encounter examples for which a stronger argument can be made that thought plays a part in deciding between alternative prewired responses.

THE BLUE TITS AND THE MILK BOTTLES

Even a clearly novel behavior may not necessarily involve creativity, insight, or planning. One of the best-known—and often misinterpreted—illustrations is the battle between birds and milk-delivery companies in Britain that began in the 1930s. Most of us are now used

Blue tits rob foil-topped milk bottles by peeling back the caps.

to buying homogenized milk in grocery stores, but not long ago milk was (as it still is in some places) delivered to the doorstep each morning in glass bottles. The milk was not homogenized, and so the milk-fat tended to separate, the cream rising to the top.

Customers in one locality began to complain that the cardboard lids on their milk had been removed and the cream skimmed off by the time they collected their bottles in the morning. The complaints came from more and more patrons, spreading relentlessly outward from the region of the first reports. The culprits were discovered: they were blue tits, a relative of the chickadee. The robbing behavior, which had spread from town to town, involved simply peeling off the lid. Foil caps were substituted, but soon they too were being removed. The practice spread to a second species of tit and, according to one report, to the Continent. Milk suppliers, working little faster than natural selection itself, finally put an end to the practice in the late 1940s by adopting different carton designs, placing the bottles into milk boxes by the customers' doors, or devising one or another of several other technological responses.

A common reading of this story is that the birds, exercising a combination of insight and planning, saw an opportunity and exploited it. But a look at the natural history of the species suggests another explanation. Tits make their living searching for insects in vegetation and on trees. Part of their behavioral repertoire is pulling back bark to look for insect larvae, and so ingrained is this behavior that hand-reared blue tits kept as pets will compulsively peel the wallpaper from the walls of their foster homes, without any reward.

Thus for blue tits the practice of peeling to obtain food is a prominent component of their innate behavior. It seems more likely, therefore, that some weary blue tit, moving from tree to tree in search of food, landed in the dawn hours on one of the thousands of milk bottles to be found in British towns and villages and, while resting, reflexively peeled the top. Investigating what it had uncovered, it found the "prey" and began to forage in this highly efficient and relatively undemanding way. In short, like many great ideas, the original step was probably an accident.

As anyone who has kept a bird feeder knows, birds are quick to investigate the sites being frequented by other foraging birds. A hungry tit spotting another feeding on a doorstep could easily have been attracted and, having landed on another bottle, might be expected to try its foraging techniques on it. Of course, the spread of cream-robbing *could* have involved a series of avian inspirations, each bird seeing the opportunity independently and devising a plan for taking advantage of the situation; but as evidence for thought in tits, the case is equivocal at best.

The caution of this story is clear: just as we saw with learning, it is essential to know the natural history of a species before evaluating the cognitive basis of its behavioral accomplishments.

KÖHLER'S CHIMPS

Wolfgang Köhler, a psychologist trained at the University of Berlin, was working at a primate research facility maintained by the Prussian Academy of Sciences on Tenerife in the Canary Islands when the First World War broke out. Marooned there, he had at his disposal a large outdoor pen and nine chimpanzees of various ages. The pen, described by Köhler as a playground, was provided with a variety of objects—"toys"—including boxes, poles, and sticks, with which the primates could experiment.

Wolfgang Köhler (1887–1967), in a photograph taken about thirty years after his pioneering work on problem-solving by chimpanzees.

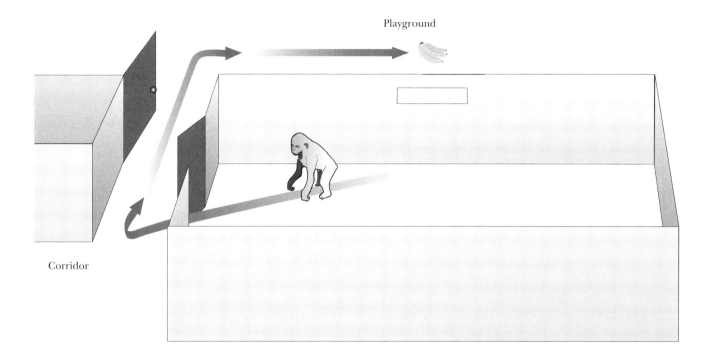

Playground

Corridor

Köhler set the chimps a variety of problems, each of which involved obtaining food that was not directly accessible. In the simplest, food was put on the other side of a barrier. Dogs and cats in previous experiments faced with such a problem found it difficult to break off visual contact with the food in order to reach it, or to move away from the goal to circumvent the barrier. The chimps, on the other hand, presented with an apparently analogous situation, set off immediately on the circuitous route to the food.

But it turns out that the other animals that had apparently failed this same test were not so stupid after all. The earlier experiments that psychologists had run on dogs and cats differed from Köhler's on chimps in two important ways: first, the barriers were not familiar to the pets, and thus there was no opportunity for using any latent learning, whereas the chimps were well acquainted with the rooms used in Köhler's tests. And second, whereas the food remained visible in the dog and cat experiments, in the chimp test the food was tossed out the window (after which the window was shut) and fell out of sight. Indeed, when Köhler tried the same test on a dog familiar with the

Köhler discovered that chimpanzees readily find indirect routes to goals when necessary. In this experiment Köhler tossed bananas out a window and then closed it.

room, the animal (after proving to itself that the window was shut), took the shortest of the possible indirect routes to the unseen food.

In fact, the ability to select an indirect (or even novel) route to a goal is not restricted to rats, chimps, and dogs; at least some insects routinely perform similar feats. What possessing this ability actually says about the underlying cognitive processing will become clearer when we look at navigation by chimps in a later chapter. For now, the point is that the chimpanzees' abilities to plan routes are not as special as they looked at the time.

Some of the other tests Köhler is justly famous for are preserved on film. In a typical sequence, a chimp jumps fruitlessly at bananas that have been hung out of reach. Usually after a period of unsuccessful jumping the chimp apparently becomes angry or frustrated,

Sultan, one of Köhler's chimps, fits two sticks together to create a tool long enough to reach food on the other side of the fence.

walks away in seeming disgust, pauses, then looks at the food in what might be a more reflective way, then at the toys in the enclosure, then back at the food, and then at the toys again. Finally the animal begins to use the toys to get at the food.

The details of the chimps' solutions to the food-gathering puzzle varied. One chimp tried to shinny up a toppling pole it had poised under the bananas; several succeeded by stacking crates underneath, but were hampered by difficulties in getting the centers of gravity right. Another chimp had good luck moving a crate under the bananas and using a pole to knock them down. The theme common to each of these attempts is that to all appearances the chimps were solving the problem by a kind of cognitive trial and error, as if they were experimenting in their minds before manipulating the tools. The pattern of these behaviors—failure, pause, looking at the potential tools, and then the attempt—would seem to involve insight and planning, at least on the first occasion.

But there is more to the story. First, Köhler's films are of chimpanzees that had repeatedly approached the problems in question; their successes, such as they were, were achieved slowly. The crate-stacking behavior, after nearly three years of practice, remains laughably inept: the animals still try to balance on a corner, or even position the crates so that the open end faces up, which makes it difficult either to stack additional crates or find stable footing on the existing pile.

Later studies, notably Paul Schiller's attempt to reproduce Köhler's work in the late 1940s, demonstrated that experience playing with the toys that later become tools was essential to eventual success. He noted that if provided with sticks, chimps poke and swing at almost anything (and frequently at nothing at all), and try to connect them into pairs with no reward in sight. Chimps love to climb on crates to provide an elevated stage for swinging sticks, and to stack crates for the apparent fun of it. Schiller reported that each tower-building chimp "climbed on the tower jumping upward from the top repeatedly with arms lifted above the head and stretched toward the ceiling. For the human observer it was hard to believe that there was no food above them to be reached. Needless to say, none of these animals had ever been tested in box-stacking problem situations."

Beyond the by now familiar lesson that the cognitive underpinnings of a behavior often seem to weaken as we learn more about the natural behavior of a species, there is the further complication that the "operant" may actually be constructed of innate motor programs

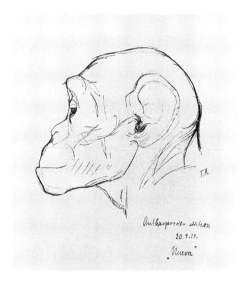

Nueva, a good-natured but obstinate member of Köhler's band of chimps, in a drawing made five days before her death.

One of the methods invented by Köhler's chimps for reaching bananas that were hung out of reach involved stacking crates beneath them.

linked together in just the $UR \rightarrow UR \rightarrow UR \rightarrow UR \rightarrow UR$ sequence hypothesized by Watson. The discovery that typical laboratory operants are actually either innate gestures or at least innately constrained (as in the pecking styles of pigeons) should already have sown the seeds of doubt. Chimpanzees may indeed have insight (and we will look at better-controlled experiments in later chapters); indeed, having the wit to realize that something done in play—as one of many possible behavioral sequences, explored apparently just for the fun of it—might solve a novel problem probably *does* qualify as insight. Of course it represents a low-level, everyday sort of insight, and if we take a hard line and require complete, from-the-ground-up novelty before conceding conscious inspiration, then Köhler's pioneering work, though charming to read and watch, does not provide much unambiguous evidence one way or the other. But by that standard few humans would get passing marks for cognitive prowess.

WASHING POTATOES AND RINSING WHEAT

One possible way around the difficulty of interpreting cases that seem to involve thought is to look for situations wholly beyond the range of situations for which natural selection could plausibly have provided useful contingency plans—in short, completely novel situations with no natural analogues. A unique problem, requiring a novel and unprecedented solution, might be expected to preclude any ambiguity presented by the possibility of innate behavior.

One of the most intriguing cases of apparent insight and innovation involves a troop of macaques living on the Japanese island of Koshima. This well-studied group is part of an island preserve and is kept well provisioned with a variety of foods, including sweet potatoes and wheat, which are simply dumped on a beach. An unfortunate consequence of this practice is that the food often becomes partially coated with sand. As most of us know from personal experience, it is almost impossible to remove damp sand completely from food or hands by brushing it off.

About 1953 scientists observed that one young macaque (known to them as Imo) would carry her potato to the water's edge and rinse it. In time this habit spread to her playmates, then to all the young macaques, then to the older females, and finally to the dominant males of the troop. Most researchers assume that the practice was picked up by the other macaques through cultural learning; however, a few

A low-ranking female macaque was the first member of her troop to discover how to remove the sand from sweet potatoes.

suggest that the spread was so slow that potato-washing must have been discovered independently several times: of the roughly 60 members of the troop, only 11 were rinsing potatoes after three years; after six years the number reached 17; after nine years a majority—36—had picked up the technique.

In 1959, Imo began dropping handfuls of wheat in the water, recovering the floating grain after the sand had sunk to the bottom. This practice spread through the troop in a similar pattern, the oldest males either the last to learn of it, the slowest to be willing to try something new, or the least likely to experiment and discover an alternative technique. After six years, 19 of the macaques were rinsing wheat.

There is nothing known in the natural repertoire of Japanese macaques similar to the sand-separation behavior, and none of the researchers is aware of having seen Imo develop the behavior. As a very low ranking female, she may well have seized a potato and fled to a protected spot to eat it. She may have retreated into the water, perhaps dropping the potato in flight or plunging it under the surface to conceal it; alternatively, she may have noticed previously that water removed the sand from her hand and deliberately tried the same trick on her potato. The last possibility, obviously, would reflect insight and planning.

The accident-based scenarios are less easily interpreted. A classical Behavioristic psychologist would have little difficulty accounting for the action through association and operant conditioning. The spread of food-washing through the troop is unsurprising, given the proclivity of primates to imitate: "monkey see, monkey do" is as true as it is trite. The independent-discovery hypothesis seems less plausible—after all, the macaques have had decades to discover that water removes sand. The self-conditioning model also seems strained: against all odds, the pioneer in potato-washing was the same macaque that initiated the wheat-rinsing revolution.

The most significant lesson Imo may be teaching us is the importance of observing the development of a behavior. As we will see in later chapters, the steps by which a novel behavior is acquired can supply powerful evidence about the cognitive manoeuvers that led to it.

THE FINER THINGS: TOOLS AND AESTHETICS

For decades the received wisdom was that only humans use tools (or, more cautiously, that only our species *makes* tools). Tool-use was said to require thought—insight, intention, planning, and so on. But such assertions depend critically on an ignorance of animal behavior. Even 120 years ago, when Darwin took up the issue, he could report in *The Descent of Man*, "It has often been said that no animal uses any tool; but the chimpanzee in a state of nature cracks a native fruit, somewhat like a walnut, with a stone. . . . and I have myself seen a young orang put a stick into a crevice, slip his hand to the other end, and use it in the proper manner as a lever." Indeed, some animals select absorbent bits of wood or other vegetation to soak up liquid food, then transport this ad hoc sponge home, a stratagem that increases their foraging efficiency by up to a factor of ten. Another species uses stones as tools to tamp down earth in an effort to conceal where it has been digging, then discards the stone, preventing it from serving as a signal that could attract parasites and predators. These two examples undercut the only-humans-use-tools argument with particular force because they involve mere insects—ants and wasps, respectively.

An example of tool use: opening nuts, chimpanzee style.

Some digger wasps use pebbles as tools to tamp down soil to seal their burrows; others close off the burrow by wedging a stone in the entrance.

Retreating from tool-using to the tool-making threshold is not much help either. One of the Darwin's finches on the Galápagos commonly modifies a cactus spine before using it to probe in holes for insect larvae; the behavior appears to be instinctive. The widely cited use of carefully chosen and highly modified sticks or long, stiff grass blades by chimpanzees in the process of fishing termites out of mounds looks both clever and cultural; photographs show young chimps sitting studiously by, apparently learning the finer points of the technique. But as many observers have noted, chimpanzees have a special fondness for sticks and whiplike pieces of grass, and routinely modify them—stripping the sticks of their leaves, for example—for no obvious reason, just as many humans pass the time whittling. And captive-born and lab-raised chimps, with no experience of termite mounds, spontaneously poke long, narrow objects such as pencils into holes—electrical outlets, for instance. Again, all the elements of this tool use seem prewired, and it is hard to see how thought would be necessary to termite-fishing, though it would probably help and could well be playing a role. Nevertheless, the behavior is readily accounted for by conventional conditioning, in which individuals learn by trial-and-error experience.

One of the most spectacular examples of animals that selectively gather and modify objects for use is the group of bowerbirds native to Australia and New Guinea. Males build species-specific bowers, some so elaborate they were taken by early explorers for pygmy huts. The birds gather and arrange colorful objects, both natural and artificial, with every semblance of care and attention to detail. Some of the objects are modified, others are held in the beak and used as signalling flags by the male in courtship. The males even gather berries of a particular color and use them to paint the inside of the bower or, in other species, mix saliva with burnt wood or charcoal to produce a gummy black plaster with which they decorate and reinforce the interior of the bower.

The bower is simply a stage; the female compares bowers, observes courtship displays, and then mates with one of the males. She leaves to build a nest on her own, and then takes care of her eggs and offspring as a single parent. Some scientists from Darwin on have supposed that beyond the use of objects as communicative tools, the attraction of bowers to females reveals an aesthetic sense not unlike our own; an aesthetic, it can be argued, implies a mind and taste and judgment. But by itself this argument is unconvincing. One of the central lessons of ethology is that beauty is in the eye and brain and feature detectors of the beholding species: an attractive cricket or toad or fish or bird or antelope depends, as it must, on species-specific criteria that aid the individuals involved in choosing not only a reproductively ready member of the opposite sex of the correct species, but in many cases the best of the available lot.

If butterfly wings, peacock tails, and bowerbird stages appeal to the human aesthetic sense more than do tarantula legs, vulture plumage, and weaverbird nests, does this mean that butterflies have more on the ball mentally than vultures? We must keep in mind that the adornments of bowerbird stages are of species-specific colors and arranged in species-specific ways; they allure only females of the appropriate species, and this before the male ever begins his own species-specific performance.

That some bowers are more elaborately decorated than others need not reflect the more highly developed aesthetic taste of certain males; in fact, it correlates almost precisely with dominance. The

The woodpecker finch of the Galápagos uses a twig or cactus spine to fish insect larvae from trees.

builders of these bowers are the males that can raid the edifice of each neighboring male, spoil his construction, and pilfer the best decorations. We are still, of course, left with the question of how the bird judges "best." We will return to this remarkable behavior in a later chapter, and look more closely at the ontogeny of bower-building and individual differences in an effort to discover if they provide a role for culture and creativity.

INSTINCT AND THOUGHT

Our goal in this chapter has been to show how careful we must be in inferring a role for thought in animal behavior. At the same time, though these cautionary tales suggest that it may be difficult or impossible to analyze the cognitive bases of many natural behaviors precisely, they suggest what to look for and in many cases allow us to judge probabilities if not absolute certainties.

There is another point to keep in mind. Donald Griffin has astutely observed that there is no reason to rule out thought absolutely when an animal is performing an innate behavior. Although it may seem implausible that a goose rolling a nonexistent egg is wondering why she is compelled to complete such a pointless behavior, it is always possible that she is actually perplexed, or even laughing at herself. After all, humans think while performing a variety of innate acts—coughing, swallowing, breathing, maintaining balance, making love.

Moreover, it is possible to spend the time performing an innate gesture wondering why we cannot readily stop ourselves. Consider our largely vain attempts to stifle sneezing, vomiting, hiccuping, blushing, smiling in embarassment, weeping at the movies (where the stimuli are illusions at every level), or experiencing one of several sorts of emotional arousal produced by a two-dimensional arrangement of tiny dots printed on a piece of paper.

In short, innate responses do not necessarily preclude thought; and given that actors can create innate emotional displays through force of conscious mental will, these elements of our instinctive repertoire can even be triggered by thought. Anyone can decide to initiate the coughing or swallowing program without needing the sign stimuli that trigger it automatically and, as we will see in a later chapter, the range of innate motor programs we regularly use in our consciously directed behavior is vastly more extensive than almost anyone real-

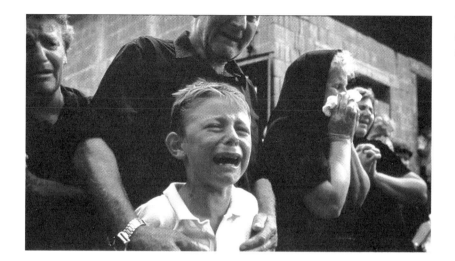

The facial gestures associated with emotional states are innately produced, and yet are connected to conscious thought and experience.

izes. Perhaps animals too can consciously weigh which innate behavioral unit to bring to bear in a difficult situation.

Thus the relationship between instinct and thought is not always either/or, at least for human animals. For the most part we will take evidence of innate elements in a behavior as a sign that higher cognitive processing is not necessary, but there will be cases in which this rule of thumb is clearly questionable. For those, we will have to look deeper to infer how behavioral decisions are being made. In particular, we will draw a critical distinction between the task-oriented responses that characterize egg-rolling, nest-building, prey-catching, imprinting, and bark-peeling—responses that under the controlled manipulation of researchers lead to obviously inappropriate behavior—and goal-directed behavior, which seems to involve a wider perspective on at least certain of the less predictable problems that animals must cope with, and which may be solved by piecing together a novel series of innate or learned responses.

Invertebrate
Cognition:
A Case Study

THIS CHAPTER WILL BE SHORT. SO LITTLE IS KNOWN ABOUT THE
MENTAL CAPACITY OF THE HONEY BEE THAT IT IS BETTER NOT
TO SAY TOO MUCH ABOUT IT.

Karl von Frisch
"The Bee's Mental Capacity," *The Dancing Bees*, 1953

f all the species that inhabit the earth—animals, plants, fungi, and microörganisms—nearly 80 percent are invertebrates; vertebrates represent less than 1 percent of the total. Most invertebrates are arthropods, animals with exoskeletons and jointed legs, and most arthropods are insects. They have adapted to a far greater range of challenges than have vertebrates, and thus this group is likely to encompass an enormous diversity of intellectual strategies.

Like vertebrates, many invertebrates build homes or other structures, hunt for food, interact with others of their species, and solve problems. In this and following chapters we will investigate those areas, looking for cases of behavior that indicate that something beyond the standard innate armory of releasers, motor programs, drives, and programmed learning may be at work. In our search we will come up against the limits of present knowledge. We will often have to live with probabilities rather than certainties, recognize that there are still missing pieces to many of the puzzles we are trying to assemble, and perhaps suggest ways in which these might be found.

Since Karl von Frisch wrote the words at the head of this chapter more than four decades ago, the honey bee has been more extensively studied than any other invertebrate, enjoying this attention in part because of its economic importance as a pollinator and a producer of honey and wax. Our present investigation of the animal mind

A FORAGER HONEY BEE GATHERING

POLLEN AND NECTAR.

Karl von Frisch (1886–1982) switched to working on honey bees early in the century, after his discovery that fish could hear was rejected by the German scientific establishment. He was awarded a Nobel prize in 1973.

benefits greatly from these studies (including work by our lab). The honey bee makes a particularly intriguing case study because the highly social organization of honey bee hives has given rise to several sophisticated systems of interaction and communication, and with those systems seem to come the most impressive cognitive powers that have evolved in insects.

NEST-BUILDING

The inability to make repairs in building, so indicative of a programmed behavior such as we saw in the solitary digger wasp, is very common but it is not universal among insects. Social insects, in particular, have what appears to be a degree of goal-directed flexibility in their architectural undertakings.

Honey bees build vertical combs out of beeswax, which is secreted in small scales from glands in the abdomens of younger workers. Bees work the wax with their mandibles and fashion it into a two-layer back-to-back structure that places the center of each hexagonal cell on one side at the intersection of three cells on the other. The result is a structure of impressive strength: though the cell walls are less than a tenth of a millimeter thick, the comb is nevertheless able to hold hundreds of times its own weight in larvae, pupae, pollen, and honey.

The sheets of comb are built in parallel, two bee-diameters apart, in complete darkness. The parallel construction, critical to the efficient use of space, is apparently made possible by the bees' magnetic sense: if a strong magnetic field is generated around a hive, the bees will build in eccentric directions. Their sensitivity to magnetic fields not only tells them what parallel is but also allows a swarm that has departed from its parent hive to build its comb in the same direction as in the previous nest, unless the geometry of the cavity dictates a more efficient orientation. This adherence to "tradition" looks a lot like an instance of cultural knowledge passed from generation to generation, while the willingness to abandon habit in the face of local conditions certainly indicates that there is no single rigid comb-orientation response.

The actual process of building is fairly well understood: the organs used to test the thickness of the wax and measure cell size are known, and experimental modification of these structures leads to predictable disruptions of the work of individual bees. Honey bees have a remarkable capacity for dealing with at least some unpredictable

The parallel sheets of comb in a honey bee nest are built two bee-diameters apart to allow for smooth traffic flow.

contingencies. For example, since the hive is built in an insulating cavity (generally a hollow tree), the interior of their protective nest site may have irregular features. Certain bees forage for tree sap and other resins rather than for nectar and pollen; they use this material (called propolis) to line the interior of the cavity, waterproofing it and smoothing out unacceptable imperfections.

Propolis is also used to narrow the entrance to a suitable size (which varies with the weather), plug drafts in the winter, and entomb any foreign objects too large to be removed (an invading mouse, for instance, may be killed and sealed off in this way). One surprising way bees can use propolis was discovered in the hot volcanic areas of Salerno, Italy, in the 1960s by Martin Lindauer, von Frisch's most famous student. He found that bees forced by commercial beekeepers to live in those hot surroundings raise the melting point of the wax they use in comb building by adding propolis to it.

The tactic of manufacturing a heat-resistant alloy of beeswax and propolis contrasts with the routine methods honey bees, termites, and some social wasps use to cool their colonies during hot weather, when foragers gather water and spread it on the cells. Evaporation, aided by fanning in wasp and bee colonies, cools the nest and protects the delicate larvae. That the propolis-mixing behavior has been observed

The strong and highly regular cells in honey bee comb are used to rear brood, hold honey, and (as here) store pollen.

only in one very unusual locale suggests (but does not prove) that this is a novel response to a novel problem. It reinforces the suspicion that the opportunistic use of propolis is a goal-oriented behavior that may reflect at least some minimal comprehension of the problem to be solved.

PATTERN-LEARNING

Until the 1970s most experts believed that insects could not learn visual images. Instead of seeing pictures, bees were thought to store a list of "parameters" including such factors as the ratio of edge to area of the target figure, the proportion of various colors in the figure, the ratio of lines of different orientations in the target, and so on. Other observations, however, hinted that bees might actually be remembering images, and when our lab performed a series of carefully controlled tests the bees readily demonstrated their pictorial memory.

Even now that the existence of visual memory in honey bees is widely accepted, a rearguard action is being fought. Some researchers still insist that bee memory is retinotopic, meaning that an image is stored exactly as it falls on the retina and can be matched to a new target only if the bee is at exactly the same distance and angle from the object viewed. Mammals and birds (and perhaps all vertebrates), on the other hand, often recognize a familiar object from a novel perspective. Part of the attraction of the retinotopic hypothesis lies in the gulf it places between insect and human vision, since retinotopic insects would necessarily fail the familiar three-dimensional-object–rotation tasks that were once a staple of human IQ tests.

Despite the large role of instinct in flower learning and recognition, we know that bees can perform at least two mental transformations on visual information. The first is the recognition of left–right reversals. Flowers, like many things in nature, are bilaterally symmetric. Like humans, honey bees readily learn to distinguish two patterns that are mirror images, a simple discrimination expected from any sort of visual learning. The cognitive point of interest is that honey bees clearly know that a mirror image is more similar to the target they have learned than is a different pattern; and as a result they will choose the reversed image when the correct target is not present. The pervasive bias against insect cognition is evident in a 1996 report demonstrating that bees can master the concept of symmetry. As we will see in a later chapter, concept formation is considered a powerful mental tool in vertebrates; in bees, the capacity was dismissed as probably innate.

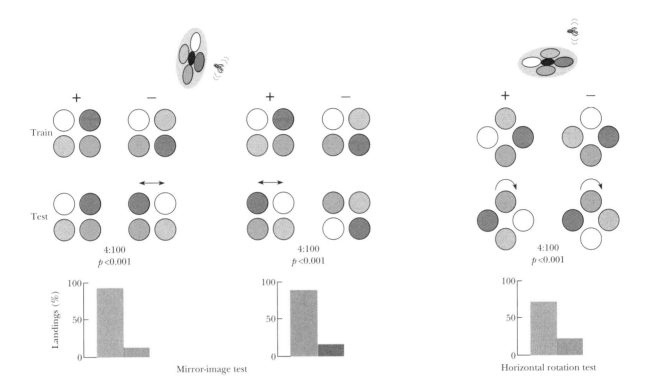

4:100
$p < 0.001$

4:100
$p < 0.001$

4:100
$p < 0.001$

Mirror-image test

Horizontal rotation test

In addition, forager bees can recognize a horizontal target from a new direction, a feat that requires the ability to perform a mental rotation of a two-dimensional figure. Like mirror-image recognition, this ability is useful for a bee in the wild as it searches for the kind of flower it is specializing on. Several other sorts of mental transformations at which humans are fairly good are beyond them, but those tasks are ones that they do not face in nature; such an ability might in fact prove a liability, predisposing them to make incorrect matches.

Some researchers argue that mental rotation is not evidence of higher-level cognitive ability in bees because it is adaptively useful and therefore possibly a result of evolutionary selection. The implicit assumption here is that equivalent abilities in humans are more impressive because they result *not* from selection but from a generalized and awesome intelligence. And it is true that some animals probably *are* specialized for certain transformation tasks. Pigeons, for example, are better at mental rotations of two-dimensional targets than we are: their response time in tests is shorter, and they are just as fast at

Foragers do not confuse a pattern they have been trained on with its mirror image (left), but they will select the mirror image over a novel pattern if the training stimulus is not offered (center). When the feeders are presented horizontally and foragers are permitted to see the pattern from only one direction, they are nevertheless able later to recognize a training pattern from a novel perspective (right).

recognizing a large rotation as a small one, whereas the time it takes humans to identify a rotated figure increases in direct proportion to its angle of rotation. It could be that pigeons have a prewired rotation-identification system while we must twist a figure around, looking at it with our mind's eye to see if it matches the original; on the other hand, maybe pigeons are simply better at this class of visual task.

Similarly, some food-storing birds (including Clark's nutcrackers and marsh tits) can remember a longer list of locations than can humans. It could be that their memory is specialized for remembering scattered sites, whereas our lesser abilities are nonetheless more significant because they derive from general intellectual prowess. As with the rotation test, the natural human response is to assume that when animals outperform us, it is because they have some sort of unfair advantage in the contest. As we will see when we consider our own species, however, a closer inspection reveals that many of our cognitive abilities and deficits are probably specializations also, ones that better suit us to our original niche as social hunter/gatherers than to our urban and mechanized modern life. Some of our mental abilities are thus probably as much a result of selection as those of other species. It seems to make more sense for us to take cognitive capacities at face value—as tools for making useful mental transformations—and ask, as we will be doing, how well and how flexibly animals use these tools to solve the larger-scale problems they often face. This approach is similar to the distinction we have drawn between task-specific and goal-directed use of innate motor programs: the raw material is the same, but the actual use of that potential can be dramatically different.

THE DANCE LANGUAGE

Until 1945 humans were believed to be the only species to have developed a language, as distinct from what was assumed to be the less specific, emotion-based communication of animals—say, the barking of dogs at strangers or the grunting of chimps at bananas. True language uses arbitrary conventions as units of communication, has a semantic organization, and can be used to refer to objects or events distant in time or space. Imagine the surprise of complacent linguists when in 1946 Karl von Frisch announced his finding that honey bees use an abstract system that is apparently the second most complex in nature: you are reading the only one that outdoes it.

This vibrating pollen forager is reporting a food source about 15° to the right of the sun's direction. Six attending bees are also being told of the distance to the food and the dancer's opinion of its quality.

Unlike human language, the bee language takes the form of a "dance" in which a returning forager moves in a figure 8. The two portions of this circuit that cross one another are the "waggle runs," during which the dancer vibrates her body from side to side 13 times a second and emits a pulsed 280Hz motorboatlike sound. Attending bees detect both components of the dance with their antennae, which act as two-channel resonant ears tuned to this pair of frequencies. The direction of the dance is encoded by the average angle of the waggle

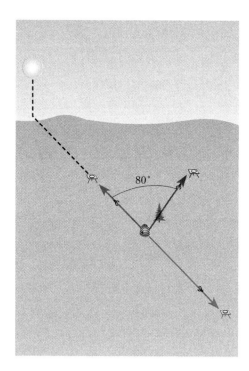

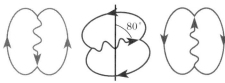

Direction is encoded in the dance as the angle between the waggle run and vertical on the comb, which corresponds to the angle between the food and the sun's direction. Thus, a dance 80° to the right of vertical means that the source is 80° to the right of the sun.

runs on the vertical comb in the darkness of the hive; "up" is taken as the direction of the sun, so that a dance 80° to the right of vertical corresponds to a location 80° to the right of the sun's azimuth in the field outside. Because the sun moves from east to west over the course of the day, the dance angle for a particular food source depends on the time of the dance; bees that dance for extended periods inside the hive without venturing back out nevertheless compensate for the unseen movement of the sun in the sky outside.

Distance is encoded as the duration of the waggle runs and their associated sounds. Like human language, the honey bee system has regional dialects: the German subspecies of *Apis mellifera*, the familiar temperate-zone honey bee, uses the convention that each waggle corresponds to about 50 m, while the Italian subspecies converts the waggles at one per 20 m; the Egyptian subspecies has a 10-m-per-waggle dialect. The three species of tropical honey bees we know of have their own conversion systems, as do the dozen or more other temperate-zone subspecies of honey bee. But unlike human language, the dialects are genetic: German larvae reared in Italian hives still "speak German" as adults, so confusion reigns.

The dance also encodes the quality of the food, and incidentally, its odor (which clings to the waxy hairs of the forager, and is learned by the attending bees whose versatile antennae are covered with olfactory receptors). The dance of temperate-zone honey bees is accurate from about 60 m out to a maximum range of 15 km. The dance could conceivably be more precise, since the dances of tropical species are about ten times as accurate. But the tropical bees forage very locally, and usually on isolated flowering trees; thus they describe small nearby targets. Temperate-zone bees forage on extended patches of flowers at far greater distances. In any event, the dance is only accurate enough to direct recruits to the vicinity of the target; from that point they must locate the flower by the odor they remember from the dancer's body. In one experiment, von Frisch demonstrated that recruits attending dances produced by foragers visiting a single species of flower were able to find that particular odor when confronted with a choice of 750 alternative scents!

The information capacity of honey bee language can be estimated by the number of distinct messages that can be conveyed; making a few reasonable assumptions for values yet to be measured directly, the total number of possible messages must be about a billion. This is far, far beyond anything seen in birds, dolphins, or nonhuman primates, for which the corresponding figures appear to be a hundred to a few thousand at most; on the other hand, it is vanishingly small compared to the capacity of human speech.

The idea that an insect might have an abstract language met considerable initial resistance. In the late 1960s and early 1970s there was a widespread rekindling of this latent skepticism when a group of American researchers led by Adrian Wenner and Patrick Wells reported experiments in which recruited bees clearly used odors rather than dance information to locate food. These researchers argued that the dance correlations were the fortuitous consequence of automatic sensory transformations. Many insects, for instance, are capable of converting visual information to gravity orientation—a curious talent that in most cases seems to serve no function. In addition, a variety of insects are known to "wind down" from demanding flights by vibrating in proportion to their exertion. Wenner and Wells maintained that the bee dances, like the agitated movements of foragers in other species of social insects, serve merely to alert potential recruits to the existence of food and provide a sample of its odor; the abstract correlations, seen in this light, would be accidental, conveying no more information about location to other bees than a cricket's temperature-related chirping rate supplies about the weather to other crickets. According to this line of reasoning, recruits simply fly out and search for the odor detected on the dancer, which includes the dancer's own odor—a scent that will have been left at the feeder. It is this latter smell, they argued, that accounts for the ability of the recruits in von Frisch's experiments to find the feeding station far more often than they discover the surrounding monitoring stations used to determine recruit accuracy.

Revealingly, their position was all or nothing: bees either have an abstract language, *or* they use odor cues like nearly all other foraging insects. This kind of reasoning pervades discussions of animal cognition: while humans may have multiple solutions to a problem, "lower" animals are lucky to have even one method for dealing with a puzzle. But we know that for important tasks many animals have alternatives to serve as backups should the primary system be unavailable; homing pigeons, for instance, can judge direction using the sun, or patterns of polarized light in the sky, or the earth's magnetic field. Bees, for their part, can navigate using the sun, *or* polarized light, *or* landmarks, depending on which cue provides the best information.

The Wenner and Wells work attracted considerable attention and initial support. Other researchers, ourselves included, were more willing to believe that von Frisch had been misled throughout the two

This robot bee seen performing the waggle run in an observation hive of the German subspecies, *A. m. carnica*, can recruit attending bees to arbitrarily chosen sites outside the hive. The central tube moves the model and causes it to waggle; the rear tube is attached to metal "wings" that are vibrated to produce the dance sound; the front tube supplies sugar water when one of the attenders demands a sample.

decades he studied the dance than that honey bees could have an abstract language. Again, the desire to see a gulf between the cognitive abilities of insects and those of humans may have played a major role. But when we look closely at the techniques that were used in the set of experiments that were meant to replicate von Frisch's work, we see that large amounts of odor were used (almost ten times what von Frisch recommended), a circumstance that is known to inhibit dancing, and the training method employed was sufficiently different from von Frisch's to confuse the issue.

In fact, we now know that the honey bee *does* have a language. We conducted a definitive test in which the feeding station visited by the trained foragers was placed well away from the array of monitoring stations. The ability to communicate false information is one of the most direct if perverse proofs that a communication system works. By using a trick that, in essence, forced returning bees to "lie" about the direction of the food, we made the dancing indicate a place the foragers had never visited, and which therefore had none of the confounding forager odor about it. Within a few minutes this arbitrarily chosen spot with no food, no odor, or anything else to recommend it, became the center of recruit activity in the field, thus demonstrating that recruits can use the coördinates encoded in the dance when they are available. In what promises to be a real breakthrough in the study of honey bee communication, a robot bee has recently been perfected. This computer-directed collection of wood, tubing, and razor blades successfully directs recruits to preselected spots, though it is not nearly as efficient as a real dancer in exciting other bees.

One of the many lessons of the dance-language controversy is that we should be wary of a seductive class of arguments about the mental abilities of animals: the presence of an automatic or relatively simple response to a problem does not, in and of itself, prove that a creature is limited to that cognitive level. More challenging circumstances may bring out other strategies that call more of the creature's intellect into play.

It is important to keep in mind that while the language of honey bees is itself innate—an individual reared in isolation still performs and interprets dances correctly—it nonetheless provides these species with a cognitive tool of remarkable potential. And there is evidence

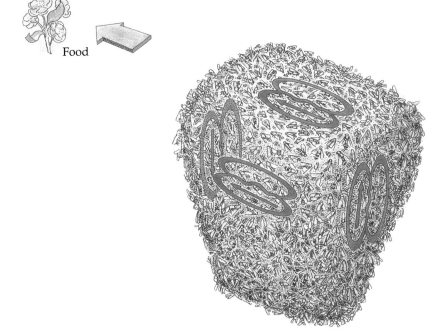

Food

In nature, dwarf honey bees always dance on the top of their exposed, bee-covered comb and aim their waggle runs directly at the food source. If they are forced to dance on the sides or end of the swarm, they reorient their waggle runs in a logical way.

that they can use the system creatively. A good example comes from the waggle language of the dwarf honey bee. This tropical species dances in the open on the horizontal top of the comb; its foragers orient their dances directly to the cues in the sky overhead. If they are forced by the manipulations of an experiment to dance on the side of their comb (which they never do in nature), they orient their dances in a completely novel way that employs the same intuitive convention used in human traffic signs: "up" means "straight ahead" (rather than the sun's azimuth, the convention in cavity-dancing species); 90° counterclockwise of vertical means "left." Future experiments may establish that this decoding is some sort of obscure innate backup routine, but if the behavior represents a way of dealing with a novel problem it is an impressive solution indeed.

FORAGING DECISIONS

When a forager returns from a food source, she does not normally dance at all: waggle dances are generally performed only when the food is of unusually good quality. The evaluation of "good" depends on the floral competition—in the fading resources of fall, dilute nectar that would have been shunned in spring elicits frantic dancing. As von Frisch and his students discovered, the forager judges the relative desirability of her load in part by the time it takes to discharge it to the younger bees that unload the returning bees. These "house" bees have been taking incoming food from many different foragers, and thus have sampled the range of the current floral market. They do not automatically unload any returning forager, nor even take a full load from those they do attend to. Instead, the unloading bees take partial loads from foragers in rough proportion to the relative quality of their food.

Because the unloaders can remember and compare, foragers returning with especially concentrated nectar are unloaded promptly, while ones with weaker fare may be unable to find an unloader and have to seek out a storage cell on their own. Foragers that are unloaded within about 45 seconds of their return usually dance; those that encounter a less enthusiastic audience response and fail to dispose of their cargo in two minutes almost never communicate their find.

This audience feedback allows the colony to respond fairly quickly to changes in the market. Foragers returning from what had been a

A returning forager (right) is unloaded by three other bees. The enthusiasm of her reception is a major factor in her decision whether or not to dance.

relatively good source stop dancing within 15 to 30 minutes of the appearance of dances for a much better source; they return to dancing after about the same latency if the better source fails. Since they do not themselves attend the dances to competing sites, they must be learning of the shifting conditions indirectly through the unloaders. The same system controls the gathering of water on hot days: when the hive temperature rises, unloading bees begin to show a preference for dilute nectar and especially water, which they have previously neglected; bees that have been gathering these are soon dancing vigorously, while the performances of the bees returning with concentrated nectar are suppressed.

Neat as this self-regulating system is, it is by no means all or even most of the story. Some foragers do not dance even when they are promptly unburdened, while others insist on advertising their source even when unloading has taken an embarrassing two minutes. The cause of the apparent variability is not the fallibility of the foragers' internal timers, but rather private information available only to them. Only the returning bee can know whether a patch of flowers is providing abundant food that can be quickly gathered, or whether time-consuming visits to hundreds of flowers will be necessary to acquire a full load. The efficiency of foraging seems to alter a bee's willingness to dance, independent of the behavior of unloaders. And only the forager knows how far away the source is. Food that is 2000 m distant is obviously a less attractive prospect than the same nectar at 100 m: more food can be returned to the colony in a given amount of time when 3800 m of the round trip can be avoided. The forager also figures in more subjective factors, which have been uncovered one by one as researchers have painstakingly varied different aspects of their bees' food sources. Flowers that provide unusually intense odors elicit less dancing; blossoms that surround the bee tend to stimulate dancing; nectar sucked out of narrow tubes is treated more enthusiastically. The adaptive basis, if any, of these almost aesthetic judgments is unknown.

Another feature of the dance-decision process, first reported by von Frisch, is even more surprising: foragers collecting food from more distant patches stop dancing (but continue foraging) at the approach of darkness or bad weather sooner than do peers frequenting patches nearer the hive. This makes sense because recruits often take an appreciable amount of time locating a new food source the first time and could easily be caught outdoors if the site being sought is too far away. Clearly, then, recruitment dances are not an automatic response to food or even to food quality; instead, they depend on a host of factors (some of which are probably yet to be discovered by humans) that are weighed one against another. When a human decides whether to recommend a restaurant, taking into account its menu, the tastes of the friend being advised, the cost of the food, the distance to the establishment, the ambiance of the dining room, the ease of parking, and all the other factors that enter into such a decision, we have little hesitation in attributing conscious decision-making powers to the calculation. When a small frenetic creature enclosed in an exoskeleton and sporting supernumerary legs and a sting performs an analogous integration of factors, however, our biases spur us to look for another explanation, different in kind. As far as we know there is no reason beyond our deep-seated preconceptions to prefer conscious choice over programmed evaluation as the explanation for either species.

While the dancing is going on, potential recruits are making their own set of decisions about where to invest their effort. It is clear that they do not simply fly to the spot indicated by the first dance they attend, or even the location specified by the most intense dances. And while attenders use a special sound signal to obtain samples of the nectar being advertised, and thus know the quality from direct experience, they do not necessarily opt for the dance offering the sweetest food. Instead, their calculations reflect the needs of the colony (nectar versus water versus pollen) and the distance to the site being advertised, weighing the time lost flying farther against the difference in sugar concentration at alternative sites. (Foragers, however, are more conservative: unless the patch being harvested completely fails, a forager usually will remain faithful to a low-quality source in the midst of frantic dancing to a better alternative. There are generally many recruits available to exploit the better patch, and the forager's own poorer source may be only temporarily depleted, or the new one ephemeral.)

It is difficult to know just how goal-oriented these intriguing economic comparisons are. Certainly a simple task-oriented response would not involve comparing many sources of information and considering several parameters from each source simultaneously. Few of us could work out the optimal choice as well or as quickly as honey bees do, though in situations more relevant to our species we can easily outperform most insects. Experiments that would determine whether the bees have any understanding of the overall goal of their multimodal evaluations are challenging both to imagine and to execute. Though all the basic facts about foraging were in hand by 1960, until recently the intellectual Umwelt in the field of animal behavior blinded nearly all researchers to the existence of any larger issue, and funding for research that does not promise an increase in the commercial value of the bee is difficult to find.

NEST-SITE DECISIONS

The bees' faculty for critical evaluation is called on again when they need to relocate. Honey bees reproduce by swarming, a process in which the old queen and about half of the hive population leave the cavity in spring and form a hanging clump on a nearby limb. In the old hive a new queen emerges, mates, and begins laying eggs. Meanwhile the swarm outside is faced with the need to find a new cavity, build new comb, and collect enough food to survive the winter.

Before the swarm leaves the security of the hive a small number of scouts scour the neighborhood in search of suitable sites, and once the hive has swarmed, the search begins in earnest. When a scout locates a cavity she explores it extensively. If it is suitable she returns

This swarm, containing the old queen and about half of the workers, has formed near the old colony. Scouts fly out to explore the region for nest sites and report their discoveries to other scouts through dances on the swarm surface.

to the swarm, which has usually established itself on the limb of a tree or in some other sheltered spot, and dances to indicate its location. Other scouts attend these dances and visit the various advertised sites. According to Martin Lindauer, who discovered swarm dancing in the late 1950s, a bee that has found a good cavity will interrupt her own dancing to attend other dances (a behavior never seen in foragers) and then investigate the competition. If one of the alternatives is clearly better, the scout will switch allegiance and begin dancing for the new site. By setting out artificial cavities and individually marking the scouts as they visited, Lindauer was able to keep track of the inspection flights and dancing of each bee. Despite meticulous records from dozens of swarms, some researchers, both then and now, reject Lindauer's results on no more substantial grounds than that they refuse to believe that scout behavior could be so flexible.

After a scout has found the best site, she will return periodically to confirm its quality. Ingenious experiments that vary multiple aspects of artificial nest cavities have shown that scouts weigh a host of factors in the search for the best site, including cavity volume, cavity shape, size of the entrance, entrance direction, height above the ground, dampness, draftiness, the cavity's distance from the home hive, and so on. Altering the desirability of the cavity before one of these revisits—say, by pouring water on the floor of the enclosure, thus suggesting that there is a leak—will immediately alter the scout's willingness to dance. Over the course of several days a consensus builds among the scouts, and finally the swarm departs for its new home.

The strategy by which the nest-site decision is made certainly appears goal oriented. Multiple cues at competing sites are weighed in an ongoing process that resembles more the way humans evaluate real estate than any simple task-related behavior like egg rolling. Scouts act as though they have a mental picture of the ideal site, as well as an overall perspective on the local market and its hourly fluctuations. But again, critical experiments to determine the actual degree of cognitive complexity underlying this remarkable behavior remain to be performed. How much do scout bees really know about the dark spaces they explore? Are they working from some innate shopping list that takes into account volume, distance, height, dryness, etc., so they could be fooled into advertising a cavity with some fatal flaw not in their catalogue? Or do their lengthy explorations generate a mental picture or map, complete with marginal notes on atmosphere and accessibility, that they can then compare with others and reach a more or less optimal decision?

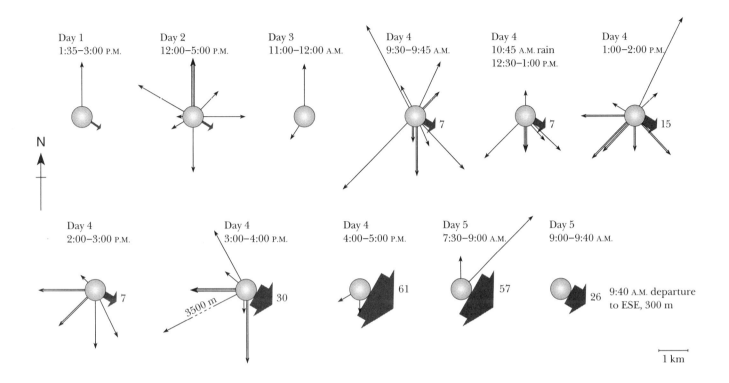

Day 1
1:35–3:00 P.M.

Day 2
12:00–5:00 P.M.

Day 3
11:00–12:00 A.M.

Day 4
9:30–9:45 A.M.

Day 4
10:45 A.M. rain
12:30–1:00 P.M.

Day 4
1:00–2:00 P.M.

Day 4
2:00–3:00 P.M.

Day 4
3:00–4:00 P.M.

Day 4
4:00–5:00 P.M.

Day 5
7:30–9:00 A.M.

Day 5
9:00–9:40 A.M.

9:40 A.M. departure
to ESE, 300 m

1 km

ROUTE PLANNING

One of the most widely accepted pieces of evidence for complex cognitive activity is a creature's ability to use latent learning to form a novel plan for solving a problem. The easiest way to test for this ability in the lab is by providing a goal (usually food) that can be reached only by an indirect route—the problem Köhler posed for dogs and chimps. If the animal is familiar with the landmarks in the testing arena, it may be able to plan a novel route if the direct path or the usual route is blocked.

For foraging insects the testing arena is the home range, which in the case of bees can encompass many square kilometers. The landmarks must be much larger and more distinct than those required by vertebrates simply because the visual resolution of insects is very fuzzy. While there have been reports of insect homing since the 1800s, von Frisch provided the first clear evidence that insects can form maplike

Scouts fly out from the swarm in search of new cavities and return to advertise their finds. They attend each other's dances as well, and visit the alternative sites. When a consensus is reached, the swarm departs for the best spot. This record of the decision-making process of one swarm covers about four days. North is up, the length of each arrow is proportional to the distance to the corresponding site, and the width is related to the number of dances for that contender.

Foragers were trained to two boats on the lake. Recruits readily flew to the shore station at the lower left but avoided the lake station until it was rowed close to the far shore.

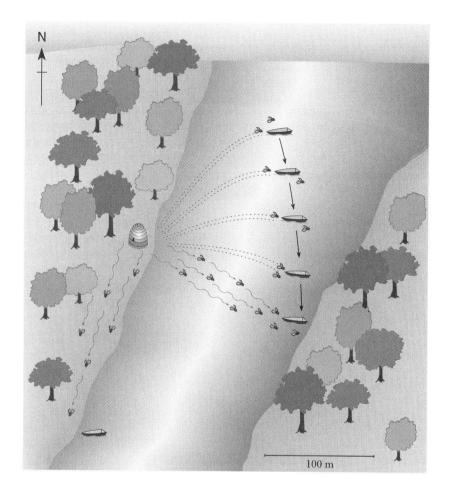

mental representations (though he did not consider this possible interpretation of his results). He set up a hive next to a tall building and trained foragers by an indirect route to a food source on the far side. When the quality of the food was increased enough to elicit dancing, the foragers indicated the shortest "beeline" distance and direction of the source, even though they had previously flown there along an indirect course.

In an effort to pin down just how sophisticated the bees' use of their mental map was, Fred Dyer, working in our lab, trained foragers to a feeding station on a boat in a lake. The idea was to see if recruits, who knew their home range, would dismiss the foragers' lake dances as implausible.

When the boat was in the middle of the lake, dancing elicited no recruitment; at the same time, dances to food of the same quality at a control station on the shore of the lake drew many new bees. Although bees are often reluctant to fly over large bodies of still water, further adjustments showed that was not a factor in the unpopularity of the lake station: when the boat was moved to within 10 m of the far side of the lake, substantial recruitment began as new bees flew (apparently 150 m across the water rather than more than a kilometer around the lake edge) to the station. It is as though the dance audience used the coördinates provided by foragers to mentally "place" the site on a neural map of the region, rejecting the middle of the lake as unlikely but accepting the far shore as a plausible location for flowers.

In another series of experiments, we captured bees departing for a feeder and displaced them in the dark to an out-of-the-way location for release. This is by no means an unnatural contingency: insects are at the mercy of thermal updrafts, sudden crosswinds, and summer storms that can displace them up to a few hundred meters. These well-controlled tests took their inspiration from other displacement experiments, the first of which were performed on social wasps more than a hundred years ago and in which many of the wasps returned home faster than the experimenter. An unplanned, serendipitous test of honey bees by Michael Brines in our lab in the 1970s involved capturing departing foragers at the hive entrance and transporting them in the dark to a site 500 m away. (We used this procedure to avoid having to train bees down the side of a building from their rooftop hive.) Young foragers, as judged by fresh wings and furry thorax, were disoriented, but older bees, whose tattered wings and bare backs testified to their experience, flew quickly back to the hive, suggesting that they recognized the release site and understood where it lay with respect to home. The all-time distance record is held by tropical bees that were kidnapped and taken 20 km from home (but still within their home range) and released; again, many returned home quickly.

To generate data that was thoroughly controlled, our lab trained a group of marked foragers (we glue tiny specially made colored plastic numbers to their backs, like little football jerseys) to a particular site and allowed them to forage there for several days. Next we captured these foragers at the hive entrance as they departed for the feeder and took them in a dark container to a release site, a location

120 m from the feeding station and out of sight of it by virtue of an intervening line of trees. The kidnapped foragers were then set free one at a time. Their departure bearings and flight times to other sites were recorded. At one release site where there was a large tree the bees could use as a landmark nearby, the foragers set off directly for the unseen goal along a direct but novel route. However, when released only 30 m farther from the landmark tree, some of the displaced foragers were confused: while many flew off toward the goal (though with less accuracy than the earlier group), others left in the same direction they would have adopted if they had still been at the hive entrance.

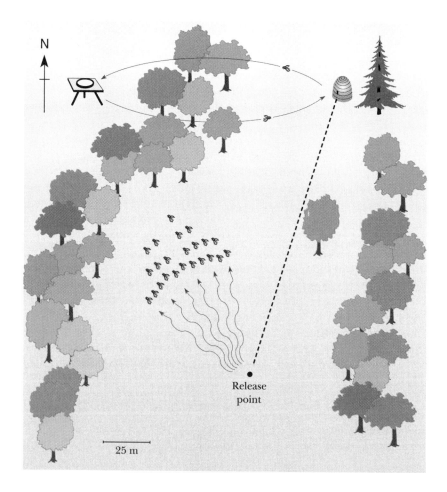

Foragers trained to the station at the upper left were kidnapped as they left the hive, transported in the dark to the release point (lower right), and turned loose. Even though the training station was not directly visible, they flew off roughly in the correct direction.

The most interesting interpretation of these results is that the well-oriented foragers scanned the landmarks (especially the distinctive tree) around them at the release site and then used a mental map to place themselves in their home range. Next, they computed the true angle to the feeding site and set off in the appropriate direction, just as a variety of mammals and birds seem able to do in analogous circumstances. The problem for bees is more challenging, however: careful behavioral experiments indicate that the resolution of their memory of landmarks is about 4.5° (equivalent to 20/6000 vision). That this performance is even worse than their visual resolution is not surprising: so far as we know, no creature remembers visual experiences at the full resolution of its eyes. (The truth of this generalization is easily demonstrated: look away from this book and try to remember the number of words in the previous sentence—a number easily worked out while looking at the page, but which is not within the level of detail of the visual memory of most people.) As a result, few features that we could use as landmarks are even stored in honey bee memory, and many objects that are large enough (trees along a forest edge, for instance) are probably so blurry and similar to one another as to be impossible to distinguish.

Many bee experiments depend on the researcher's ability to recognize individuals. The bar-coded tags allow this process to be automated.

The mental-map hypothesis is one of three possible explanations advanced to account for the behavior of kidnapped bees. Some researchers believe that the bees successful in setting course for the unseen goal were merely using routes remembered from previous trips to the feeder. This route-based system, championed by the Swiss entomologist Rudiger Wehner, supposes that individuals remember a series of scenes along a familiar path—itself an impressive cognitive achievement (and a strategy we also use at times), but still something less than a map-based ability to plan. To use a route-based system in the kidnapping experiment, each of the 25 bees would have to have flown a highly indirect dogleg route to the feeder that happened to include the release site; moreover, each forager would have to have made this particular circuitous approach so often that it had been firmly entered into her album of route-specific snapshots. This does not seem likely, particularly since the home range was large, and the bees were originally trained to the feeder along quite a different route.

The third explanation, favored by Dyer, supposes that the released bees attempted to match their memory of the landmark panorama seen from the hive on departure with the panorama available at the release site. The bees would have to perform some sort of computation to determine which direction they must fly to reduce the discrepancy between the two images. Alternatively, the degree of discrepancy might be calculated at various points in a departing bee's circling; comparing these values could then allow the bee to choose the direction on the circle that corresponds to the point of minimum discrepancy. The bee would then repeat this "getting warmer" computation periodically, and thereby be drawn ever closer to the perfect match and thus the goal.

The discrepancy-minimization strategy is certainly different in kind from most models of vertebrate navigation. It suffers from a lack of any concrete mathematical basis: no one has been able to suggest how the problem could even be approached, much less to develop a set of equations for actually accomplishing these calculations. Bats

The poor quality of honey bee vision makes it unlikely that kidnapped foragers can use distant landmarks as orientation cues. The bee's-eye view on this page shows what foragers can see from the release site; the training site is behind the trees near the center of this panorama. The illustration on the facing page gives the view from the hive; the training station lies behind the trees to the right. These representations were created by blurring actual photographs until details smaller than honey bee visual resolution (indicated by the smaller, dark oval over the panorama on the facing page) were lost; the resolution of honey bee landmark memory (the larger oval) is even worse. Comparing these views suggests that bees cannot see or recognize distant landmarks near the training station or match them to the view remembered from the hive. The landmark tree near the release site, however, appears critical to displaced bees attempting to get their bearings: when the release site is moved away from this tree, the foragers are less well oriented.

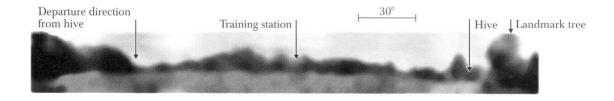

Departure direction from hive   Training station   30°   Hive   Landmark tree

and cruise missiles do something analogous, so the task is probably not completely impossible, but a discrepancy-based system seems to require more complex circuitry than either of the other two hypotheses currently in vogue.

There are two further difficulties with the discrepancy-minimization hypothesis. First, the actual behavior of released foragers seems much more accurate than this model would predict. Comparing the panorama seen from the release site with the one visible from the hive, it is hard to conceive what could draw a bee toward the unseen feeder. Second, experiments extending the work that led to the discrepancy hypothesis indicate that bees must know the *distance* to the landmarks they are using rather than just the relative angles between the markers as seen from the goal or starting point. But knowing both the azimuths *and* distances of a set of landmarks is exactly what constitutes a map representation of a locale. Thus the very work that led to the discrepancy-minimization theory now seems to provide independent evidence that bees use a mental map.

Attempts (beginning in 1989) to replicate the kidnapping experiment have met with mixed success. One set of tests in Germany found that recruits flew directly to the unseen goal only under overcast; on sunny days they used celestial cues. Researchers have known since the 1950s that bees familiar with an area prefer to use any prominent landmarks that are available even on sunny days, and later work by Dyer showed (not surprisingly) that on cloudy days their dependence on landmarks increases dramatically. Thus it is possible that the landmarks at the German site were good enough to use under overcast skies but not sufficiently prominent to tear the foragers away from celestial cues when the sun was visible. This may well account for the substantial effect of the 30-m move in the original kidnapping experiments, which reduced the apparent size (and thus the usefulness) of the landmark tree.

Wehner altered the protocol by kidnapping foragers from the feeder rather than as they left the hive. When released at other sites

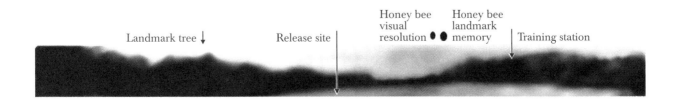

Landmark tree ↓   Release site   Honey bee visual resolution ● ● Honey bee landmark memory   Training station

they flew off in the appropriate celestial direction. But von Frisch had shown as long ago as the 1950s that honey bees rely more on landmarks on their trip *to* a feeder, switching to celestial cues on the way back. Thus foragers trained to a station along a dogleg that passes a prominent landmark en route will, even days later, fly out to the feeder via the dogleg (or some shortened version of it) and then depart directly for home after filling up with sugar water. Thus the Swiss test was no test at all.

Dyer reported in 1991 that bees kidnapped to a site next to a prominent stand of trees departed directly to the unseen feeder they had been visiting. But when bees from the same colony were carried off to another location in the middle of a field or at the base of a 6-m-high cliff, they adopted a celestial course. Again, it looks like kidnapped foragers

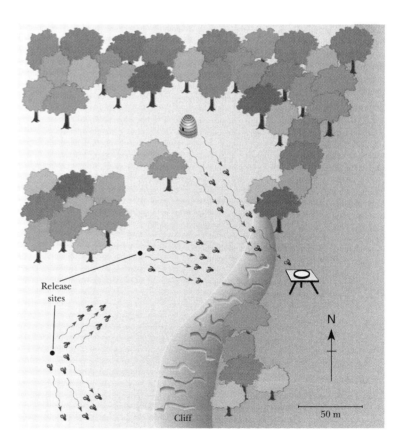

Kidnapped foragers were well oriented when released near a prominent landmark (a stand of trees), but were unable to depart directly toward the training station (hidden at the foot of a quarry cliff) when turned loose in the middle of a featureless field.

have a map-based system for navigation, but simply cannot use it unless they have suitable landmarks to provide bearings. A 1997 test by the German neurobiologist Randolf Menzel provided a large unambiguous landmark for bees to use; under these conditions, foragers kidnapped from the hive were indeed able to select correct novel headings.

The complications inherent in testing the cognitive abilities of unrestrained animals in the wild, particularly when they have more than one way of solving a problem, is well illustrated by the bee-map saga. Equally apparent is the difficulty we have in taking seriously the mental powers of phylogenetically remote organisms. There is a widespread inclination to seek an explanation different in kind rather than degree for indications of imagination, language, complex decisions, and planning in invertebrates. To a lesser extent we will encounter the same difficulty with vertebrate behavior: with the team spirit and group loyalty so evident in our species during times of war or sporting events, we tend to look down on outsiders. It seems obvious that the "lower" orders simply must be mentally inferior, beginning with the cold-blooded classes (fish, amphibia, and reptiles), but including the nonmammalian taxa, the mammals that happen not to be primates, those primates that are not among the great apes, and finally the nonhuman apes.

In fact, however, honey bees and fish have been evolving to meet the intellectual challenges of their niches for many more years than has our species. Natural biases aside, it seems only fair to assume that the cognitive equipment of bees is at least as well adapted to the challenges they face as ours. Despite a widespread unwillingness to take indications of insect intellect at face value, there is good evidence that even a few milligrams of highly specialized neural wiring can accomplish a limited set of individually impressive cognitive tasks essential to the natural history of the animal in question. We should not forget that most of the mass of an animal's brain is devoted to operating the creature's muscles, and scales directly with body size; thus a large brain in a large animal is no surprise, but a high ratio of brain to body weight (like that seen in humans) *does* suggest that there is extra computing power not devoted to the overhead of controlling motion. This sort of comparison implies that social insects have a substantial surplus of brain tissue compared to, say, flies and moths. The excess brain power of social insects may well have evolved to solve problems based on goal-oriented strategies—strategies that require a level of cognitive finesse far beyond anything imagined in invertebrates by most researchers as recently as two decades ago.

Animals
as Architects

A SPIDER CONDUCTS OPERATIONS THAT RESEMBLE THOSE OF A
WEAVER, AND A BEE PUTS TO SHAME MANY AN ARCHITECT IN
THE CONSTRUCTION OF HER CELLS. BUT WHAT DISTINGUISHES
THE WORST ARCHITECT FROM THE BEST OF BEES IS THIS—THAT
THE ARCHITECT RAISES HIS STRUCTURE IN IMAGINATION BEFORE
HE ERECTS IT IN REALITY.

Karl Marx
Capital, 1867

e have seen that innate motor programs can choreograph the process of nest-building among wasps and bees. Even among vertebrates, animals reared without the opportunity to learn about their natural homes nevertheless select appropriate material and produce a species-specific structure. We saw that some of the construction is organized as a strict series of task-oriented steps; intermediate criteria signal the animals to cease one task and begin another. Any flexibility in the behavior was limited to specific steps and contexts. In these sequences there was little to suggest much in the way of cognitive powers.

But when we looked at honey bees, we saw a genuine flexibility, an apparent ability to modify or choose among innate behaviors to solve problems. This enhanced flexibility seems to require an animal to understand the *goal* of an undertaking; only then can the creature determine what must be done to complete or repair or modify a structure. This sort of goal-oriented flexibility is probably what underlies the limited but impressive ability of bees to plan routes or design ad hoc solutions to novel challenges. It certainly seems to inform the nest-building behavior of many social insects as well as certain vertebrates, ranging from a few remarkable species of fish to a number of birds and at least one aquatic mammal.

THE NESTS OF SOCIAL INSECTS CAN BE LARGE AND

INTRICATELY BUILT. THIS ANT MOUND IN

NORTHERN GERMANY STANDS 1.2 M HIGH; IT

INSULATES THE NEST BELOW, WHERE TENS OF

THOUSANDS OF WORKERS COÖPERATE TO BUILD

CHAMBERS AND REAR BROOD.

TERMITE NESTS

The nests of certain termites are so massive that elaborate provisions must be made for ventilation, cooling, and defense against specialist mammalian predators. Species whose colonies comprise hundreds of thousands or tens of millions of individuals remove so much earth that, like human miners, they must reinforce the walls and ceilings of the tunnels to prevent collapse. Instead of timber, these insects use mud mixed with their own secretions, a compound that dries to the consistency of concrete.

Some termite species construct enormous aboveground structures of vaguely totemic appearance. The air-cooling chimneys of certain rainforest species look like multiroofed pagodas, the layering providing protection from tropical downpours. The mounds of the compass termites (*Amitermes meridionalis*) of Australia, up to 5 m high, suggest the standing stones left by the early inhabitants of Britain and are, like them, oriented to the sun: facing east and west, the broad sides catch the early and late warmth and avoid the heat of the noonday

The massive aboveground portions of these Australian termite mounds act as heating and ventilation devices. The warmed air in the attic chimneys draws cooler air up from the basement.

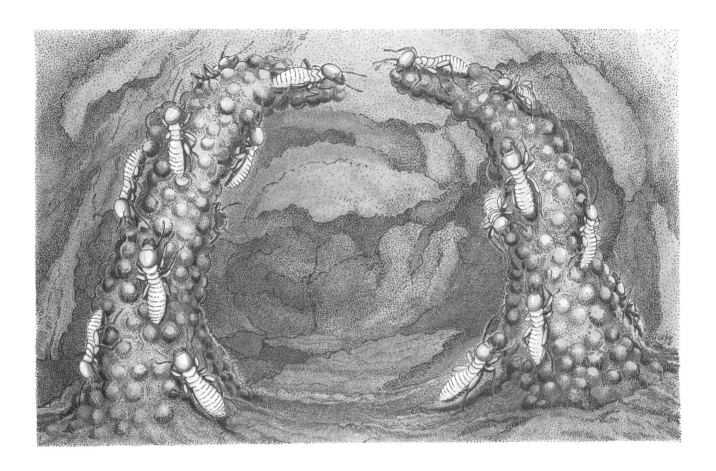

sun. Whatever the aboveground specializations, all nests begin as underground excavations that create a chamber for the two reproductives (the king and queen), increasing numbers of brood chambers for the eggs, and still other chambers for storing or growing food.

Termites thrive because they harbor symbiotic microörganisms that live in the gut and digest cellulose. Some species also farm a fungus that can digest the lignin in vegetation; the termites then eat the fungus. The nest may be built in a tree, which is slowly consumed, or in the ground, in which case the workers tunnel up to 50 m to forage for vegetation and seeds. As a termite nest grows, so too do the problems of ventilation and cooling: the CO_2 and heat generated by the larvae and adults (and, in some species, fungi) must be dissipated if

Blind workers coördinate the work on the variously sized internal buttress arches in the dark so that they begin curving in the right direction at the right height to meet at the top of the arc.

the colony is not to suffocate. The solutions to air-management problems suggest a degree of planning beyond anything we have yet seen.

Consider, for example, the African species *Macrotermes bellicosus*, whose nests in the Ivory Coast were studied in detail by Martin Lüscher. The nests are built so that air may circulate: cool air is drawn up from a cellar into an attic by the heat produced by metabolizing termites and growing fungi, and the air is then shunted to the ten or so buttresses that project from the base to near the top of the above-ground portion of the nest. In the honeycombed buttresses warm, CO_2-rich air from the attic is exchanged through pores with the cooler, O_2-rich air outside, and this cooler air descends through the buttresses, growing cooler still as the exchange continues, until the air enters the cellar, where it is cooled further by contact with the subsoil.

The coördinated building of these elaborate structures by millions of blind insects strains or exceeds the limits of conventional behavioral programming. No two nests are ever alike. It seems simpler to account for the feat by supposing that the individual termites have some functional picture of the end result and, from an array of innate motor programs, choose the behavior most appropriate in the circumstances to bring the work closer to that goal. The same mechanism probably controls the construction of the many internal support structures: in total darkness, individuals begin the two sides of an arch with the appropriate separation and, by moving from one of the growing pillars to the other, begin the curves at the same height, in the correct direction, and with the appropriate degree of curvature. It is possible that the workers involved have an image of both the developing structure and the eventual goal; alternative scenarios for coördinating such projects—the use of pheromones, for instance—seem much more complex and even less plausible.

More remarkable, though, is the possibility that the design is at least partially cultural: nests in Uganda built by the same species employ a flow-through strategy of ventilation radically different from the one used in the Ivory Coast. Air in the Ugandan nests is drawn into the cellar through a tunnel from the outside, rises through the nest, enters the attic, and then is vented to the outside through pores at the top of a kind of chimney; there are no buttresses. The seasonal patterns and temperatures of the two habitats are similar, but Uganda is drier and less forested. No work has yet been done to see whether this dramatic architectural difference involves learning or regional specializations in behavioral programming. Transplanting new colonies from one habitat to the other could settle the question.

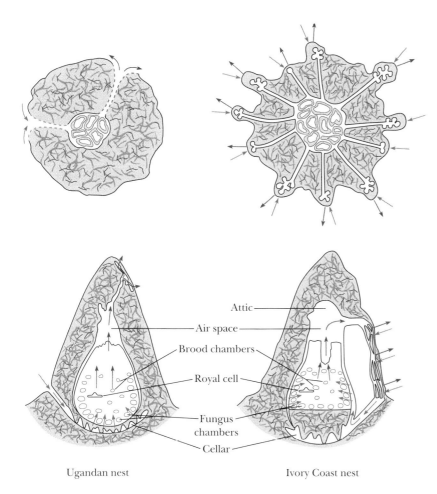

Attic

Air space

Brood chambers

Royal cell

Fungus chambers

Cellar

Ugandan nest   Ivory Coast nest

In Uganda, this termite species used a flow-through strategy for circulating air in its nest (shown in drawings representing both vertical and horizontal sections through the brood chambers): cool, O_2-rich air (blue arrows) is drawn in through an opening into the base of the nest, passes through the chambers and galleries, and leaves as warm CO_2-rich air (red arrows) from a chimney near the top. In an Ivory Coast nest of the same species, however, air is recycled: warm CO_2-rich air is drawn into the attic and then descends through a set of peripheral buttresses, where it is exchanged through vast numbers of pores with cool fresh outside air.

Whether or not the difference in styles is genetically based, the ability of termites to remodel their ventilation systems in unusual ways both frustrates the efforts of the scientists seeking to learn about them and suggests, though it does not prove, some level of understanding. When researchers draped a plastic sheet over a large nest that prevented the normal flow of air essential for cooling and CO_2 disposal, the insects devised a novel emergency system of cone-shaped chimneys that saved the colony.

Termites must maintain a high humidity (typically well above 90 percent) in the nest. In arid climates where cooling is also a problem, unrestricted flow-through ventilation would remove badly needed moisture along with the excess heat and CO_2. Termites modify the ventilation system to confine the heat- and gas-exchanging flow to the periphery, thus conserving the water in the core of the nest, and they usually also dig a well down to the water table—a distance of up to 40 m—to resupply the moisture that is inevitably lost. In less arid regions, colonies of the same species do not bother with wells and restricted peripheral exchange.

Again, this variation within a species in response to different conditions suggests a more goal-directed behavior rather than a program of preordained steps. But there has been no systematic work to establish the nature of the cognitive processing, simple or sophisticated, that makes this adaptability to changing challenges possible. The well-entrenched bias against the possibility of any degree of creativity or insight in insects, once a useful defense against the excesses of anthropomorphizing rampant in the last century, has deflected investigation or, more often, blinded researchers to the possibility that there might be any issue to be resolved.

FISH NESTS

Although by far the most impressive nests found among vertebrates are constructed by birds, three examples of fish nests suggest the possibility of goal-oriented behavior in this distant class of chordates. The simplest is the shelter created by the sand goby. The males of this bottom-dwelling fish search for empty bivalve shells. When a male finds one he turns its convex side up and then begins to excavate under it, removing mouthfuls of sand and carrying them off to a safe distance. Then he uses his fins to scoop sand on top of the shell, burying it except for an entrance groove. Finally, he rubs sticky mucus from his skin on the sand lining the entrance, reinforcing it against collapse and slippage. The shell is now his camouflaged nuptial chamber: females that he courts enter the chamber, turn upside down, and deposit their eggs on the "ceiling," the concave inner surface of the shell. The male fertilizes and then guards the eggs until they hatch. Since any damage to the structure is repaired, the behavior may well be goal oriented, but experiments to determine this have not been performed.

Three-spined stickleback males also build nests, excavating a shallow pit in a sandy area and then collecting filamentous algae or tearing off threads of other plant material. After gluing the algae with

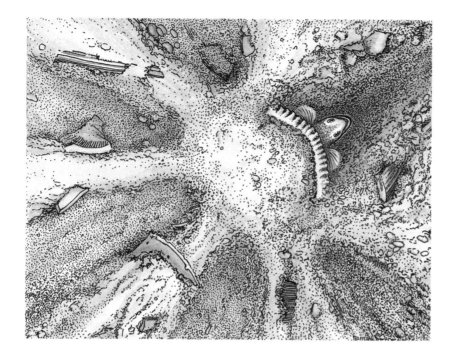

A sand goby in the nest he has excavated under a shell. He has also dug an entrance ramp in the front and hidden the shell under sand (the radiating depressions were created as he gathered the camouflaging sand).

a sticky substance secreted from his kidneys, he bores a tunnel through the mound. (A close relative, the nine-spined stickleback, makes a similar nest above the bottom in large aquatic plants.) The male then courts females, induces them to lay eggs in his nest, fertilizes the eggs, and guards his developing offspring, circulating water through the nest by fanning his fins to insure a sufficient supply of oxygen. Even after the fry hatch, the male guards them for a few weeks (particularly from the attentions of hungry female sticklebacks). Like the goby, the stickleback makes any needed repairs promptly, suggesting (but not proving) a goal-oriented strategy and some kind of mental picture of what the end product should be.

By far the most impressive of the fish nests are constructed by jawfish, whose structures serve as year-round homes. Both males and females excavate a vertical tunnel up to a meter long with a chamber at the bottom that provides room for turning around. Rather than using glue, jawfish reinforce their wells with stones and shells, just as humans construct theirs. The jawfish then waits concealed near the top of its masonry-lined home and ambushes unwary prey. The nest's

Jawfish line their excavated tubes with shells and stones, creating a strong and durable well.

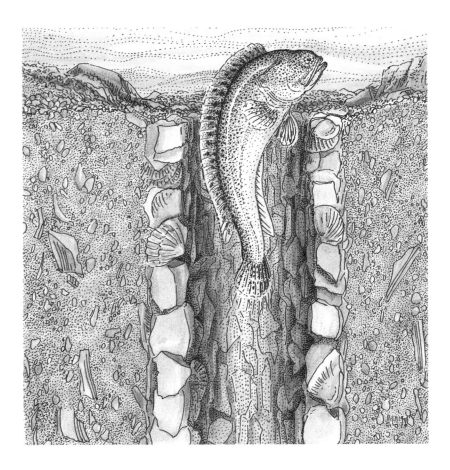

construction involves frequent repair and constant decision-making in the choice of an optimal place to position each newly gathered stone or shell. Again, the behavior looks goal oriented, but direct experiments tampering with the structure of the well or manipulating the materials available for construction remain to be performed.

BIRD NESTS

Intricate bird nests are more familiar to most humans than the dwellings of insects or fish, but Donald Griffin puts them into useful perspective: "[W]hen allowance is made for the difference in size of the builders, most bird's nests are rather small and simple compared to the elaborate nests of wasps, bees, and ants." And to the extent that the building is task oriented, the cognitive underpinnings seem less impressive as well. Indeed, there are cases that suggest that birds can be very stupid about the design and purpose of their nests. Hummingbirds, for instance, build tiny nests out of species-specific materials—moss, lichens, and so on—which are often held together by cobwebs. While incubating her eggs, a female hummingbird may ignore the activity of other hummingbirds as they fly up and remove material from her nest. Even when a hole begins to appear she pays no attention, and eventually the eggs or even chicks may fall out and perish. Similarly, mallard duck pairs that have built their nests on the roofs of buildings have been observed to lead their hatchlings mindlessly off the edge on their way to the nearest water.

But such task-oriented blindnesses may exist alongside behavior that does appear flexible and goal oriented. True, the weaverbird's complex nest is produced through a series of subroutine tasks, and a hand-raised male weaverbird will select appropriate material and construct a species-specific nest without learning from others of its kind.

A weaverbird's first step in constructing a nest is the creation of a sturdy circular perch. An adept builder will work so quickly that most of the early parts of the structure will still be green when he begins his courtship display at the nest-cup entrance. The long nest tube will be added if a female accepts the male.

But just as important in the developing picture of an animal mind is the observation that the first attempts of even wild-raised weavers are very clumsy. The initial circular perch—essential to the overall support of the finished structure and as a foothold for many steps in construction—is rarely made strong and tight enough the first few attempts: again and again the bird and his perch fall to the ground together. Through experience, when he has gained some sense of what is to be achieved, the young male perfects the perch and begins the next step of the process.

Similarly, a male's early attempts to create a roof or nest cup are not very satisfactory, and the entire structure is frequently torn down and completely rebuilt. This self-critical attitude serves the males well because females compare nests, selecting the sturdiest and greenest. Since the vegetation in a nest begins to turn brown as soon as it is collected from living plants, there is a premium on speed, which comes only with practice. Moreover, male weaverbirds repair their structures and show a modest degree of consistent individual variation. All these signs point to the possible existence of a sense of the overall object of the activity, achieved through a mixture of innate motor programs and learning. But as with fish nests, the critical experiments necessary to dissect higher-level cognitive processing from programming have yet to be performed.

Rehearsal—and thus possibly learning—is a prominent part of bowerbird behavior. Young males build "practice" bowers that are initially rather crude. This preliminary stage lasts for up to two years and often involves groups of young males working together; it takes place before the adult plumage appears and is never accompanied by any attempt at courtship. Juveniles also frequently visit completed bowers, observing the building, the finished products, and the courtships. Though there is as yet no evidence that this experience serves them in any way, it seems possible that the youngsters might be learning something about what females value beyond the species-specific information provided by their genes. Even as adults the quality of their work improves year by year, and females tend to mate with that small subset of older males with the best-built courtship edifices.

A finished bower is constantly under repair by its owner; damage is inflicted not only by raiding males but also by weather (particularly heavy rain) and most of all by episodes of mating, which tend to be violent and can level a bower. The male also appears to be constantly experimenting with and optimizing his bower. Males observed from blinds over extended periods are seen to fuss over their ornaments,

The Lauterbach's bowerbird builds a bower with two parallel covered avenues. The white and green decorations are placed on a stick mat in front of one of these tunnels. The male holds a favorite ornament in his beak during the courtship display, alternately showing and hiding it from the female's view.

repositioning one, moving back to look at it from a different angle to judge the effect of the redecoration; then, more often than not, returning the ornament to its original position and shifting another. They are alert for the first signs of fading in the flowers they gather, and search out fresh blossoms as often as necessary.

Males seem just as alert as females to what constitutes a good bower, and they focus their raids on the best-built and most attractively decorated bowers in their neighborhood, thus enhancing the comparative ranking of their own. Many bowers are unique in their detailing, suggesting a role for individual judgment in the optimal design. The bird immediately adjusts the slightest change in design (caused by the wind, another bird, or an experimenter), and if an entire bower is picked up and rotated slightly (an experiment that incidentally testifies to the strength and careful construction of these structures), the returning male, unable to rotate the bower back, tears it down and starts all over again.

Beyond these individual preferences, there is evidence of a kind of cultural aesthetic, as seen in the different styles of two groups of the same species. The Vogelkop bowerbird found in the Wandamen

Mountains of New Guinea constructs a thatched hut 60 to 80 cm high and 100 to 200 cm in diameter, complete with doorway; this structure protects an interior project, which consists of a decorated maypole supporting a moss cone placed centrally on a large moss mat. The mat itself, as close to a perfect circle as seems possible, is made by weaving strands of moss tightly together. At the base of the cone, lying on the mat, is a precise array of radially arranged sticks, and farther out on the mat are the decorations. They are mainly black: black fruits, black fungi, and shiny black beetle wings; some males customize the array with a few red and orange fruits.

In contrast to these bowers, males living just 200 kilometers away in the drier Kumawa Mountains of New Guinea build the identical style of maypole but dispense with the thatched protection of the hut. The local color of choice is not black, but brown: brown acorns, brown stones, brown snail shells, brown sticks, and shiny brown beetle wings. Experiments that involve leaving colorful poker chips near the nest have shown that Kumawa birds inevitably remove them, but some Wandamen birds add them to the display, preferring not only orange and red, but blue and purple as well. The difference in style between the two groups may be genetic, but given the time the birds dedicate to observation and practice, cultural transmission of "taste" seems much more likely.

There has been considerable debate about the cognitive powers of bowerbirds. Even the staunch advocate of the overwhelming role of instinct in behavior, Karl von Frisch, comments that "some people are convinced that our mental states differ fundamentally from those of animals and that only we humans possess the faculty of thought. Even in displays as elaborate as those of bowerbirds, they see the working of innate instincts and the effects of natural selection. Such a theory cannot be refuted. But I myself do not much believe in it." The ontogeny of bower-building, its flexibility, the role of individual variation, and the (very likely) cultural dimension, all suggest that this behavior goes at least one step beyond even the goal-directed building of other species. The individuals are not only able to escape from rote task-oriented programming to achieve a goal, they are able to some extent to set that goal for themselves, or at least the details of the goal—to the extent that these individual details consistently differ from some species-specific default model. The temptation to invoke the word "thought" here is almost overwhelming.

MAMMALIAN NESTS

Because the developing embryo is carried by the mother until birth, mammals have less need than birds to make nests. But if the young are helpless and immature, which is the case for most rodents (the most numerous order of mammals), they need a refuge for postnatal development. Field mice, for instance, build elegant little nests, but like birds they recognize the appropriate material innately, and the design is preordained. At one time this seemed the universal case, but Donald Griffin's recent reëxamination of the literature on the construction of beaver lodges and dams indicates that the handiwork of at least this one species is unlikely to be the mindless product of innate guidelines.

Beavers live on the twigs and young branches of trees, tree bark, and the roots and tubers of water plants. Symbiotic microörganisms in the intestines of these aquatic rodents help digest the cellulose;

Beavers often tunnel into high banks from under water to create nest chambers above the waterline. The water may rise after the dam is built, requiring the beavers to create a new chamber inside the mound of sticks they have already positioned above the putative location of this second den.

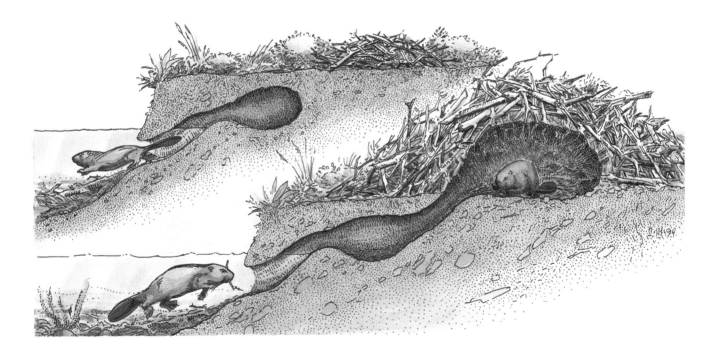

without these bacteria beavers, like termites, would starve. Beavers are usually found in habitats with cold winters where the ponds and streams they inhabit freeze over. Nearly all their construction behavior is directed toward regulating water levels during the winter.

The heart of beaver family life is the lodge, which can be built on land or in the middle of the pond. On land, the beaver pair or family chooses a bank sufficiently high to permit the construction of a large underground chamber above the water level of the pond or stream, and steep enough so that the tunnel that will connect the chamber to the adjacent water is not too long. The lodge must be above water so its inhabitants can breathe and dry themselves. Beavers excavate the upward-slanting tunnel to the lodge from well below the waterline so that their access to the water will not be blocked in winter by ice.

Because the beavers pile sticks and branches above the lodge chamber, they can excavate upward from within the lodge and thus stay above water even if the water level rises. They stockpile sticks under water for the winter, and when the food supply in the lodge runs out during the cold months, more is brought in from underwater storage depots.

Collecting enough material for this larder and the family's various construction projects takes considerable organization and teamwork. Often two beavers take turns working to fell particularly large trees in order to get at the higher bark and edible upper branches. Trees along shore often lean out over the water where there is more light for their leaves, and so when they are felled they conveniently drop into the pond or stream. Trees in from the shore provide a more difficult challenge, and beavers clear roads into the woods along which branches of felled trees can be dragged to the water. Sometimes they even dig long canals into the forest; though they are a great deal of effort to excavate, they make transport much easier.

Beavers must contend with fluctuating water levels: high water can flood the lodge, and low water can leave the entrance tunnel open to predators or clogged with ice during the winter. The solution is to dam the stream or pond to generate stability and an extra measure of safety. The dam creates a minimum water level (except in times of severe drought) as well as a safety valve, since during floods the beavers open holes in the dam and thus lower the water level. Beavers sometimes also make gaps in the dam after their pond has iced over, producing an air space between the surface ice and the water that al-

After the dams are built, beavers may be able to create a new lodge protected by water on all sides.

lows them to forage farther from the lodge without having to return home just to breathe.

The structure of these multipurpose dams depends greatly on the local topography. If the stream is narrow, the beavers may be able to begin with a fallen log (either already in place or felled by them) that lies across the flow of water. They then drive branches vertically into the streambed immediately downstream of the log (thus bracing it in place) and upstream of it (these branches are stabilized by the log). If sizable rocks are available, the beavers may use them to reinforce their structure and make it watertight with mud, clay, smaller stones, and sticks.

In the absence of a starting log, beavers take advantage of existing boulders or trees on the bank to use as foundations. In these cases, however, they usually have to cut long branches to act as downstream braces on the vertical branches driven into the stream bottom. The scale on which beavers can operate is remarkable: some dams are over 100 m long, and the record is 700 m.

Ideally the dam raises the water enough to surround the lodge with water, making it safe from terrestrial attack. Alternatively, a family may undertake to build a new lodge in the middle of its pond by piling up stones, mud, clay, and sticks to create a platform and then constructing a superstructure of sticks and branches, usually beginning with a radial teepeelike array of load-bearing branches. When the lodge is complete, the family moves in.

This natural history makes it hard to believe that dam-building behavior is not, at the very least, goal oriented rather than task directed. It seems likely that beavers are operating with an idea of ends that need to be achieved and have an ability to think, at some level, about how best to go about accomplishing them. This is not to say that, as we have come to expect, most of the basic techniques are not innate: hand-raised beavers fell trees and build simple dams. But innate micromanagement of each necessarily changeable step in producing dams and lodges is extremely unlikely.

This capacity for flexible problem-solving is reflected in various interactions between beavers and humans. Beavers will take over suitable buildings on shore, for instance, and use them as lodges; clearly they understand what they need and are not locked into some sort of computerlike routine that compels them to *make* lodges. Similarly, they will use human-built dams, adding an additional course of stones cemented with their usual mud, clay, and twig plaster where appropriate; there is no compulsion to build the usual substructure of reinforced vertical branches or to work mainly in wood and earth. When humans attempt to fence off particularly valuable trees, beavers can build the sort of ramp structures used in medieval sieges to surmount the protective outer rampart.

One group of researchers attempted to keep beavers in an artificial pond that was drained by a pipe with 8-mm holes in its protective cap. After a few weeks the beavers began cutting and modifying branches with sharpened points, rather like enormous pencils, which they used to plug each hole.

Beavers have a remarkable grasp of the way water works, which aids them not only in repairing the inevitable leaks, but also in placement and general structural work. Their apparent understanding of hydrodynamics may also help them manage emergency repairs in case of massive damage to the dam. In such situations the beavers show more presence of mind than do some humans in analogous situations, discarding familiar techniques as they prove futile and trying what

Beaver dams help prevent fluctuations in the water level that would expose the burrow entrance. The structure usually has a framework of branches, trunks, and stones, filled with mud and sticks.

seem to be novel strategies in an effort to find quick solutions to grave and unexpected problems.

Beavers are not infallible: pairs working together sometimes begin cutting through trunks at different heights, often let the trees fall in what we would consider the wrong direction, and even build small dams that appear to be extraneous. But given their general finesse at what they are about, if beavers do not have a general understanding of the tasks they face, then the power of innate programming extends far, far beyond anything we yet have evidence for.

The consensus among anthropologists is that the challenges of our early hunter-gatherer niche led to the runaway increase in human brain volume that has left us with the highest brain-to-body-mass ratio in the animal kingdom. It should come as little surprise to discover that, even in proportion to its massive body size (20 to 30 kg), the beaver brain is easily the largest among rodents. It seems likely that this extra ratio of neural mass has evolved to help beavers meet the enormous cognitive challenges their unique life style poses.

7

Hunting
and Escaping

ay to day, finding food and avoiding predation are undoubtedly the top two priorities for most organisms, and as such are likely to provide a strong impetus for the development of intellect. Some animals specialize on a single type or even a single species of animal or plant, and there is rarely much evidence of planning or innovation in their foraging behavior. Similarly, survival techniques can be fairly straightforward: stay alert and either hide or move away as rapidly as possible in the face of a threat. But some animals employ deceit rather than escape, an approach that may require more subtle calculation than simply running away. By the same token, for animals with more catholic diets there is a potential advantage for individuals that can locate and exploit a new food source, or that can develop a novel technique for getting at a known food more efficiently.

DECEPTION STRATEGIES

The animal world is full of deceptions that have no cognitive basis whatsoever or, like camouflage, are completely passive. Drone flies, for instance, look like stinging bees and therefore enjoy a measure of protection from insectivorous but wary birds; some tropical praying mantids look like flowers and capture the nectar-feeding insects they fool. Even when the deception is active, many cases are probably no more than species-typical behavior, either innate or learned—that is,

CHEETAHS AFTER OUTRUNNING A

THOMSON'S GAZELLE.

there is nothing to suggest that the individual deceiver is "reading" the dupe and adjusting its behavior accordingly. The females of one species of firefly, for instance, after mating mimic the sexual responses of another firefly species; these siren females eat the males they lure in this way, obtaining extra nutrients that permit the production of additional eggs. But the false alarm calls uttered by shrikes in mixed-species flocks of foraging birds do suggest something more.

The major selective advantage of mixed-flock feeding is increased vigilance: flocks have more eyes than individual birds for both aerial and terrestrial predators, and because the species making up these flocks have slightly different feeding niches, the costs of competition are minimized. In tropical mixed flocks the range of species is wide, including birds specialized for a variety of heights from the forest floor to the canopy top, as well as for differences in hunting techniques and food preferences.

The species usually fall into two classes: one focuses on the understory plants while the other works the trees. Each group has a typical lead species, the one that forages higher than all the others, that flies ahead and calls, inciting the others to follow. The lead species—often antshrikes in the understory and shrike-tanagers in the canopy—spend much of their time perched, watching for the opportunity to swoop down and capture flying insects.

The perch-and-search strategy enables the shrikes to act as sentinel birds, spotting aerial predators before any of the other species do; since hawks and other raptors are the major threat to the flock as a whole, the other birds follow the sentinels when they move to new positions. And because most of the insects the sentinels catch are flushed by the other birds, it is not surprising that the sentinels wait for the rest of the flock to follow and then give them time to feed before moving on. Since the shrikes have the advantage of gravity-assisted speed and are more agile fliers than any of the other flock members, they are successful in capturing most of the insects they choose to swoop for.

When a sentinel spots a hawk, it emits an alarm call; the other birds stop what they are doing to look up or head for cover, though they will not actually drop an insect they have already captured. When, as occasionally happens, an especially large or desirable insect is flushed *and* one of the lower-foraging birds appears likely to capture it, the pursuing shrike sometimes emits a hawk alarm call. The bird that had been chasing the insect interrupts its attack and takes cover, and the shrike gets the insect.

The shrike's use of its alarm call is therefore not simply an automatic response to hawks. Additionally, there is a flexible component to the behavior. If the lower-foraging bird manages to capture the prey, the shrike can abort the alarm in mid-call and turn its vocalization into another kind of signal—a sensible strategy, since too many false alarm calls might discourage the shrike's staff of prey-flushers. Other animals with separate terrestrial-predator and aerial-predator calls, like chickens and ground squirrels, take the size and makeup of their audience into account before emitting even a genuine call; here too, judgments of some cognitive complexity intervene between stimulus and response.

Researchers have reported the use of false alarm calls in other situations: great tits, for instance, sometimes use bogus alarm calls to scare sparrows from a feeder. A boundary dispute observed between two groups of vervet monkeys was ended prematurely by a member of the losing side when he produced the species' terrestrial-predator call: the opponents fled from a phantom leopard before the issue had been decided. A skeptic could argue that false calling is a built-in backup strategy that animals are programmed to use when competition for highly desirable food or status is keen. But the behavior shows none of the characteristics of a task-directed ploy; instead, the flexibility, restraint, sensitivity to context, and infrequency of use all suggest that the animals understand how the call can be used to achieve larger and longer-term goals.

A very different sort of deception is practiced by many ground-living birds and chicks that are unable to fly. When a predator such as a fox catches one in its jaws, the prey may struggle, then cease to move. If other birds are still scurrying to escape, the predator will often drop the one it has apparently already killed and pursue a second victim. After a moment, the dropped bird gets up and runs away.

When observed and tested in our laboratory, the bird's behavior, known as tonic immobility, appears to have elements of both innate programming and individual risk assessment: death-feigning can be induced by trapping the chick and exposing it to a pair of eyes—marbles on the ends of a pair of sticks will do, but realistic eyes mounted on an object are better. A pair of forward-looking eyes that provide the binocular vision necessary for judging distance to prey is a pretty reliable indication that an animal is a predator; but in a prey species usually only one eye can be seen at a time: the second eye is on the other side of the head, watching for danger from a different direction. Two eyes rather than one, then, seems to signal danger. The

A hognose snake feigning death. The snake can also exude blood from special glands near the mouth.

interesting lab discovery is that after beginning its death-feigning, the bird slowly opens its eyes every half minute or so and looks for the predator. If the paired eyes are still present, the bird slowly recloses its eyes. When a check reveals that the coast is clear, the bird is more likely to get up and head for cover.

No one as yet has posed the necessary experimental questions to determine whether the bird understands the situation it is in, or whether it is endowed with a set of risk–benefit rules to guide its behavior. For example, a pair of 1 cm "eyes" set 5 cm apart on a brown head shape is very effective in eliciting death-feigning; would a chick find the same pair with the same spacing as effective if each eye were mounted on a *separate* head shape? If not, would that indicate it understood it was seeing two prey animals rather than one predator? What would happen if the predator closed one eye after grasping the chick?

More is known about a set of chick-saving stratagems employed by ground-nesting birds. Though formerly written off as mindless innate ploys, they are now known to be highly flexible in use. The most thoroughly studied cases involve plovers and the closely related killdeer, small birds that typically nest on beaches or in open fields. Their nests are mere scrapes in the sand or earth, and plovers have an effective repertoire of tricks for distracting potential nest predators from their exposed and defenseless eggs or chicks.

The ever-watchful plover can detect a possible threat at a considerable distance. When she does, the nesting bird moves inconspicuously off the nest to a spot well away from eggs or chicks. At this point she may use any one of at least four ploys. One technique involves first moving quietly toward an approaching animal and then setting off noisily through the grass or brush in a low, crouching run away from the nest while emitting rodentlike squeaks. The effect mimics a scurrying mouse or vole, and the behavior rivets the attention of just the sort of predators that would also be interested in eggs and chicks.

Another deception begins with quiet movement to an exposed and visible location well away from the nest; once there, the bird pretends to incubate a brood. When the predator approaches, the parent flees, leaving the false nest to be searched. The direction in which the plover "escapes" is such that if the predator chooses to follow, it will be led still farther away from the true nest.

In a third possible manoeuver the bird begins calling loudly once it has moved quietly well away from the nest. The distracting parent

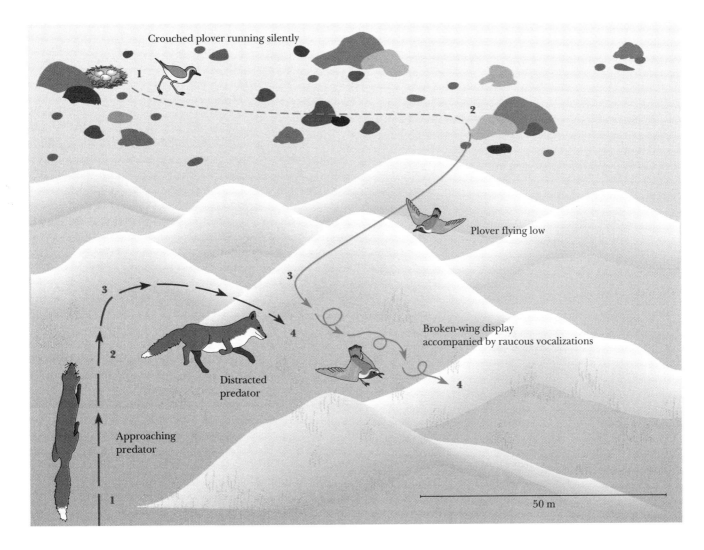

Crouched plover running silently

1

2

Plover flying low

3

3

4

Broken-wing display
accompanied by raucous vocalizations

4

Distracted
predator

Approaching
predator

2

1

50 m

alternates between moving toward and away from the predator, always providing various vocal and visual stimuli that cannot fail to attract attention. The movements away from the threat are oriented away from the nest as well. As with the other displays, the predator is often lured 300 m or more away from the eggs or chicks before the plover returns to the nest inconspicuously by a roundabout route.

As a human intruder, or theoretically a predator, approaches the nest, the plover moves rapidly but inconspicuously away, then walks or flies to an exposed location and begins a broken-wing display, complete with raucous sound effects. As the intruder begins to stalk the seemingly helpless bird, the plover moves steadily away from its nest.

A plover beginning its broken-wing display.

The plover's most famous stratagem is the broken-wing display, actually a continuum of injury-mimicking behaviors spanning the range from slight disability to near-complete helplessness. One or both wings (and perhaps even the tail) are held in an abnormal position, suggesting injury; the bird appears to be attempting escape along an irregular route that indicates panic. In the most extreme version of the display the bird flaps one wing in an apparent attempt to take to the air, flops over helplessly, struggles back to its feet, runs away a short distance, seemingly attempts once more to take off, flops over again as the "useless" wing fails to provide any lift, and so on. Few predators fail to pursue such obviously vulnerable prey. Needless to say, each short run between "flight attempts" is directed away from the nest.

At one time these distraction displays were thought to be the incidental result of strong conflicting emotions in the parent bird—fear (the desire to flee from danger), aggression (the desire to protect the nest), and brooding (the desire to incubate the eggs or remain near the chicks). Cases of conflict behavior are well known among animals, but they usually take the form of an inappropriate but otherwise normal part of the behavioral repertoire of the species. This redirected or displacement behavior seems to satisfy the animal's need to do *something* even though all the relevant responses are inhibited. Thus a male gull defending his territory may be caught between a desire to attack a neighbor who is close to his border and fear of being attacked himself if he steps off his own territory. In the face of this kind of conflict the male often vents his apparent frustration by pulling bits of grass, part of the innate behavior used to gather nesting material. But flapping just one wing is not normal plover behavior; nor is it very plausible to suggest that the behavior is an abnormal result of the conflict between flight and defense, with the resulting "compromise" the use of only one wing for escape while the other is kept ready for attack.

Thanks largely to the recent work of Carolyn Ristau, we now have some idea of what is going on in the mind of the plover. One telling observation is that, like the death-feigning chicks, the displaying plover periodically looks at the predator; if the threatening animal has not moved toward the parent bird, the plover moves to another spot and begins a new, usually higher intensity, display. Only once the predator is beginning to follow does the plover commit itself to a particular role and begin to maintain a relatively consistent course away from the nest. Ristau found these displays so effective that 87 percent of the time the threatening animal never came any closer to the nest and was ultimately led away in essentially all instances.

In this study and follow-up work, Ristau also found that plovers come to recognize individual humans (by their dress and manner) and learn which are threats—that is, which ones approach nests and which ones ignore both displays and nests. The "safe" humans soon elicit much less distraction activity. Killdeer, the field-nesting relative of the plover, learn that grazing cattle ignore *distraction* displays and are uninterested in finding nests; they produce instead a *warning* display that serves to prevent the clumsy animal from stepping on the nest.

Plovers are not perfect dissemblers: they are not always successful and they sometimes misjudge the degree of the threat posed by an approaching animal. But humans also frequently make errors of judgment and fail in their aims. The essential point is that plovers perform very well in a task that seems to require a fair degree of cognitive power. By apparently analyzing the motives of the animal in its habitat by species (as with cattle) or as individuals (as it does at least with humans), the plover protects its eggs or chicks both from predation and the unnecessary risk of chilling or overheating in an uncovered nest. The highly graded and flexible nature of the behavior strongly implies that these birds have some understanding of the subtleties that are involved in the achievement of their goals.

NOVEL TECHNIQUES

Most birds have a fairly well-defined feeding niche or foraging style. Blue tits look for insect larvae under leaves and bark; purple martins take flying insects on the wing, many finches crack seeds on the ground, woodpeckers drill into trees for grubs. The beaks, feet, wings, and tails of most species provide strong clues about an animal's feeding niche.

But the morphology of predatory birds (hawks, for example) that capture any of a number of species of relatively large moving prey, and generalists, including crows and ravens, that forage on a variety of foods ranging from grain to the nestlings of other birds, is less specialized, and there is an obvious need for greater behavioral flexibility. It may be no coincidence that these two groups have the highest avian brain-to-body-mass ratios.

The most intriguing evidence for some degree of insight comes from the problems faced by birds attempting to take unusual prey. Individuals of three different species of hawk, for instance, have been observed to take birds they could not readily kill to nearby bodies of water (in one instance, a puddle) and hold their victim's head below the surface until the animal ceased to struggle. In another well-substantiated case white pelicans at the Cairo zoo habitually seize, drown, and then swallow unwary ducks. So far as we know, pelicans have never been observed hunting anything but fish in the wild. But these data, though intriguing, are anecdotal, and nothing is known of the events leading up to the behavior.

The extreme rarity of these incidents suggests that drowning prey is not part of the innate repertoire of these species but appears to have been discovered independently by different birds. Almost any scenario, including forms of operant conditioning, seems to require the

One of Heinrich's ravens solving the meat-on-the-string puzzle.

bird that discovers this tactic to understand that animals held under water eventually stop struggling.

Generalist birds offer a far better opportunity for controlled study. A recent set of experiments by Bernd Heinrich provides some insight into the ontogeny of novel behavior in ravens. Heinrich raised nestlings by hand and, when they were mature, hung small pieces of meat on strings from horizontal poles in their aviary. At first the ravens attempted to take the meat on the wing, but the food could not be detached. Then they tried standing on the pole and reaching for the food with their bills, drawing the long string up partway; but they still could not reach the meat.

After six hours one of the birds performed the entire series of actions necessary to solve the problem. He drew the string up with his bill, caught it with a foot, and let it fall from his beak; he then reached down with his bill, drew up more string, caught the next bit with a foot, and so on until the meat was within reach. In a few days, a second raven solved the problem, and ultimately four of the five birds learned how to get the food, though they used two strikingly different techniques. Two birds stayed in one place on the pole and piled up the loops of string; the other two moved laterally on the pole, leaving the string stretched out lengthwise.

Heinrich concluded that the birds understood the problem and that in spite of the opportunity to observe one another each solved it independently by what we have called cognitive trial and error—that is, each was able to execute the complete successful behavior pattern without experimental intermediates. Analogous string problems posed to more specialist feeders have either gone unsolved or have required extensive experimentation before an individual discovered an answer; this difference underscores the apparent ability of ravens to *imagine* a solution. Moreover, the ravens seemed to comprehend the very unnatural relationship between the food and its constraining string. In nature, a startled raven flies off with whatever is in its beak; in Heinrich's aviary, birds that had solved the string problem would drop the meat before taking flight if it was still attached to the string when he startled them. Birds that had yet to work out a solution would take off with the food in their beaks, only to have it yanked out jarringly when their flight took them beyond the string's reach. Heinrich's raven study, which gives hand-raised, inexperienced animals puzzles to unravel, should provide a model for future work on how animals solve problems.

Perhaps the most compelling example of apparent innovation among free-living birds comes from observations of green herons. On five separate occasions during the past three decades, in five different places (separated by thousands of kilometers) one or more green herons has initiated the practice of bait-fishing.

A bait-fishing heron tosses a small, low-density object like a piece of bread or a twig into the water. As any angler knows, a variety of fish will dart to the surface and inspect anything that lands in case it might be prey. The watchful heron lunges at any fish that rises to the bait.

Very few herons use this ploy, and the practice has been observed to die out in some places, indicating that cultural transmission may be relatively inefficient. In other locations where groups of herons live together, only a few birds ever pick up the practice, but the tradition seems to be relatively stable. In one area bait-fishing appeared briefly in a group near some bait-fishers, though the herons were not tagged and this may have been a case of emigration.

One suggested explanation is that the practice is an artifact of exposure to humans: a bird might have picked up the practice by observing children tossing bread crumbs to fish. But human efforts to teach herons in this way have consistently failed, and it seems more

A green heron casting its breadcube upon the water.

likely that the technique was discovered independently by individual birds.

Since all herons must see things fall into the water, and many must also see fish briefly inspect them, the rarity of the behavior indicates that the association is an exceedingly difficult one to make. It is not difficult to suppose that bait-fishing is discovered by the Einsteins among the herons, and learned from them by only the brightest of their neighbors. Skeptics, however, would argue that the behavior is a conventional piece of operant conditioning involving no special insight. They would account for its rarity by noting the infrequency with which herons normally drop debris in the water; operant conditioning can occur only if the bird itself performs the dropping behavior (observation of other birds could play no role) and then makes the association between dropping the bait and the arrival of prey. The definitive answer depends on the unlikely circumstance of observing the de novo acquisition of the behavior in the wild. For now, we must use our intuition to infer the most probable scenario.

FOOD CACHING AND RECOVERY

The foraging behavior of many birds and mammals provides clear evidence for the use of cognitive maps. Studies of marsh tits, a species that caches seeds and later recovers them, indicate that these tiny birds can remember the location of scores of hidden seeds. The memory relies on a landmark-based map. In the most conclusive of many experiments, David Sherry and his colleagues covered one eye of a bird foraging in the laboratory. Because the eyes of this species are on opposite sides of its head, it has almost no binocular vision. Thus when the bird was allowed to become hungry and was tested a day later with the same eye covered, it searched accurately; when the cover was moved to the other eye, however, the bird searched randomly. It was evident that the bird was neither using olfactory cues nor leaving behind subtle clues while hiding the seeds. Moreover, the bird's memory of its caches was relatively flexible, as opposed to the fairly rigid rote learning and recall behavior seen in some insects: the bird recovered seeds in an order different from that in which it had stored them, tending to move to the next-nearest seed.

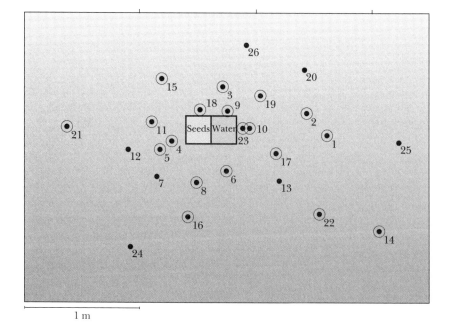

In one experiment, a Clark's nutcracker was given 26 seeds and hid them in the order indicated. The experimenters removed half the seeds from their hiding places so that the birds would have no olfactory cues. When the bird was allowed back a month later, it probed 20 locations, 18 of which (the sites circled) were cache sites; 10 were sites from which the seeds had been removed.

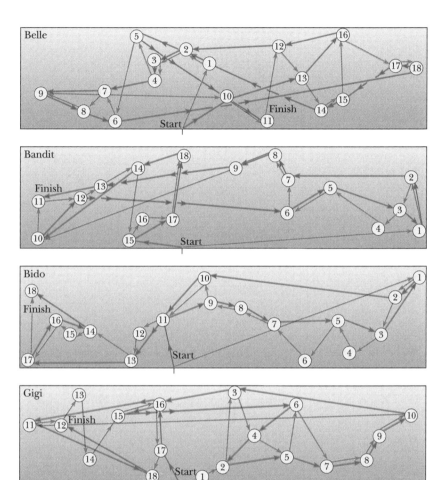

Individual chimpanzees were shown food caches in the order indicated by the numbers and the red arrows. When released later the chimps located most of the caches, but in a completely different order (blue arrows).

15 m

Chimpanzees display equally clear evidence of landmark-based map memory. In an experiment typical of the sort first performed by Emil Menzel in the early 1970s, a chimp is carried about an enclosure and shown a series of hiding places containing food. The order of sites visited in this tour is deliberately random, to make the task as difficult as possible. When allowed back after varying delays, the chimp chooses a much more direct route between sites and searches only in the baited areas. It is indisputable that the animal is remembering the relative location of each, just as we would.

Similarly, in an experiment designed by David Olton, rats interrupted in their exploration of a maze with eight radial arms, each baited with food, remember for hours or even days which corridors they have searched. They manage this task even though they do not explore the arms in any systematic order. The rats' knowledge of which arms they have explored is based on their memory of landmarks in the maze or cues visible above it; moving these cues reorients the animals' searches. The ability to construct and use maps seems to be prevalent throughout the species of birds and mammals thus far studied. As our exploration of the honey bee Umwelt has suggested, the use of cognitive maps is likely to be based on an internal representation of the outside world, and an ability to plan behavior based on this representation and the animal's prior experience in the area. And planning is the essential ingredient in nearly any definition of thinking.

COÖPERATIVE HUNTING

The coördination essential in coöperative hunting strongly suggests a degree of planning. Groups of pelicans sometimes hunt by forming first a line, then an arc, and finally a circle around a school of fish; only when the prey has been herded and trapped do the pelicans begin to feed.

Coöperation in hunting is often seen when prey are too large to be captured by a lone hunter. A single hyena is unlikely to bring down a wildebeest, but a pack can separate a victim from its herd, take turns running it until it becomes winded, and then attempt to injure it by attacks on several fronts. Even some predatory birds coöperate to take prey larger than themselves—hawks can kill rabbits twice their weight

These pelicans have coöperatively rounded up and encircled a school of fish.

if they coördinate their efforts at hunting, flushing, turning, and killing the victim.

The best-known group-hunting species is the lion. Even though these enormously powerful animals can kill most prey without help, group hunts increase their chances of success. Records of hunts show that lions frequently employ a division of labor in which some animals routinely occupy the center or flanks of a hunting group; flanking animals are the ones most often in a position to encircle target herds. Some of the lions distract the herd's attention while other members of the pride wait in ambush; still others take up positions from which they drive the prey toward their hidden colleagues. Lions would be more successful if they were to discover the importance of wind direction: these otherwise canny hunters do not seem to avoid hunting from upwind, even though prey are quick to flee when they catch a lion's scent.

A telling characteristic of coöperative hunts is that the animals do not seem to have a leader to organize matters. Because a pride hunts together daily, it seems likely that its members know one another's habits and preferred techniques. During a hunt the lions seem to take cues from one another's behavior, judge from that what the various hunters intend to do, and plan their own behavior accordingly. Even though hunt scenarios can vary widely, the members of the pride generally carry off a creditable (though not always successful) attack. In short, an ability to judge intentions and to plan seems essential to lions.

In perhaps the most remarkable example of group hunting two different species coöperate to locate and harvest a resource. The African honeyguide feeds on insects, insect larvae, and beeswax. The ability to digest wax is a very unusual metabolic trait, and thus a priori evidence that honeyguides are specialists on bees. But honey bee nests in Africa are almost always enclosed, usually in tree cavities; honeyguides have no way of breaking into these nests. (In tropical Asia, on the other hand, most honey bees live on exposed comb. It seems likely that the honeyguide evolved its wax-digesting specialization in association with exposed-comb bees, either in Asia or, when the climate there was more hospitable to exposed-comb living, in Africa.)

The answer to this problem is the honey badger, a powerful mammal capable of tearing open tree cavities, where it feeds on the honey in the nest. The honeyguide, as its name suggests, leads badgers to bee colonies. When it has located first a nest and then a honey bad-

A honey badger, whose powerful claws can splinter wood to get to honey combs, is used as a "tool" by the African honeyguide, which locates the wild honey bee nests and eats the wax and larvae.

ger, the bird begins a noisy display that attracts the badger's attention. The guide then makes a short display flight away and begins calling again. If the badger begins to follow, the pattern continues until the badger has been led to the hive, which may be up to 2 km away. Then the guide perches and remains silent, and the badger goes about his work. When the badger finishes the honey, his scout and guide moves in to consume the larvae and wax.

Honeyguides also attempt to lead humans to honey bee nests. The pattern is the same, and the persistence of a guide that is being ignored is remarkable: in some cases a bird has followed a human many kilometers attempting to attract his attention, trying a variety of different strategies to induce following. Studies of an African tribe that regularly coöperates with honeyguides show that unaided human searchers take about nine hours to locate a colony, as opposed to three hours with the help of a honeyguide. Clearly the relationship is mutually advantageous.

The question, then, is what sort of cognitive processing underlies honeyguide behavior. Obviously the birds are using some sort of internal maplike representation that allows them to lead in the correct direction. One incident reveals just how sophisticated this map is: A guide attempted unsuccessfully to recruit a group of workers, and followed them as they travelled by truck to a location 8 km away. Once at the site, one of the workers began to follow the bird on foot and was led to a nest only a kilometer away. Since no honeyguide has ever been observed to lead humans or honey badgers much more than about 2 km, it seems very likely that this particular bird knew the locations of at least two nests, switching targets when its intended helpers moved.

The more interesting question is whether honeyguides (or honey badgers) understand what they are doing. The ontogeny of the behavior in honeyguides is unknown; presumably the guiding is learned from the parent birds, since the display varies between individuals (some mimic a honey badger call, a few mimic the sound of breaking wood, and there are other tactics). The persistence of honeyguides in attracting the attention of badgers and humans, the context-dependent flexibility of the accompanying behavior, as well as the apparent ability to switch targets all suggest that the birds have a fairly clear picture of the goal of their behavior.

The conclusion that some animals *do* understand the essential elements of their foraging behavior seems a simpler and more parsimonious alternative to the baroque explanations required if conventional conditioning theory is invoked. It seems more likely, for instance, that the rattle of a food box that brings a pet running does so not as a result of an elaborate combination of classical and operant conditioning (though that may have had a role initially), but rather because the sound calls to the animal's mind a picture of the food or its odor, and its cognitive map of home allows it to select the most efficient route to the goal.

As we learn more about the natural behavior of certain species, programming and conditioning seem to explain less and less. And yet the fact remains that most animals in most contexts do not appear to need, have, or use any understanding, nor do they attempt innovations. To the extent that cognitive powers have evolved, they seem to be focused on the kinds of situations that require them. It is as though thinking is a potentially dangerous backup strategy, too slow and error-prone to be applied indiscriminately.

Social and Personal Knowledge

KNOWLEDGE IS POWER.

Francis Bacon,
Meditationes Sacrae, 1597

ost behavior is, as natural selection predicts, selfish. Yet animals do help one another: dolphins keep injured members of the group afloat, vampire bats share food with starving inhabitants of their colony, childless elephants help form a defensive circle to protect the young of the herd. And if all animal behavior is ultimately self-protective, why are some pets apparently despondent when their owners die? What do these seemingly altruistic or emotional responses, observed almost exclusively in social species, tell us about the animal mind? Are some animals empathetic, or are our untutored impressions deceiving us?

In fact, most apparent altruism and sympathy is essentially selfish, benefiting the giver directly or indirectly. Often the recipient is a relative: if the benefit an animal receives from protecting a niece or nephew from a predator, for instance, is worth much more than it costs in terms of, say, wasted time or risk of injury, selection will favor this behavior. Or if the recipient of help can be expected to repay the favor when it is needed—to share food when the original lender is starving, for example—then selection will work to induce sharing on the part of those with a temporary surplus. Nevertheless, these two kinds of selfish helping, which are known as kin-directed altruism and reciprocal altruism, require animals to understand a great deal about social relationships and group dynamics. In this chapter we will look closely at the way animals manage the necessary social calculus. We

A FEMALE VERVET GROOMS A MALE AS PART OF

HER STRATEGY TO RISE IN THE DOMINANCE

HIERARCHY OF THE TROOP.

will find evidence of cognitive processing so sophisticated that individuals in at least certain species can deliberately trick and manipulate each other. This ability for flexible dissimulation may provide evidence for some degree of self-knowledge or awareness.

INDIVIDUAL RECOGNITION

We have seen that at least some animals alter their alarm-calling in response to their audience. Chickens are more likely to call if there are other chickens nearby, and ground squirrels tend to remain silent unless the individuals in the vicinity are close relatives. In each case the behavior is suited to the context: the ground squirrels' fine relational discriminations demonstrate that a fair amount of social knowledge is also involved.

By far the clearest examples of social awareness come from primates, particularly monkeys (including vervets, baboons, and macaques) and chimpanzees. The key to interpreting primate social interactions is understanding, as they clearly do, the social hierarchy and bonds of kinship in a group. An individual normally works to appease a dominant animal but can usually harass a subordinate with impunity; primates aid kin more often than they help unrelated animals, and close relatives more than distant kin. There is no doubt whatever that these animals are intimately familiar with their own place and that of every other member of the troop.

The most thorough study of the extent and consequences of social knowledge, the work of Robert Seyfarth and Dorothy Cheney, has

The alarm calls of vervets are specific to particular classes of predators. These sonograms show the calls elicited by eagles, leopards, and snakes.

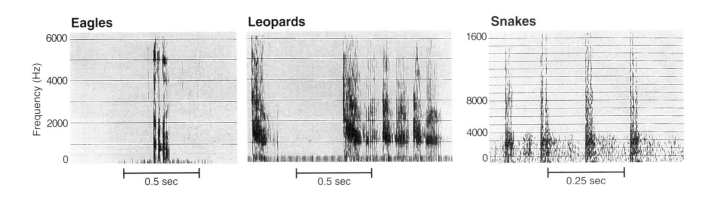

Eagles

Leopards

Snakes

Frequency (Hz)

6000

4000

2000

0

0.5 sec

0.5 sec

1600

8000

4000

0

0.25 sec

focused on the vervet monkey of East Africa. This species has a number of distinct vocalizations, including four alarm calls. One call is for aerial predators such as eagles and hawks; it causes the troop members to look up, seek cover in bushes, or drop from exposed positions in the tree canopy. A second call sends vervets into the trees to avoid leopards or other terrestrial predators. A third call signifies snakes, a slow-moving class of animals of which only a few are dangerous; vervets hearing this warning stand and look down at the grass. A fourth call seems to be associated with humans or other group-hunting predators. Playback experiments using hidden speakers and a tape recorder confirm that each distinctive action is in fact a response to the call, not to the threat itself: the vervets react directly to the recording without needing to see the predator.

The calls are innately produced and innately recognized, and young vervets seem to have some instinctive idea of the categories: they give aerial alarm calls for a variety of harmless birds and even falling leaves, and terrestrial calls for nearly any mammal. The adults, for their part, distinguish between the calls of juveniles, which elicit a casual look around, and the alarms of other adults, to which they usually react by redeploying first and looking second. Juveniles seem to learn which animals are genuine threats from the reactions of the adults, and they soon become more discriminating. In the case of aerial alarms, individuals can learn from the adults to focus on a single dangerous species—in most areas the martial eagle. Though some elements of the behavior are innate, it seems clear that the vervets understand exactly what each call means, and how credible each caller is.

Vervets have a number of other calls, two of which are used to draw the attention of group members to the approach of another group; the more serious "chutter" call frequently causes the troop to coalesce. When one of the "chutter" calls recorded from a single individual was played repeatedly, the troop members came to ignore it, usually by the eighth repetition; but when the same call recorded from another vervet in the group was then played, the troop responded normally by looking for approaching monkeys. This was not a simple case of habituation to a particular version of the call; when the "wrr" call (a less serious warning of a nearby group) recorded from the individual that had apparently been "crying wolf" was played back, the vervets ignored that too; playback of the same call from another member of the troop, however, was fully effective. In short, the vervets must be able to recognize each other as individuals by voice alone, and they learn whose messages are unreliable.

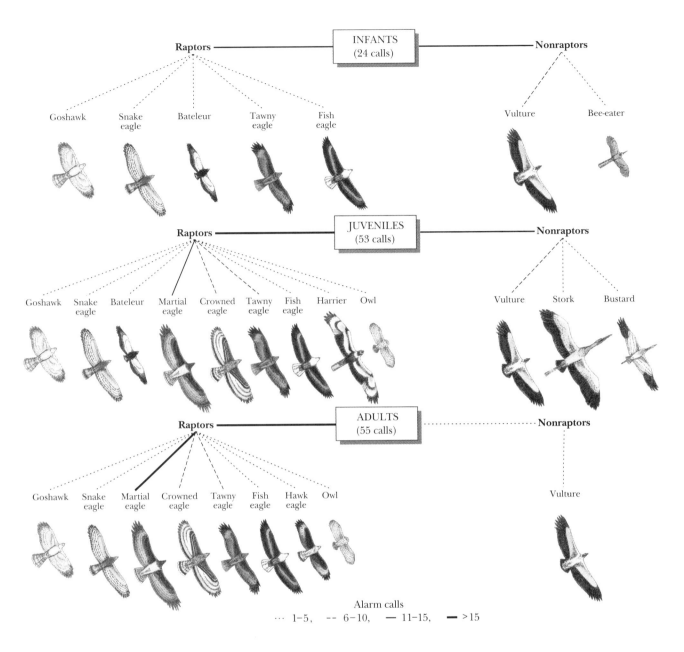

INFANTS
(24 calls)

Raptors ——— Nonraptors

Goshawk Snake eagle Bateleur Tawny eagle Fish eagle

Vulture Bee-eater

JUVENILES
(53 calls)

Raptors ——— Nonraptors

Goshawk Snake eagle Bateleur Martial eagle Crowned eagle Tawny eagle Fish eagle Harrier Owl

Vulture Stork Bustard

ADULTS
(55 calls)

Raptors ——— Nonraptors

Goshawk Snake eagle Martial eagle Crowned eagle Tawny eagle Fish eagle Hawk eagle Owl

Vulture

Alarm calls
··· 1–5, -- 6–10, — 11–15, ▬ >15

The alarm calls of vervets show both innate recognition and cultural learning. Eagle alarms are given by infant vervets in response to virtually any flying bird, and sometimes to butterflies and falling leaves; adults, on the other hand, direct the vast majority at martial eagles, the species that takes vervets in the region where these data were collected. When adults make mistakes, it is usually because the bird is so far away that it is little more than a dot in the sky.

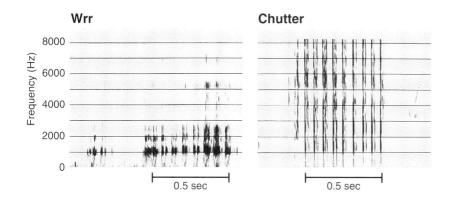

Wrr **Chutter**

Frequency (Hz): 8000, 6000, 4000, 2000, 0

0.5 sec   0.5 sec

Vervets also have distinct calls specifying two different degrees of threat from other troops, the "wrr" that signals the initial sighting of another group and the more serious "chutter" that accompanies aggressive interactions.

Vervets, baboons, and macaques show individual recognition in yet another way. Playbacks of infant distress calls produce an immediate reaction from the older females in a group: the mother of the recorded infant looks toward the source of the sound, while the other females look toward the mother.

In each of these cases, the behavior of animals demonstrates that they understand their own and one another's social standing and kinship relations and adjust their behavior accordingly. Does this imply that monkeys have a self-image, or is it that they are simply very smart about group dynamics?

SELF-IMAGE

The question of self-awareness is very touchy, evoking extreme emotional responses from many students of animal behavior. The Clever Hans fiasco still haunts us. Nevertheless, privately many primatologists (and publicly a few) concede that they assume that their subjects are to some degree self aware. In part this view may arise not because primates are so much smarter than other species, but because it is much easier for humans to read primate gestures and emotional expressions than the equivalents in, say, beavers or dolphins. It is also easier for us to empathize with behavioral responses to situations that could touch our own lives.

A primate behavior that strikes most observers as indicative of some form of interior experience is the apparent expression of grief.

When a wildebeest calf dies, its mother loses interest in it within minutes; when a juvenile baboon dies, on the other hand, the mother's behavior undergoes a long-lasting change. She becomes morose and withdrawn, and may carry her dead offspring with her for weeks. (To a lesser extent, the same behavior can be seen in a few other species—cheetahs, for instance.) The mother's unwillingness or inability to accept the death of her young could reflect an awareness of what it was to her; the behavior is certainly not an adaptive innate response to an inevitable fact of life.

A more objective approach to the question of possible self-awareness has been pioneered by Gordon Gallup. He became interested in the apparent ability of chimpanzees, reported first by Wolfgang Köhler, to recognize themselves in mirrors. When he studied the ontogeny

Frans de Waal photographed a young chimpanzee discovering the nature of a mirror image without the help of experimenters.

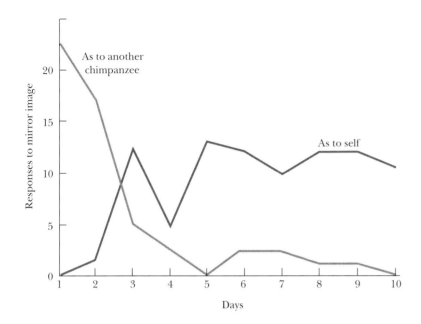

Chimpanzees respond initially to a mirror image as though it were another chimp, reacting with social gestures. Within a very few days, however, the chimp figures out what is going on and begins using the mirror for self-grooming.

of this behavior, he found that some (but not all) chimps stop treating mirror images as other chimpanzees within about four days; instead, they use the mirror as an aid in grooming themselves. Other researchers have found that some chimpanzees are quick to recognize themselves on video screens, and when the scene is live will use the camera and screen to explore themselves; in one case a chimp even used a flashlight and the television camera to inspect its throat.

Gallup showed that chimpanzees seem to understand that the image is of themselves by anesthetizing several and applying paint marks to their foreheads. When the animals awoke they showed no sign that they felt the marks, but when they caught sight of themselves in a mirror, each immediately began to rub at the spot on its own body and attempted to remove it.

Gallup tried the same experiment on a variety of large primates. Orangutans showed the same behavior, but gorillas (a species more closely related to humans than are orangutans) and baboons did not. This may suggest that the capacity for self-recognition may have arisen at least twice in primate evolution. Since staring is threat behavior in gorillas, however, the context surrounding Gallup's tests may have led

Chimpanzees in Gallup's experiments learn how to use mirrors for grooming or amusement.

his gorillas to avert their eyes from the image; Penny Patterson's gorilla Koko, living in very familiar surroundings, has been observed using a mirror to apply makeup. In any event, there is probably little selective advantage favoring the ability to use mirrors, and these results suggest to us that self-recognition may emerge as a secondary consequence of some other ability, or perhaps as an artifact of a high ratio of brain to body mass. Some other researchers, however, think these results can be explained in terms of operant conditioning: the animals are learning by trial and error how to groom themselves.

CIRCUMVENTING THE SOCIAL ORDER

The possible self-awareness of chimpanzees may be critical in enabling them to use a variety of social ploys that exploit their ability to manipulate others. These stratagems require an understanding of what signals mean, as well as the relative social status and special interests of the other animals involved. In general, social tricks are the refuge of the least-dominant individuals; those near the top of the hierarchy usually do not need to resort to subterfuges to get what they want.

The simplest manipulations involve food. As Jane Goodall and others have reported from the field, subordinates that find food and are noticed by dominants usually have it taken from them. The lesson is quickly learned. When Goodall first gave a young male some bananas, he uttered loud food barks; these signals promptly attracted older males, who took the bananas for themselves. The next day Goodall again gave the same male bananas; now he made only "faint, choking sounds in his throat . . . and ate his allotment undisturbed."

The innate food call can alert chimpanzees at a distance, and this clarity serves the group when an abundant supply such as a fruiting tree is discovered. When chimps are together, they monitor each other's behavior directly, in particular following one another's gaze in an apparent effort to discover what has caught an individual's attention. Thus if a subordinate spots a food item, others will almost always see it too and claim the meal first. Emil Menzel tried carrying one member of a small group of chimpanzees repeatedly into an enclosure and showing her hidden fruit. When the group was released together, this chimp would lead the others to the food. (Control experiments showed that the food could be discovered by chance only about 2 percent of the time.) In time, as soon as the informed chimp so much as looked toward the hiding place, the other members of the group would race ahead.

So long as there was plenty of food or the informer was not at the very bottom of the hierarchy (and thus would get nothing to eat after her "betters" had fed), all went well. But when the chimp that had been shown the caches was very low ranking, she employed a variety of tricks. One was simply to look in the wrong direction; once the troop had set off on the false scent, the subordinate would race to

Dandy, observed by Frans de Waal, solving the grapefruit problem in another way. As the only chimp in the group unafraid of water, he hurries with his prizes to a pool where, safe from the approach of more dominant males, he can eat the grapefruit at his leisure.

a cache and begin to feed. Obviously this ruse did not work for long. Another trick was to walk slowly past the food, and then quickly turn back and seize it. Still another was to walk slowly to the piece of fruit and sit down on it, eating it only when the group began searching nearby. Again, each new ploy was only briefly successful.

Goodall's subordinate male invented similar strategies once the dominants figured out that he had a private source of bananas. The male would stride purposefully into the woods, the dominants following and soon racing ahead; then the subordinate would circle quietly back to the bananas. In another case a banana was placed on a tree branch; the subordinate spotted it first but suppressed any attempt to retrieve it or keep his eye on it; instead, he sat looking studiously away until he was alone, then fetched down the fruit.

Similar behavior has been observed in captive chimpanzees not pretrained with food caches. Dandy, a particularly crafty subordinate male studied in detail by Frans de Waal, happened to walk past some concealed grapefruit; he so suppressed his surprise that the researchers felt sure that he had not noticed the food. But three hours later, when the dominants were asleep, Dandy returned to the cache and ate the fruit. Of course such reports are anecdotes, but the behavior in question was observed by experienced researchers. Because of its novelty, each inventive ploy is by its nature a unique event.

Chimpanzees are by no means alone in their ability to work out ways of circumventing the hierarchy. A low-ranking female baboon, for instance, often ingratiates herself with a high-ranking male by providing regular grooming services, then safely threatens her superiors from the vicinity of her friend, the alpha male. Because each baboon knows his or her rank relative to every other individual, the middle-rank baboons dare not respond to the female's threat for fear that the dominant male will see it, take it as a personal insult, and retaliate. In time the female rises in the hierarchy because of her exalted patron. A fair degree of mental sophistication seems necessary to set up and exploit this ploy.

Baboons sometimes outwit the hierarchy when a female comes into estrus. In general the most dominant males have undisputed access to these females, but the females and less-dominant males can conspire to foil the seniority system. One tactic is for two subdominant males to coöperate to force a dominant away from an estrous female. When the female is left unaccompanied, one male keeps the dominant at bay while the other mates, if the female is willing. The

A subordinate male checks to make sure no dominants are watching before attempting to mate with the female.

roles may later be reversed, suggesting that monkeys understand the rule that favors must be repaid to ensure future coöperation.

TRICKERY AND DECEPTION

It is clear that primates can manipulate their own behavior and that of others to mislead and to keep secrets about food. Chimpanzees have also been observed to feign injury to deflect aggression or solicit attention, a tactic that seems to require some insight into the likely responses of others. A similar pattern emerges in a variety of other contexts, and the tricks employed are particularly cunning when love and sex are at stake. For instance, female baboons may attempt to thwart the hierarchy by sneaking off to consort with particular subdominant males. This requires great care since the dominant keeps a pretty close eye on estrous females and may go looking for any that are missing; pairs attempting unauthorized assignations are promptly punished. If a female has a rendezvous with a male behind a tree or boulder, she peeks out periodically to check on the alpha's movements, or exposes her head and shoulders and pretends to be foraging.

Female chimpanzees may feign indifference when solicited by a subordinate male within sight of a dominant, since alpha males usually interfere with any attempted copulation between an estrous female and a subordinate male. But when out of sight of the alpha, the same females solicit copulations from the favored subordinate and suppress the normal screams that accompany climax, presumably to prevent dominant males from knowing what is going on.

De Waal's Dandy understood well the logistical problems posed by the alphas, and he would sometimes create a distraction by calling the attention of the troop to an unusual object or occurrence and then slip off hurriedly for an assignation. He demonstrated similar cleverness when he found his favorite female surreptitiously copulating with another subordinate: instead of exploding in a jealous fit (thwarted chimpanzees frequently throw tantrums), he raced off to the nearest dominant male and brought him over to witness the forbidden contact; the alpha promptly broke up the pair. These plot devices are straight out of the *Decameron*, and there is little reason to suppose that Boccaccio's characters are any more or less aware of what they are attempting to achieve than the baboons and chimps.

Subordinates must also play their cards right when they have angered a dominant. One tactic is to pretend not to notice a threat until the dominant calms down; canny subordinates sometimes look around casually in every direction except the one from which the threat is coming, giving every evidence of being deaf and nearly blind.

If the subordinate is truly afraid but is attempting to stand his ground, he must display no fear. In a tactic observed in chimpanzees, the subordinate turns briefly away when he can no longer control his expression and turns back when he can again suppress his overt response. Alternatively, he may cover whatever symptoms of terror he is showing with his hands. If the other chimp perseveres in his threat, the tension can sometimes be relieved if the subordinate feigns an interest in something completely different; the other animal may welcome the distraction, and the situation is defused.

Even dominants may need to manipulate interactions. When a dominant male is seriously challenged by an up-and-coming subordinate, it may make sense to pretend not to notice the threat; as his challenger becomes more and more exercised he is likely to make a mistake and redirect a violent gesture at a potential ally. Frans de Waal reports that when the dominant male in his troop was threatened, he frequently feigned benignant nonchalance and played with the young of the group, while appearing not to notice the threatening subordinate. The dominant's tension while acting out this maddening charade would be evident to observers by a variety of subtle behavioral signs, but they were too subdued for his enraged challenger to notice. If, in the end, the subordinate persisted, the dominant would suddenly drop the pose and respond at full intensity.

Smart-chimp stories can be marvelous. A chimp named Kanzi, a participant in a language-learning project at the Language Research Center in Atlanta, was notoriously mischievous, and thoroughly frightened a new keeper by disappearing; a complete search of his quarters, roof and all, failed to locate the chimpanzee. As it turned out, Kanzi had flattened himself on a bed, covered his body with blankets, and lain completely still for 20 minutes, only to emerge laughing when unable to contain himself any longer.

On another occasion, after he asked to leave and was refused permission, Kanzi hid the tool used to open the outside gate of his compound. The researchers thought they must have dropped the tool and searched thoroughly for it. As a veteran of language-learning experiments, Kanzi understood the researchers' request for aid in the search, and he showed every sign of helping them look. Finally, after the scientists had given up searching and were no longer watching, Kanzi recovered the tool and let himself out.

These anecdotes could just as well be stories drawn from a local junior high school. The mixture of hormone-driven aggression, sexual and social lust for power, deceit and gamesmanship, friendship and spite, and good- and ill-natured fun ring familiar chords. Though cynics may argue (plausibly) that teenagers are not fully aware or in control of their actions, the fact remains that there is no reasonable way to account for much of primate (and especially chimpanzee) behavior without assuming that these animals understand a great deal about what they are doing and seeking to do, and are inferring almost as much as humans do about the intentions and attitudes of their peers.

Young chimpanzees experiment with ways to make unique play faces. Frans de Waal photographed this example.

THE ROLE OF PLAY

How do animals come by the social knowledge they require to understand and manipulate the behavior of others? In chimpanzees at least, the answer seems to be that much of the social polish is picked up during play. As anyone who has had a kitten or puppy knows, though, animals other than primates engage in spontaneous play; moreover, given that cats are basically solitary, the purpose of play cannot be solely the learning of social finesse. Nevertheless, play seems a fairly consistent characteristic of the species we see as unusually intelligent, and thus it seems likely that it is connected to some important aspect of cognition.

It is difficult to define play objectively. We need something more tangible than the I-know-it-when-I-see-it approach most of us use to identify those hard-to-quantify concepts like bad taste and pornography. The attempt to identify a phylogenetic line between the species that play and the ones that don't is even more problematic. Nevertheless, there are some characteristics common to play behavior that allow us to define it as apparently purposeless activity with no immediate adaptive goal, utilizing species-typical motor programs that are exaggerated in intensity or number of repetitions, or misordered compared to mature behavior, or mixed together with behavior appropriate to different contexts.

Thus when kittens play, they combine elements of prey-stalking and fighting. They make exaggerated leaps, begin but do not finish bites, produce disemboweling movements without extending their claws, interrupt one sequence with an irrelevant run to another spot (and perhaps up a tree), and so on. As a whole, kitten play is a satire on adult behavior. Even most adult cats play to some degree, and nearly all tolerate play initiated by kittens. Indeed kitten play, like dog play, horse play, and chimpanzee play, is accompanied by species-specific invitation gestures.

Studies of play have led to three major ideas about its function. One suggestion is that play assists the development of behavioral flexibility and calibration to the environment; another is that it aids in the development of cognitive and motor skills; finally, play could be important in promoting kin recognition and social learning (including the development of dominance relationships). In each case play would allow these skills to develop or be perfected in relative safety before they are needed in critical situations.

Documented examples of play are rare outside of birds and mammals. Perhaps the best-known invertebrate case is the play-flight behavior of honey bees: around noon on sunny days workers between two and three weeks of age emerge for brief looping flights near the hive entrance. These bees have spent the previous two weeks performing

The drive to play is especially evident in certain breeds of dogs.

chores in the hive—tending brood, building comb, unloading foragers and storing food, and so on—and are nearing the time when they will begin their work as foragers. The play flights, which range successively farther and farther from the entrance, may enable bees to learn to recognize the hive entrance, to land gracefully, and to become calibrated to the direction and rate of movement of the sun, their prime navigational landmark. If this is the goal of the behavior, though, it is not completely effective: attrition among foragers on their first day of serious food-gathering is nearly 50 percent.

Among birds the evidence for play is stronger. The fledged but immature young of ravens as well as many shore-living species carry inedible objects into the air, drop them, and then catch them before they hit the ground. A pair of birds may even play this game together, alternating the roles of dropper and catcher. Juvenile raptors engage in similar play with inedible objects and small prey. Play fighting and play-flying dogfights are evident in the juveniles of many species of birds; the most complete accounts to date are of ravens.

Juvenile parrots engage in object-oriented play: they manipulate inedible objects with their feet while lying on their backs, and some have even been observed to make snowballs. Young parrots have also been observed swimming on their backs and otherwise fooling around. If play does have something to do with cognitive skills, it is surely significant that it is most evident in ravens (whose remarkable problem-solving ability was touched on in the last chapter) and parrots (whose language-learning capacity will be described in the next).

Mammalian play most often takes the form of play fights and exaggerated chasing and jumping. The cavorting of foals is familiar to many of us, and mirrors the social games of tag and king-of-the-mountain seen in the young of feral goats and mountain sheep. All the elements of dominance-contest behavior that will appear in earnest years later are evident among juveniles. Carnivores add stalking and prey-capture behavior to this list, with the young taking turns as hunter and hunted. Each of the explanations of play—development of cognitive and motor skills, calibration to the environment, and building social skills—seems to fit a variety of species, and there is no reason to

Mountain goats playing in the Canadian Rockies.

Pygmy chimpanzees at the San Diego Zoo have been observed by Frans de Waal playing their own version of blindman's buff. Each player covers its eyes (with a banana leaf, as here, or a bag, an arm, or by holding the eyelids shut with the fingers). The object is to negotiate a dangerous-looking climbing frame that stands 5 m off the ground.

suppose they are mutually exclusive. In social species, including humans, the early dominance patterns that take shape in play tend to persist into adulthood.

The social role of play takes center stage among the primates. Play is the major occupation of the young, and though their parents do not otherwise play as adults, they seem to encourage and participate in it with their offspring. While play is by its nature spontaneous and wholly lacking in the sort of overt reinforcement that operant-conditioning theory requires (play must be its own reward), the active involvement of (as opposed to toleration by) adults is unusual in other kinds of mammals and unknown in other vertebrates. It is as though parents are programmed to provide a head start for play learning before the young can begin their self-reinforcing interactions with each other.

The fullest range of natural primate play, first described in detail by Goodall, is seen in chimpanzees. Her introduction to the phenomenon was abrupt: the troop she was studying ransacked her camp and carried off a substantial quantity of equipment to use as toys.

"They climbed, jumped, swung and dangled from branches of trees," she observed, "chased round tree trunks, broke off and waved or carried branches, leaves, or fruit clusters, grappled with each other for an assortment of small objects, dragged and hit each other with branches, and so on."

Friendships and dominance relationships formed during adolescence provide the major social glue among adults. The playful experimentation with objects and tactics probably forms the basis of the innovation and deceit that become more apparent as chimpanzees mature. In short, play is probably an important means for developing cognitive potential—thinking, planning, imagining—just as it seems to be in our species. Small wonder then that captive juvenile chimpanzees take as readily to joystick-driven video games as they do to more conventional children's pastimes like hide and seek.

DO ANIMALS DREAM?

If at least some animals understand enough about the world around them to make plans, then it follows that they may have some ability to imagine. Indeed, many of the examples of behavior we have touched on in this and earlier chapters seem to require a relatively sophisticated ability to think out the consequences of behavioral alternatives. This raises the very difficult question of whether nonhuman animals can experience those unconscious flights of imagination we know as dreams.

Until recently, about the best evidence for dreaming in animals came from casual observations of pets, who sometimes in their sleep exhibit body movements (including running, biting, and mating) and produce subdued vocalizations that suggest they are reliving an experience. Awakening an animal during one of these episodes can produce what seems like striking disorientation, as though the creature is not sure where it is. Darwin thought that observations like these indicated a continuity of mental experience through the mammals.

Fortunately, there are more objective indices of dreaming. Humans have sleep episodes called REM (rapid-eye-movement) sleep. When awakened during REM sleep a person is much more likely to recount an interrupted dream than when roused from non-REM sleep. This correlation raises the question whether other animals also undergo REM sleep (the question is irrelevant for nearly all invertebrates, whose eyes are fixed). In fact, at least some birds and higher mammals *do* have phases of REM sleep, which appear to correlate with the episodes of subdued body movement that first suggested animal dreaming.

If indeed animals dream in their REM sleep, we have of course no idea what they are dreaming about. At the very least they could be recalling an event, though the adaptive value of such dreaming is not obvious. Some researchers have speculated that dreaming is a way of sorting through a day's recollections before committing portions to memory, but they must be studying exceptionally mundane dreams. Most people report dreams that tend to go well beyond memory or reality, exploring instead what might have been or what still could be.

If natural selection has led to dreaming, it seems reasonable to think that an animal might benefit more from exploring in imagination the consequences of alternatives, rather than passively replaying the day's mental videos. Again this suggests some degree of imagination and planning, but as yet there is no way to ask an animal what it is dreaming. As we will see in the next chapter, though, the day may be rapidly approaching (and some would say it has arrived) when researchers may be able to ask at least a chimpanzee what it is thinking about while it is awake.

Logic and Language

ASK THE BEAST, AND IT WILL TEACH THEE, AND THE BIRDS OF
HEAVEN AND THEY WILL TELL THEE.

Job 12:7

When it comes to the skills that make us able to dominate other species, humans are clearly the smartest of all animals (with the possible exception of the domestic house cat). And through the centuries the consensus has been that our intellectual superiority is the result of our capacity for logic and rational thought, as expressed in, and perhaps engendered by, our ability to use language.

Extensive studies of animal communication systems have made it clear that, at least in the wild, no other species uses our sort of language, and so we are at a disadvantage in trying to assess the capabilities of other animals. Do some species, though lacking the vocal machinery, still have our capacity for rational deduction? Might some other communication systems express much the same mental processing in very different ways? Perhaps other species have the potential for language and logical thought but have never been under the types of environmental stresses that selected for language in early humans. To discover the extent of at least a few other species' ability to make logical connections, researchers need a window into the animal mind. Some have tried to teach animals our kind of language system, and others to find out through more traditional means whether (and if so, how) animals categorize, formulate concepts, and link ideas. Their successes—and to a great extent their failures—have given us much to consider.

ALEX, AN AFRICAN GREY PARROT, CAN ANSWER—IN WORDS—QUESTIONS ABOUT THE NAMES, SHAPES, COLORS, AND NUMBERS OF OBJECTS.

CATEGORIZATION

In the early 1960s, Richard Herrnstein tried a radical departure from the relatively simple and unambiguous stimuli normally presented to pigeons in discrimination and memory experiments. Instead he showed his laboratory-raised birds slides of various outdoor scenes. He reinforced pecks during slides showing a particular stimulus, such as a tree, and did not reinforce ones without it.

Because the slides were actual photographs taken in a variety of locations, the trees varied in size, location, shape, color, and prominence from one scene to another. Moreover, each picture included numerous other stimuli—people, houses, cars, buildings, clouds. After training them on a limited set of examples, Herrnstein tested the pigeons with a large and completely new set of slides they had never before seen.

There are two ways to solve the puzzle the pigeons were given: one is to memorize all the reinforced slides; the other is to deduce what they have in common. Deduction is much easier once the animal has worked it out (whether consciously or through some sort of automatic neural filtering) that a visual category is being reinforced. However, since no one tree is exactly like another, isolating the characteristics common to such a conceptual category is no trivial matter: until recently there has been considerable debate over how even humans learn categories like "tree." The consensus now is that there is no single set of defining characteristics common to all the members

Four examples of the hundreds of different shots used in Herrnstein's experiments on concept formation in pigeons. Two of these pictures have trees; two do not.

of a category, but rather a constellation of characters, each with a certain probability of being associated with a particular example of the target group.

In control experiments pigeons were trained on slides with nothing in common, and their ability to memorize large numbers of different pictures ran into the hundreds. Moreover, they could remember photographs virtually without error for months. In the wild, many animals must remember large numbers of scenes over long periods in order to navigate through familiar areas, and free-living pigeons probably have more landmarks to remember than most species. Perhaps the ability of a bird to store an enormous mental inventory of miscellaneous pictures is essential to its survival. In any event, pigeons should have no trouble solving the is-there-a-tree-in-this-picture problem by rote memorization if they choose to do so; if this were their approach to the problem, however, their responses should be random when they are shown new slides. In fact, though, when presented with novel scenes the birds typically responded to members of the correct (tree-containing) set about 75 percent of the time.

Herrnstein's pigeons had apparently created a rough mental category for trees. In many cases, in fact, their "errors" turned out not to be mistakes at all: on closer examination it proved that human experimenters categorizing the slides had failed to notice a tree in the background, or part of a tree intruding from the edge. In other instances the lab-raised birds, with no experience of actual trees, had lumped in telephone poles and television antennas.

Skeptics argued that since trees are objects of special importance to birds, pigeons might have an innate representation of them, and Herrnstein's tests might not have required deduction at all. This interpretation has been soundly refuted by a series of similar tests using other target stimuli. The categories that pigeons have successfully identified include people (even particular individuals, or people expressing a particular emotion), fish, bodies of water, alpha-numeric characters, flowers, automobiles, and leaves of white oak trees. Their levels of accuracy paralleled the difficulty humans have in quickly categorizing the same stimuli.

While pigeons can learn to respond to "tree" as a conceptual grouping—indeed, they learn this concept faster than they master simple colored-light tasks—some other categories turn out to be harder. Pigeons have had trouble with the concepts "drinking cup" and "wheeled vehicle." The symbol for the letter A is easier to learn than the symbol for the number 2. Line drawings are much harder for pigeons to work from than photographs. These instances suggest that there may be another level of complexity or abstraction or real-world experience, which pigeons lack, necessary to formulate concepts about human artifacts.

It seems clear that while categorization is necessary for human language, language is by no means necessary for categorization. It also seems clear that the ability of animals to form concepts about the objects and individuals in the world about them ought to be essential to rapid generalizing about food and predators, as well as efficient thinking, planning, and the other mental manipulations that at least certain species appear to be capable of. In short, an ability for conceptual organization has probably been favored by natural selection.

LOGICAL THOUGHT

For any object or concept A, the following must be true:

> A is A
> A is not not-A
> Everything is either A or not-A

These three essential and deceptively simple rules, the foundation stones of Aristotelian logic, are at the basis of our everyday human reasoning. For many years nonhuman animals were thought incapable of understanding them. In part, the difficulty was technical: no one had discovered how to ask logic-based questions of nonverbal creatures. Another problem, though, was conceptual: few researchers *expected* animals to be able to demonstrate logical reasoning.

Perhaps the first task that any animal mastered that clearly depends on logical exclusion was a same–different paradigm. In tests first developed by David Premack in the late 1970s, chimpanzees were shown first one symbol or signal and then given a pair in which one member was the same as the initial stimulus and the other different. The chimps were reinforced for selecting the stimulus that differed from the sample, and they mastered the first set of stimuli after a little training. By itself this accomplishment is not impressive: they could have been memorizing each particular different stimulus rather than responding to the concept of difference (that is, to the non-A aspect of a stimulus).

As the training proceeded with different sets of stimuli, there came a point at which the chimpanzees began to respond correctly to new sets of stimuli from the outset; they had learned that food was

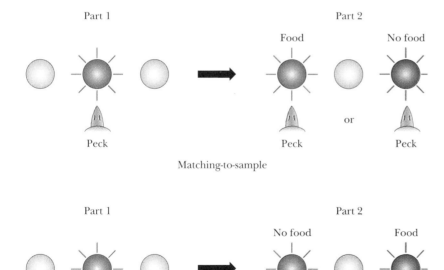

Pigeons can be taught rules that are independent of particular training stimuli. When consistently reinforced for pecking first an illuminated key and then the key of the matching color when a choice is offered (top), pigeons are able to apply this learned rule to novel colors. Conversely (as illustrated at the bottom), they can also be taught to choose the key with a different color. Some researchers believe that the birds must have (or develop) a concept of "sameness" and "difference" to solve these problems.

associated with *any* non-A. The concept of oddity, so readily learned by chimpanzees, was much harder to teach pigeons until one group of psychologists discovered that if the choice is between a non-A and several A's, all presented simultaneously, pigeons pick up the concept very quickly.

Researchers have so far discovered that the essentials of Aristotelian logic are accessible to at least one other species: the sea lion. The first task presented to the seals was to learn that two icons are equivalent: X = Y. Next they were taught that Y and Z are equivalent: Y = Z. Then they were asked if X and Z were equivalent: does X = Z? (In a verbal analogy, *elated* means *happy; happy* means *joyful;* therefore *elated* means *joyful*.) Sea lions readily mastered this logical train.

Children are able to work through such equivalence sequences at an early age (though there can be serious regression during adolescence), but many researchers had assumed that language is a necessary mediator of this kind of thinking. The results of a classic Soviet study of the 1920s seemed to support this view. The following syllogism was posed: Ivan lives in Siberia; in Siberia, all the bears are white; what color was the bear Ivan saw? Illiterate (and therefore uneducated) adults usually responded with statements such as "I've never been to Siberia" or "I've never met Ivan," whereas children emerging from a decade of schooling answered the conundrum without hesitation. Illiteracy is not, however, a lack of language, but of education: for humans, as for sea lions, it seems that the classroom experience of dealing with the hypothetical is the essential element.

The point is that logic does not require language; apparently language is only needed to *discuss* logic. The seeming inability of other species to perform the same syllogistic feat (as yet) may suggest that Aristotelian connections push the limits of animal cognition. However, it is more likely that the researchers rather than their subjects are to blame. The training used with the sea lions, for instance, employed a novel approach developed by Ronald Schusterman that is yet to be tried on other animals: they were first taught to choose symbol B rather than an alternative when A had been presented moments earlier; then they were rewarded for choosing A when B had been presented; then they were reinforced for selecting C when B had been presented, and vice versa; finally, when they were shown A they immediately selected C over an alternative.

If the concept-learning tests have taught us anything, it is that finding an approach to training that builds on an animal's natural

One of Ronald Schusterman's sea lions solving a simple problem in logic that seems to require category formation.

frame of reference is often the key to reaching the animal mind. We are, naturally, much better at this with humans, though if the current acrimonious debate over intelligence testing is any indication, we have not even figured out an effective way to test all members of our own species.

SPOKEN LANGUAGE

It would be much easier to study the operation of animal minds if we could just interview their possessors, a Doctor Dolittle approach that was considered impossible until about 1970—at least if talking to the animals is defined by speech. Attempts to teach chimpanzees human speech were doomed from the outset since the chimpanzee vocal tract cannot form the necessary range of vowels. But attempts to teach human sounds to birds have a long history of success.

Parrots can mimic a variety of sounds, including telephone bells and flushing toilets. Not surprisingly, parrots can produce reasonable copies of human speech, but few people supposed that they could have any understanding of words—indeed, we describe mindless repetition as "parroting." But the owners of parrots know that once a bird learns the word for a piece of desirable food, it will ask for it by name and usually reject substitutes.

Working from this hint that parrots understand something about the sounds they make, Irene Pepperberg used a training technique with an African grey parrot called Alex that reflected the way in which vocalizations are picked up in the wild. In nature, juveniles usually learn sounds from other animals; in contrast, attempts to train parrots in isolation in the lab using operant techniques have consistently failed, probably because there was no feedback from other animals. In the late 1970s Pepperberg began to place training in a social context.

In the Pepperberg tests, two trainers spoke slowly and clearly to each other in Alex's presence. One "teacher," holding an object, would ask "What's this?" If the other trainer, acting as the "student," answered correctly, using the object's name or identifying one of its obvious characteristics, such as color, the "student" was given the object. In these interactions, the "student" was thus a rival with the parrot for the "teacher's" attention. As anyone with children knows, jealousy for attention is one of the most powerful motivators of juvenile behavior. Alex began to learn the code, apparently so that he could participate. Food was not used as a reward, but presented only if the bird specifically asked for a piece of something edible. Getting the object he wanted, either to play with or just to maintain the attention of his trainers, was sufficient reinforcement.

After about ten years of training, Alex had mastered a 70-word vocabulary that included thirty object names, seven color adjectives, five shape adjectives, several substance adjectives (like "paper"), the names of five numbers, the phrases "come here," "want to go to," and "how many," and the words "color," "shape," "matter," "what," "same," "different," "none," and "no." Beyond picking up the words, Alex has learned how to apply them in order to get food by answering questions: if a trainer asks what color a poker chip is, Alex will name it correctly about 95 percent of the time.

The most interesting results so far involve same–different questions: when asked what characteristic two objects have in common or how they are different, Alex can reliably identify the relevant parameter—shape, color, or material—or point out that the two do not differ at all. Moreover, the parrot does just as well with novel objects

IRENE (acting as trainer): Bruce, what's this?

BRUCE (acting as model/rival): *Five* wood.

IRENE: That's right, *five* wood. Here you are . . . *five* wood. (hands over five wooden popsicle sticks; Bruce begins to break one apart, much as Alex would)

ALEX: 'ii wood.

BRUCE (now acting as trainer, quickly replaces broken stick and presents the five sticks to Alex): Better . . . (briefly turns away, then repositions himself in visual contact with Alex) . . . How many?

ALEX: No!

BRUCE (turns from Alex to establish visual contact with the principal investigator): Irene, what's this? (presents sticks)

IRENE (now acting as model/rival): 'ii wood.

BRUCE: Better . . . (turns, then resumes eye contact) . . . How many?

IRENE: *Five* wood (takes wooden sticks) . . . *five* wood. (now acts as trainer, directs gaze to Alex, and presents sticks to him) . . . How many wood?

ALEX: Fife wood.

IRENE: OK, Alex, close enough . . . *fivvvvve* wood . . . Here's *five* wood. (places one stick in the bird's beak and the other within his reach)

Excerpt from a training session with Alex to review and improve his pronunciation of "five." The other participants are Dr. Irene Pepperberg, principal investigator, and Bruce Rosen, secondary trainer.

as with familiar ones, proving that he really understands the concepts and the logical connections involved.

If parrots can comprehend concepts, we must ask if the language-based training merely served to reveal an ability regularly used by parrots (and presumably many other species) in the wild. Or, as some linguists still argue, does language produce conceptualization as a kind of side effect? Is language necessary to teach distinctions that cannot be learned otherwise? Taking together the experiments we have looked at, it seems most likely that the ability to form conceptual categories and use logic is present even when language is not, and is probably used in the wild to deal with the most challenging problems animals face. The word-based communication being taught to animals is probably serving simply as a window into the minds of the few species

At Pepperberg's request, Alex correctly selects the blue object.

researchers have to date discovered how to reach. As we will see, though, there remains the lively possibility that language instruction greatly amplifies the ability of an animal to make logical deductions.

UNDERSTANDING GESTURAL LANGUAGE

Dolphins and sea lions have proven apter students of language than the African grey parrot. Ronald Schusterman has taught a sea lion called Rocky a vocabulary of more than 190 human gestures, each hand or arm signal corresponding to a noun, adjective, or verb. Unfortunately, the gestures are one-way signals: humans tell the animal what to do and not, as is possible for Alex, vice versa. Nevertheless, the ability of the sea lion to remember so many distinct signals, and to interpret their meaning according to a word-order grammar (adjective, subject-noun, verb) is highly thought provoking.

Because of the degree of spontaneous play behavior they initiate and their capacity to imitate, dolphins strike many humans as the most intelligent of the marine mammals. Bottle-nosed dolphins are generally considered the easiest species of this group to train, and therefore the smartest—at least by this very pragmatic standard. They produce an enormous variety of sounds during social interactions, encouraging some enthusiasts to suppose they have a vocal language. The widely reported efforts of dolphins to help injured swimmers as well as each other to stay afloat suggest to many that they have empathetic feelings as well. There is no concrete evidence for either supposition: innate programming could easily account for these behaviors. What *is* known of their intellectual abilities comes mainly from language-learning experiments.

Louis Herman has trained bottle-nosed dolphins to respond to abstractly coded instructions. One dolphin was taught using acoustic signals for words while a pair learned a gestural vocabulary. The dolphins learned to interpret both gestural and acoustic signals according to a word-order grammar; two different sequence rules have been used successfully in the gestural experiments: subject-adjective, subject-noun, verb, object-adjective, object-noun ("bottom pipe place-in surface hoop"), and subject-noun, subject-adjective, object-noun, object-adjective, verb ("pipe bottom hoop surface place-in").

The first word-order sequence is typical of the simplest English sentences; the second sequence is similar to basic German. Unlike

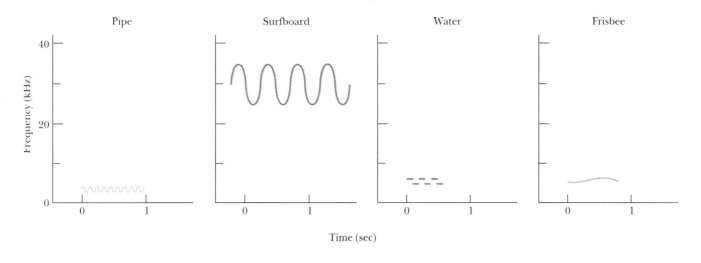

Time (sec)

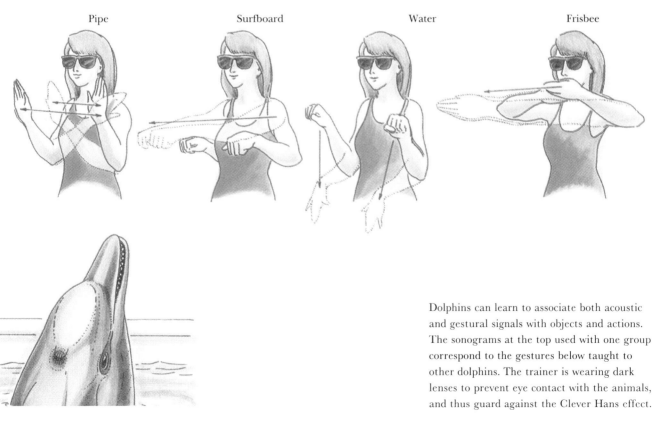

Dolphins can learn to associate both acoustic and gestural signals with objects and actions. The sonograms at the top used with one group correspond to the gestures below taught to other dolphins. The trainer is wearing dark lenses to prevent eye contact with the animals, and thus guard against the Clever Hans effect.

Louis Herman giving the "pay attention" gesture to two of his students.

English and German, however, most human languages are highly inflected—that is, the grammatical role of a word in a sentence depends not so much on its location as on its ending. The end-of-utterance modulation essential to meaning in inflected language often involves subtle changes in frequency and tone. The same pattern is common in the natural calls and gestures of animals, but (perhaps because nearly all the researchers in this field have been English-speakers) no one has attempted to incorporate inflected flourishes to help convey meaning in the abstract languages taught to animals.

Although the vocabulary taught to the dolphins is relatively small (about three dozen words), their ability to decode five-word sentences correctly is remarkable. Moreover, the dolphins clearly understand what the words mean: "hoop" is used to identify not only the training hoop but an entire class of novel objects that satisfy our concept of "hoop" regardless of color, size, or shape. As yet, however, Herman has not used his technique to explore the capacity of dolphins for logical reasoning or problem-solving, or even to answer acoustic commands with their own sounds.

USING GESTURAL LANGUAGE

The breakthrough in teaching an abstract language to a nonhuman animal came with the work of B. T. and R. A. Gardner and their chimpanzee, Washoe. Using a gestural language taught in a social context, the naturalistic approach of the researchers mirrored some aspects of the range and acquisition of cultural communication in the wild. The language they used was based on standard American Sign Language (ASL), a gestural version of English that incorporates a fair degree of manual inflection to help overcome some of the limitations of sign language. Washoe's eventual vocabulary (after four years of instruction) was about 130 words.

Using similar techniques, the Gardners and others have taught several more chimps roughly the same number of signs over about the same period. An orangutan was taught more than 50 gestures, and a gorilla was reported to have mastered nearly 200. As with the studies of parrots and marine mammals, the testing methods ruled out the possibility of any Clever Hans effect: the objects to be named were projected on a screen visible only to the chimpanzee, whose responses were scored independently by two observers (one of whom was sometimes a deaf person fluent in ASL and who had no previous contact with the experiment); even the photographs used of each object were new shots not previously seen by the animals, and the order of presentation in these tests was never the same. Clearly, the apes really connect the signs with the objects, individuals, attributes, or actions they refer to.

The most impressive demonstration of true understanding of the connection between abstract gestures and the objects, properties, or actions they signify came when one of the chimps learning sign language was instructed for a time with spoken words. After mastering the association between ten words and the objects to which they referred, the chimp was trained to associate the same words with ten new signs. One new object–word–sign connection was taught each day. For instance, in the morning a chimp that already understood that the word "spoon" referred to that object would be told "this is the sign for spoon" and shown the appropriate gesture; no physical spoon would be present. In the afternoon another observer, unaware what sign had been taught earlier, would show the chimpanzee five objects, including a spoon, and ask in sign language of each, "What is this?" The chimp would use the new gesture to identify the spoon. At the end of ten days the chimp knew all ten new signs. This is the same logical series we saw demonstrated by sea lions: $X = Y$, $Y = Z$, therefore $X = Z$, where X is the object, Y the sign, and Z the word.

The evidence is also fairly convincing that the signing chimps understood that their gestures corresponded to conceptual categories rather than specific objects; for example, the verb "open" was taught only in the context of a door, but was used spontaneously by the animal to request that books, water faucets, and drawers be opened. Some creativity in sign use was also observed: Washoe "named" a swan with the two-sign combination "water bird" (though both water and a bird were present, and thus the chimp *could* just have been naming two separate objects). Other chimps created combinations like "metal hot" to identify a cigarette lighter, "listen drink" for Alka-Seltzer, and "candy drink" for watermelon.

Some of the chimps in these projects even communicate with one another to a limited degree using signs, and there is some evidence for cultural transmission. For instance, Washoe's adopted son, Loulis, acquired more than 50 signs from Washoe over a five-year period during which humans were forbidden to use signs in Loulis's presence.

In contrast to the impressive gestural vocabulary of these apes, there is far less evidence that they learned much about grammatical organization—that is, that they proceeded from learning names to understanding grammar. About half of the signing consisted of one-word "utterances," and most strings of signs showed no obvious organization, as "give orange me give eat orange give me eat orange give me you." Can it be that the chimpanzee mind is limited mainly to one-word thoughts and plans? Or did the training technique merely fail to equip the chimps to use a mixed inflected/word-order system, so that our idea of proper grammar, whether innate or conditioned, continued to be a closed book?

SYMBOL-BASED LANGUAGE LEARNING

Two other approaches to teaching language to chimps have produced evidence for an ability to pick up grammar. One technique, developed by David Premack, used colorful plastic shapes as words; these "lexigrams" were placed in sequences on a magnetic board in an effort to teach both vocabulary and a word-order grammar. His early student,

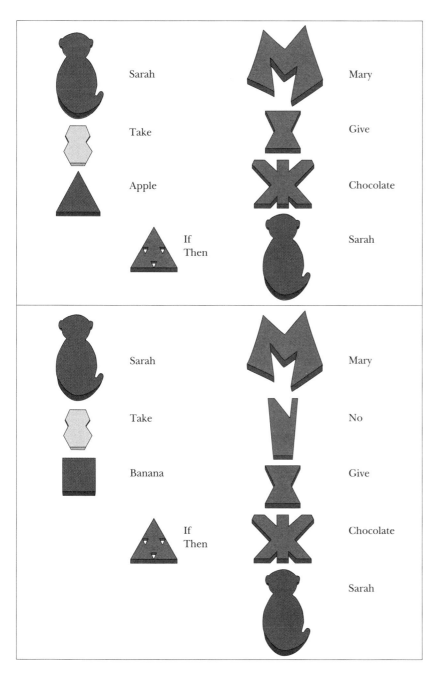

After the chimpanzee Sarah was taught to use a language based on plastic shapes, she learned to interpret conditional sentences. The first sentence reads, "If Sarah takes the apple, then Mary will give chocolate to Sarah"; the other, more sinister, outlines a different consequence: "If Sarah takes the banana, Mary will not give chocolate to Sarah."

Sarah, gradually learned the meaning of about 130 symbols, which she could use in simple three- or even four-word sentences that related one object to another or conveyed an instruction.

Critics of chimpanzee language work have devised alternative operant-based explanations for Sarah's linguistic behavior. These hypotheses, however, do not account for the pattern of learning in ape-language research. For instance, we can train a pigeon to associate a colored shape with a particular food in 30 to 40 trials, and chimps are far faster than this. But the same chimpanzees needed hundreds of trials to connect a lexigram to its referent in the linguistic context, and some never learned a single word.

Moreover, once a plastic word became associated with an object (as opposed to an operant for obtaining a reward), its use with other descriptive or action lexigrams took less time to learn, and the ability to generalize the symbol to a class of objects (or actions or modifiers) was faster still. In short, the chimpanzees clearly acted as though they were learning *language* rather than a set of conditioned behaviors. Still, it's important to keep in mind just how slowly even the best students in these tests learn: Alex the parrot picked up about a word every two months, while the chimps never acquired more than about two words a month. Human children, by contrast, can learn dozens of words a day without any overt reinforcement.

The most ambitious project to teach language to chimpanzees was initiated by Sue Savage-Rumbaugh and Duane Rumbaugh. With their colleagues they developed a keyboard-based language. Each key is marked with an arbitrary symbol. When pressed, a key lights up and its symbol appears in sequence on a screen, so the chimpanzees can keep track of their lexigram sequences. The researchers used a word-order grammar with a generic interrogative symbol to initiate question sentences. The chimpanzees in these experiments are typically taught a vocabulary of 75 to 90 words.

The computer-mediated keyboard approach allows unprecedented accuracy in recording the linguistic progress of chimpanzees. Analysis of the painful transition from the one-word stage of using a lexigram to identify an object to a two-word level that permits interrogation (by both humans and the chimps) shows that in these experiments the symbols initially *are* learned as operants for obtaining things (usually food). But once the two-word concept is mastered for, say, asking the name of a particular food, the chimp realizes how it applies to all other objects. This kind of mental breakthrough opens

One of the Rumbaughs' chimps uses a portable representation of its laboratory keyboard to communicate when outdoors.

new horizons for the chimp and at the same time demonstrates that they understand concepts like "food" and "tool."

In a further extension of language use, the keyboard-based approach has allowed two chimpanzees to communicate with each other. The chimps had to learn that the keyboard and screen could be used for two-way exchanges; just mastering the techniques for answering researchers' questions or making requests was not enough. But once the chimpanzees grasped the idea of exchanging information, they were able to coöperate to solve problems. To take a typical example, one chimp would figure out what sort of tool it needed to get at food left by a researcher, and then use the keyboard to ask the other animal (in an adjoining room) for that implement; the second chimp, who was unaware of the particular problem, would pass the requested tool through a small opening. Again, there was every evidence of a conceptual threshold having suddenly been reached: training accelerated and error rates plummeted. Moreover, the chimps began to engage in what seems to be interactive play via the keyboard link.

All the chimpanzee work we have described so far involved the common chimp, *Pan troglodytes;* there is a second species, the pygmy chimpanzee or bonobo (*Pan paniscus*) that, though rarer, is clearly quicker than its larger relatives. One pygmy chimp, Kanzi, has provided significant insights into the fuller capacities of nonhuman primates. Kanzi's mother began as a student in the keyboard-based experiments when he was about six months old; he was with her during about two years of training but never received any formal instruction himself. After the researchers gave up on Kanzi's mother, the young chimp spontaneously began using the keyboard to make requests.

Kanzi acquired an 80-word vocabulary by the time he was four and used it with more grammatical consistency than any other chimp has ever demonstrated. His keyboard exchanges with humans have been more frequent, more spontaneous, and much more fluent; his communication skills are roughly equivalent to those of a 30-month-old human. There seems no doubt that Kanzi understands the symbols and their use as tools for exchanging information and communicating wishes and intentions. He may be smarter than the other chimpanzees that have been used, or the inadvertent opportunity to learn by observing an older chimpanzee may have been the key to his success. In any event, the lexigram language provides a tool for exploring in unprecedented detail what a member of another species is thinking, and how those thoughts are organized.

CHIMPANZEE LOGIC

Though the reasoning abilities of keyboard-trained chimpanzees have not yet been explored in any systematic way, Premack has tried teaching a variety of logical operations to both language-trained and untrained chimpanzees. In the simplest tests, the chimps were faced with the task of labeling pairs of objects as either "same" or "different." This problem is unlike the same–different concept tests described earlier. In the usual form of the task the experimenter shows an example and then a pair of objects, one of which is the same as the example and the other different; the animal is rewarded for choosing the member of the pair that is different. In the Premack study, however, the two objects to be categorized were presented simultaneously. Language-trained chimps learned this discrimination, whereas untrained chimps did not.

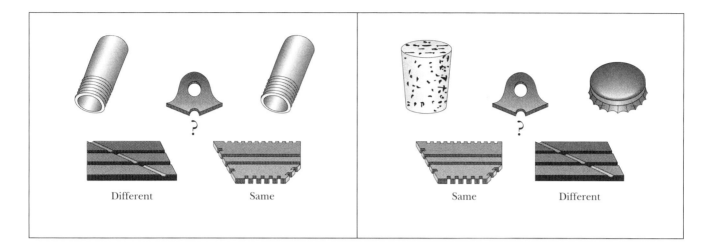

Premack also attempted to teach the concept of analogies: A is to B as C is to D—lock is to key as can is to can opener, to choose one of the most abstract examples he used. The usual format of the test was to present an incomplete analogy and offer a choice of three different objects to finish the verbal equation. Language-trained chimpanzees eventually handled these tasks with nearly an 80 percent accuracy rate; chimps without language training, on the other hand, never mastered even the simplest analogy: "apple is to apple as banana is to —————."

Another task familiar to students of child development is proportionality. Language-trained chimps could choose an object—a half circle rather than a full or three-quarter circle—that corresponded to the proportion visible in the test object (a half-filled glass of water, for instance). Chimps without language training could master this task only so long as the choice objects they had to select from were similar to the test object. Interestingly, Premack found that his language-trained chimp had no difficulty with a related concept that proves very difficult for children: conservation of volume. Young children judge the amount of liquid in a glass or the mass of clay in a lump by its height or length; thus they behave as though there is more water in a tall, thin glass than in a short, squat tumbler, even if they have seen each filled from identical containers of liquid. The language-trained chimp tested on this task required no instruction: from the

Sarah was able to use symbolic language to show that she understood the concepts of "same" and "different" by choosing the correct plastic shape to describe the relationship between the two objects she was asked to compare.

outset she recognized the two amounts as being the same. To be fair, though, this chimp was nearly 20 years old at the time, and she had had plenty of opportunity to learn the basic facts of fluid physics before testing ever began.

Finally, Premack has taught language-trained chimps to complete cause-and-effect sentences of the form "whole apple plus X produces cut apple," offering three objects (a bowl of water, a knife, and a pencil, for instance) as possibilities for X; in other tests, the goal was to supply the final item, as in "dry sponge plus bowl of water produces Y." The language-trained chimp mastered these tasks with a minimum of training; untrained chimps failed.

Premack interprets these results as indicating that language makes animals smarter by allowing them to think in terms of abstract symbols rather than only visual images. This is a plausible explanation, but it is also possible that language training makes it easier for chimpanzees to figure out what the researcher is getting at in the testing. The latter alternative reminds us that attempts to create "culture-free" intelligence tests have generally failed. People from non-Western cultures, for instance, often perform poorly unless they have had experience with Western-style schooling and its emphasis on multiple-choice quizzes. Success on such tests, it seems, depends both on native intelligence *and* on knowing how to take such tests.

It is possible, therefore, that the chimps that had not had the benefit of a decade or more of daily training and testing performed poorly because they had not deciphered the true nature of the testing game. Certainly chimps in the wild understand similarity and difference, analogies, cause and effect, and a great deal more besides. They are able to formulate fairly complex and subtle plans. The issue is whether they accomplish their thinking and planning solely by manipulating visual images—actual or mental pictures of objects—or if they also have more abstract conceptual tools available. Does an untrained chimpanzee comprehend such concepts as "opening" or "stacking" by picturing these specific operations as performed on the particular objects to be used, or can the animal reason in terms of both object and action concepts, complete with appropriate adjective- and adverb-like modifiers?

Perhaps there is a middle ground, in which generic category icons are used in visual thinking. Concepts would be manipulated mentally in some way, and thus would probably have some kind of representation independent of a specific canonical example. A model based on something like mental icons—generic category images that might act as a mental alphabet for objects and actions and characteristics—would help explain the ease with which chimpanzees form and use conceptual categories, as well as their limited ability to learn language. Certainly there is no compelling evidence that language-trained chimpanzees are quicker at solving real-world problems than their untutored peers; abstract words and symbolic thinking, so essential to much of our culture-based behavior, do not seem to be powerful intellectual tools for chimpanzees except in situations specifically designed by researchers to make word-use necessary.

The issue of what conceptual tools are available to animals in the wild is central to understanding the animal mind. Language studies provide only a dim window into the cognitive processing that goes on inside the brain, but it is a unique perspective that remains to be fully explored. At the very least, language-based studies confirm many of our earlier deductions that were based only on behavioral observations; at best they promise a fuller appreciation of the intellectual powers of other species.

Human Cognition

PLAC'D ON THIS ISTHMUS OF A MIDDLE STATE,

A BEING DARKLY WISE, AND RUDELY GREAT:

· · · · · · · · · · · · · · ·

HE HANGS BETWEEN; IN DOUBT TO ACT, OR REST;

IN DOUBT TO DEEM HIMSELF A GOD, OR BEAST.

Alexander Pope
An Essay on Man, 1733

n argument first proposed by Darwin suggests that just as human anatomy and physiology are part of an evolutionary continuum that stretches back millions of years, so too the human mind is a product of stepwise natural selection. As the complexity of our brain differs only in degree from the neural structures of other animals, so the nature of the thinking it generates differs only in degree from the mental processing performed by other creatures. In this view, our abilities are the result of selection for specific capacities, and our cognitive powers are no more remarkable than the ability of bats to form precise mental pictures of flying insects in total darkness. Because of differences in our evolutionary trajectories, we are terrible at catching moths with or without light, and bats are inept when it comes to long division.

Another perspective suggests that humans are different in kind from all other animals, and there is no bridge across the cognitive gulf. At some point in the explosive growth of human brain volume over the past 3 million years, we crossed a neural threshold that made higher-order thinking possible. Perhaps the essential element of brain growth was connectivity: with "excess" neurons, those above and beyond the number needed for processing sensory data and controlling muscle movement, the number of possible connections among cells increases rapidly: there are 20 possible one-way connections among 5 cells, 90 among 10 cells, and so on. This tremendous growth of

HUMANS AND CHIMPANZEES HAVE MORE THAN

99 PERCENT OF THEIR GENES IN COMMON.

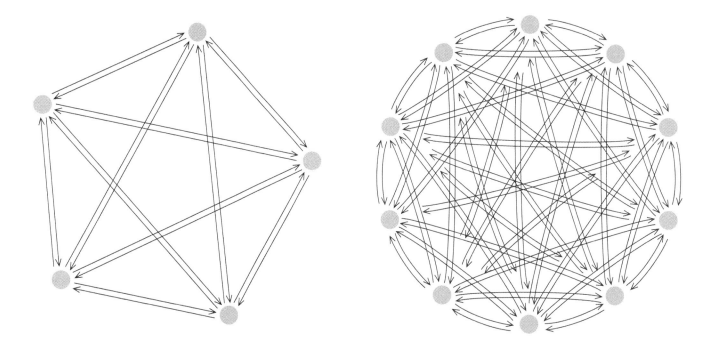

The number of potential connections between neurons rises as the number of cells increases: for example, the network of five cells has 20 connections, whereas the group of ten neurons has 90.

potential associations results in spectacular increases in cognitive power. (This argument is analogous to the demonstrably correct cultural-multiplier effect: each invention makes subsequent innovations easier, and so the rate of invention speeds up.)

Each position is plausible and has empirical support: if language is the touchstone, it is true that other primates have simple languages and can be taught symbolic communication systems; on the other hand, do the languages of other primates differ only in degree from ours? Many linguists argue that primate languages are nothing like human communication, having only a thousandth of our vocabulary, a billionth of our ability to formulate novel sentences, and almost no capacity to create new words. But if human language is a species-specific specialization, like echolocation or nest-weaving, then the in-kind arguments lose much of their force. As in our earlier investigations, before we can ask intelligent questions about cognition we need to know something about the niche and the evolutionary history of the species concerned—in this case, ourselves.

THE HUMAN NICHE

Continental drift and climate changes gave rise to the savannahs of Africa, which border the tropical forests in which our primate ancestors lived (and where our nearest relations live to this day). About 17 million years ago dry forest began to appear, which over the course of the next 5 million years gave way to grassy plains. The savannahs provided a new niche for grazers (primarily antelope), which evolved from small forest-dwelling animals. The appearance of the antelope created in turn a niche for large or group-hunting carnivores. About 8 million years ago the line that led to humans was also moving into the savannah.

The heat and dryness of the plains required major physiological changes in these early hominids, but it is the behavioral developments that concern us most. The design and composition of human teeth testify to an omnivorous diet, a mixture of flesh and vegetation. Experts differ over how our ancestors came by the meat they ate. Modern chimpanzees ambush smaller primates and eat them, but animal flesh is only a minor part of their diet. One popular theory is that early hominids scavenged meat from sick or dying animals and the

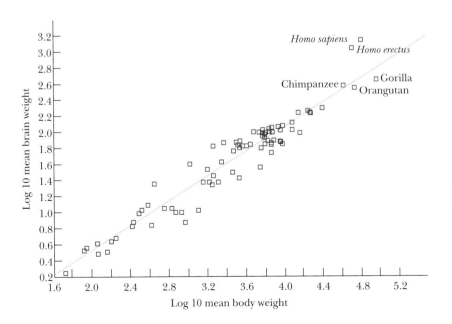

Most of the brain's mass is devoted to muscle control. All things being equal, therefore, an animal's brain weight should be proportional to its body weight. This brain-weight/body-weight plot of 85 species of primates shows that humans have anomalously large brains, while gorilla brains are surprisingly small.

kills of other hunters, perhaps attacking in groups to drive off the carnivores that had caught the prey. There is evidence that some small, slow prey was clubbed to death.

A million years ago our ancestor, *Homo erectus,* was using stone axes to kill animals, including elephants and giraffes, that had no other enemies: hunting had become a powerful technique. Planning and cleverness must have been necessary to overcome the disadvantages of limited size and speed. These early humans had enormous brains (about half the volume of modern *Homo sapiens*), and there is no more potent weapon than thought.

We know something about this early way of life from studies earlier in this century of a few isolated societies that still maintained the hunter/gatherer way of life, the best known of which were the !Kung people of the Kalahari desert of southern Africa. The men hunted, usually in small groups; the women, less mobile because of the young (who nursed for as long as three or four years), gathered fruits and

The brain volume of the line leading to humans increased dramatically over the last 4 million years, suggesting strong selection pressure for a large nervous system.

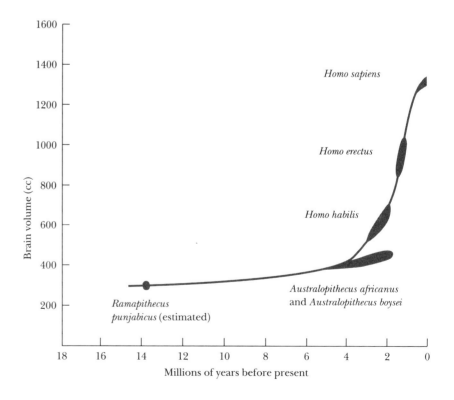

other edible vegetation. Gatherers used digging sticks, ostrich-egg canteens, and woven nets; hunters made bone knives, flint scraping tools, spears, snares, bows with sinew strings, and arrows with heads shaped from bone or flint and tipped with poison from toxic grubs or plants. Both hunters and gatherers made use of fire and cooking implements. Passing this range of technology from one generation to the next depended on cultural learning.

When our ancestors began to grow crops and herd animals, this hunter/gatherer lifestyle disappeared in all but the most isolated groups, and even they are gone now. The domestication of plants and animals, a development at most 20,000 years old, meant that groups no longer needed to follow game and range widely to find suitable vegetation. The upper limit to group size had been set mainly by the practical extent of the foraging range from a base camp (the more members of a group, the wider the areas that must be scoured to feed them all); now populations could grow. Consequent developments include the appearance of cities, the division of labor by craft, and centralized government, with its relentless by-products of taxation and large-scale warfare.

Humans have passed through only about 250 generations since cities rose on the plain. Some researchers believe we have not had time to make major evolutionary adjustments to our novel, self-created habitat; thus the incompatibility between behavior adapted to life in small groups of hunter/gatherers and behavior necessary to get along in large, dense societies creates a stress that sometimes gains pathological expression. Others—exponents of the flexibility of human behavior and the adaptability of our minds—suggest that we have slipped the bonds of natural selection, and can shape our destinies as we will.

The sociobiologist Edward O. Wilson has enumerated cultural universals that appear in otherwise diverse societies, whose constancy suggests innate proclivities: some of these recurrent elements are property rights, body adornment, incest taboos, sexual roles, rites of passage, intraspecific war, and belief in the supernatural. He also points out that the mind is prepared to generate strong and immediate phobias after a single unpleasant experience with a few special stimuli (closed spaces, heights, thunderstorms, running water, snakes, and spiders, for instance) but not to realistic modern threats like electrical outlets and automobiles; again, this may be taken as evidence of the innate nature of much of our cognitive experience. However, it is also possible to emphasize the diversity of *other* cultural practices among groups of humans and consider Wilson's list of "univerals" as inevitable societal adaptations to widespread human challenges that transcend tribal needs. In this argument, diversity represents a cultural version of the character displacement seen when selection acts on two closely related groups of animals living in the same region to make them more distinct—a pattern often seen, on a smaller scale, between siblings.

One fruitful way to circumvent the ambiguities of the debate is to attempt to isolate aspects of human activity that are genetically determined. In our species there are two groups of individuals that provide a practical field for such investigation.

IDENTIFYING INNATE BEHAVIOR AND KNOWLEDGE: NEWBORNS AND TWINS

Although enculturation begins very early in the life of a human, the behavior of newborns offers at least partial evidence of the innate component of human activity. Though their cognitive capacities are immature, they are sufficiently distinct to permit useful comparisons with the mental abilities of other animals. But because human infants lack a language, investigating the workings of their minds requires as much ingenuity as it does with other inarticulate animals.

As parents will remember, one of the most annoying characteristics of infants is their overwhelming tendency to be bored in the absence of constantly changing and novel stimulation. Researchers have put this propensity to good use. By tracking an infant's eye movements, they can ask newborns what stimuli they can discriminate. If substituting one stimulus for another does not reawaken interest, then it seems likely that the baby cannot distinguish them. If an infant is accustomed to a violet light, for instance, switching to one that is blue-green (a change of more than 50 nm in wavelength) does not catch a baby's attention, but changing blue-green to green-blue (a difference of less than 25 nm) rivets the infant's eyes.

By making a series of such comparisons, researchers have shown that newborns innately categorize the world into four colors: red, yellow, green, and blue (black and white were not tried); all the other color distinctions are learned later. It is possible that the programmed knowledge of these different colors permits infants to make adaptive discriminations from the outset. The color names taught to other animals in language experiments have all been one or another of these

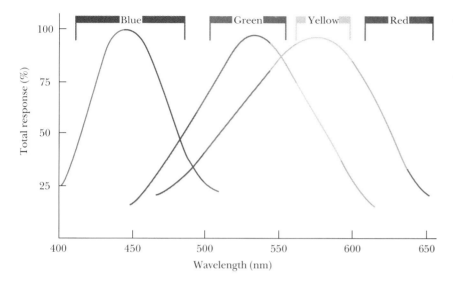

Although humans have only three visual pigments (which respond best to blue, green, and yellow-green), infants subdivide the full range of hues into four categories whose boundaries are shown by the brackets labeled "blue," "green," "yellow," and "red."

four; would it be possible to teach a chimpanzee different words, or signs, for violet and blue?

Infants also seem to be able to recognize facial expressions. This allows them to mimic adult gestures like smiling, frowning, surprise, and so on. Human facial gestures are one of our cultural universals; they make use of striking but otherwise rather useless structures such as eyebrows and pigmented lips. It seems likely that infants understand and accurately categorize these species-specific signals.

An understanding of the rules of frictionless momentum also seems to be innate in humans. If an object traveling at a constant rate disappears behind a screen, an infant's eyes track its presumptive location, and the baby is surprised—that is, its eyes widen in apparent amazement—when the object reappears too soon or in the wrong place. Again, this ability to apply unlearned rules to the world must help to sort out what would otherwise be chaotic stimulation.

If newborns can make these distinctions and have innate sets of conceptual rules for dealing with their perceptions, it seems reasonable to imagine that nonhuman animals might—indeed, probably must—have analogous mental rules and initial assumptions about how their world works. The nature of this early epistemology must color any later learning, thinking, and understanding that may develop in an individual.

Another window into the extent of innate programming in humans is provided by studies of twins reared apart, nearly all of which have shown evidence for some degree of genetic influence on cognitive abilities. About one in every 85 births produces twins; of these, about a third have developed from the same fertilized egg and thus are genetically identical. The rest are fraternal twins, no more closely related than any nontwin pair of siblings.

The strategy behind the analysis of twin studies can be seen in this simple example: the correlation in height between identical twins compared to the similarity between unrelated individuals of the same sex and age is about 0.93; for unrelated individuals it is 0.0. Since a perfect correlation is 1.0, about 93 percent of the factors contributing to height are genetic. Fraternal twins, on the other hand, who share only half their genes, show a correlation of about 0.47; doubling a fraternal-twin figure provides a reliable measure of the genetic component of at least some traits.

If the determinants of a trait are 93 percent genetic, it follows that the other 7 percent come from environmental influences. What this example assumes, however, is that *any* correlation between identical twins is entirely genetic. While this is a reasonable assumption for eye color, it is less so for traits that can be influenced by learning, nurture, and social interactions. To note a high correlation in acting ability between identical twins would not lead most of us to conclude anything definite until we asked whether the parents were actors or had provided both siblings with classes. In fact, the assumption isn't even quite correct for height: identical twins reared apart have a height correlation of 0.86. Interfamily environmental differences (such as nutrition) generate an additional 7 percent variation over and above the 7 percent that results from intrafamily effects.

Of course, when a correlation appears before cultural influences could have any impact, we must take the data seriously. In fact, the importance of cultural influences and learning on most aspects of child behavior and development are usually greatly overestimated. Although parents agonize over their efforts at toilet training, for instance, actual studies in which one twin is coached and the other is left to his own devices show that the ability appears so spontaneously that determined teaching advances the onset of the behavior by only a week.

In theory, we could compare the correlation between the identical twins reared apart (for example, 0.9 for height) with the correlations between each twin and his or her adopted siblings (0.0 for height) to get a rough idea of the genetic basis of the trait. In fact, the analysis is not quite this simple for a variety of reasons, three of which are especially important.

First, parents tend to be more genetically similar than we would expect by chance; this results from assortative mating, a phenomenon that might be described as "like attracts like." Thus to say that fraternal twins share only half their genes is not quite true for some traits; for characteristics that are subject to assortative mating (such as parental weight and intellectual ability), fraternal twins will be slightly more similar than would be expected by simply halving the correlation observed in identical twins.

The second complication involves the frequent synergistic interaction between genetic propensities and environment; for example, children with some native musical ability will tend to be given more training than those with little, and so the genetic basis of the trait may be exaggerated when correlations are measured later in life.

The third problem is a possible correlation between the environments of the two separated twins: the more alike the adoptive households, the less difference in environmental inputs, and the relative importance of genetic contributions is correspondingly enhanced.

All three of these factors tend to increase the apparent role of genes in the development of cognitive traits. Fortunately, there are ways of controlling for or measuring and accounting for these complications. As a result, modern estimates of the genetic basis of mental and personality traits are considered fairly reliable, but older data, still widely quoted, are somewhat suspect.

The most general measure of cognitive ability is IQ, "intelligence quotient." IQ correlates exceedingly well with school performance, for example, and is relatively stable after age 12. A variety of modern studies, correcting for all the potentially important biasing factors, indicate that about 30 to 35 percent of an individual's IQ can be attributed to environmental influences; 65 to 70 percent seems to be genetically determined. It is, of course, important to realize that these values account for the *variance* observed in a given population; the same study comparing humans and chimpanzees would conclude that IQ is 99.9 percent genetically determined.

These results demonstrate that the enormous differences we observe in human intelligence are largely the result of genetic effects, which means that cognitive ability in our species is genetically shaped—it is not a simple and inevitable spinoff of excess brain mass. The data also suggest that if there are differences in gross cognitive ability, there may be differences in more specific aptitudes as well. Indeed, twin studies have shown major genetic influences in every kind of intellectual test—box-folding, object-rotation, mathematical reasoning, perceptual speed, memory (the lowest correlation, but still 50 percent genetic), visualization, verbal reasoning, verbal comprehension, and so on. The two categories in which environmental input is more important are, not surprisingly, vocabulary size and creativity.

Several psychological traits that are important to an individual's cognitive "style" are also largely shaped by genetic influences. These include the two broad categories of extroversion and neuroticism. More specific traits with large genetic components include shyness, optimism, leadership, ambition, aggression, alienation, conservatism, and imagination. Of course, no one has tested for weaving ability, navigational accuracy, or the capacity to echolocate; when researchers talk about cognitive ability, they mean the species-specific capacities of *Homo sapiens*. In fairness, then, the cognitive abilities of other species must, as we have already seen, be measured by different yardsticks. The studies also demonstrate the flaw in the oft-heard argument that particular animal abilities cannot imply intelligence or thinking because they are genetically based. By this standard, we could rule out the possibility that intellect or thought has any role in human testing.

Another important lesson from test-based research on our species is that there is no best combination of cognitive abilities and personality traits; if there were, selection would have operated to produce

Trait	Number of Studies	Average Correlation between Twins	
		Fraternal	Identical
Extroversion	30	0.25	0.52
Neuroticism	23	0.22	0.51
Masculinity–femininity	7	0.17	0.43
Conformity	5	0.20	0.41
Flexibility	7	0.27	0.46
Impulsiveness	6	0.29	0.48
IQ	8	0.70	0.97
Height		0.50	0.93
Weight		0.43	0.83

Source: T. J. Bouchard, Twins reared together and apart, in S. W. Fox, ed., *Individuality and Determinism* (New York: Plenum, 1984). IQ data added.

far less variance in these characteristics than is regularly observed. It is obvious that frequency-dependent selection would work to balance the proportion of aggressive morphs, for instance, since too many fighters would lead to a self-inflicted reduction in their numbers, whereas too few might lead to the demise of a kin group. So too it must be for intellectual abilities: IQ tests tap a set of abilities whose relevance to hunter/gatherer survival, or agricultural expertise, or skill at herding and ranching is not entirely obvious. Our current society tends to test for and reward traits that may have had less value formerly—characteristics with a certain utility to be sure, but less important in the long run perhaps than patience, physical strength and endurance, loyalty, and empathy, none of which has any place in college entrance examinations.

LANGUAGE ACQUISITION: SPEECH, MEANING, AND GRAMMAR

One really compelling argument for our uniqueness in a world of inarticulate organisms is our communication system, one supreme intellectual achievement that stands as a triumph of cultural transmission over natural selection. Logic, thought, reasoning, planning, and even self-awareness are all variously said to depend on language. Though at least some species manage these cognitive triumphs without language, it might be that language has a multiplier effect on intellectual abilities. The questions for us are whether human language is a consequence of general intellect or is a species-specific adaptation, and how our language affects cognition.

At birth, human infants move their limbs in synchrony with human speech, but not in time to music. The ability to react specifically to language suggested that human speech might be innately recognized. Skeptics countered that the response resulted from learning: the fetus heard its mother talking and came to respond to it (though what the reward might be is unclear; habituation seems a more likely consequence of prenatal exposure to speech). Tests to determine if language contains innately recognized sign stimuli take advantage of the boredom technique and the nature of our consonants.

Human languages share a relatively small set of roughly three dozen consonants, produced by combining the distinct vocal gestures we can form with our mouths with different positions of whichever structure—lips, tongue, or soft palate—stops the flow of air. Vowels

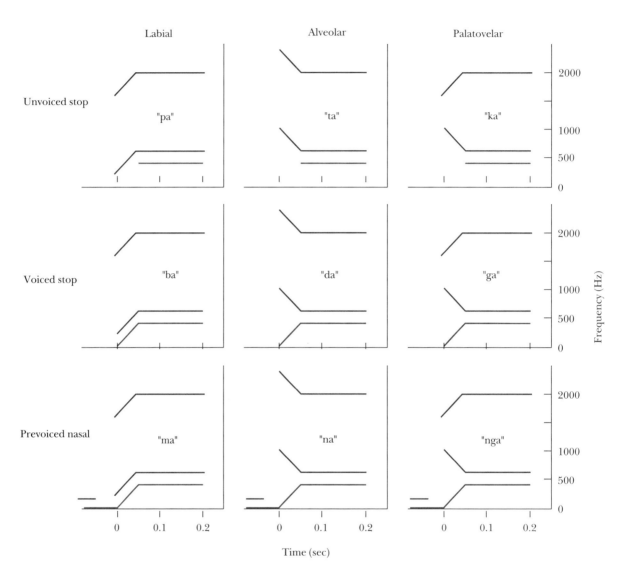

These nine consonants are distinguished by the location in the mouth where the airflow is manipulated (the labial, alveolar, and palatovelar groups) and the relative timing of the airflow change and the voicing of the vowel in the throat (prevoiced, simultaneous voicing—"voiced"—and delayed voicing—"unvoiced"). The airflow manipulations mainly alter the form of the second and third "formants" (the upper two lines in these sonographs), while the timing of voicing is reflected in the lowest (first) formant, shown in blue.

are produced by vibration of the vocal cords. Superimposed on the location variable—the position of the lips in pronouncing [b], for instance—is the timing of the vowel sound. Consider, for the contrast they present, the syllables "ma," "ba," and "pa," introduced by the labial consonants [m], [b], and [p]. The entire range of difference in timing to produce these sounds is only about a tenth of a second. If the synthesized vowel-production time is varied by small steps from an exaggerated prevoicing ("mmma") to an extended delay ("p . . . a"), adult listeners still hear only the three standard consonants of the labial group; moreover, they agree very closely about where the voicing boundary falls.

When the same graded series of consonant sounds is played to newborns, they become bored by sounds that fall within a consonant group, but perk up when a sound is played that falls just on the other side of the consonant boundary. In short, they already parse sounds into the full set of consonants used in human language. The observation that a newborn makes consonant distinctions that may not exist in its mother's language makes short work of the skeptics' concern that these distinctions might have been learned in the womb.

It is interesting to note that many birds and primates have about two dozen distinct, innately recognized calls. It is possible that human language developed from a conventional set of innate calls—that is, auditory sign stimuli. Whether consonant production depends on innate motor programs is unknown; certainly there is a strong drive to experiment vocally, and it is out of this auditory play that mature consonant production emerges.

The generation of vowels involves creating two separate, resonant cavities, one in the throat and the other in the mouth; the two frequencies produced are called formants. The necessary separation between the throat and mouth critical to producing two formants simultaneously appears to have arisen as a by-product of our upright posture and the consequent right angle between the neck and the mouth.

Vowels are clearly cultural—the boundaries are defined by use—but the processing of vowels appears to be innate. We can recognize vowels spoken by different people, regardless of the pitch of their voices, because our auditory circuitry automatically compares the ratio of the two formants produced by the two cavities in the vocal apparatus.

The total number of distinct sounds the combination of innately recognized consonants and innately processed vowels makes possible

Vowels are distinguished by the frequency ratio between their lowest two formants. The boundaries between vowels in any particular dialect are culturally determined. The use of ratios allows us to identify a vowel in our own language regardless of the average pitch of a speaker's voice.

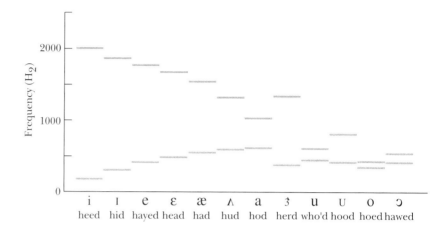

is quite large. Each syllable can have the form consonant–vowel–consonant, which means the total syllable repertoire, at least in theory, is 36 × 12 × 36 (roughly 35 consonants plus the option of omitting a leading or trailing consonant, and about 12 vowels), for a total of something like 15,000. This greatly multiplies the potential number of communication sounds in human language. And of course most English words generally have two or more syllables. A language exclusively composed of one- and two-syllable words would have a potential total of more than 100 million distinct words; by comparison, a well-educated speaker of English has a vocabulary of about 50,000 words.

Virtually all humans learn language, and they do so with little or no overt reinforcement or correction. On the other hand, the intellectually far simpler tasks of addition and subtraction are rarely picked up spontaneously; instead they require constant training, encouragement, and correction of error. Clearly one task involves drive and programmed learning, and the other does not.

The degree of innate help in the acquisition of language is now known to go far beyond the syllable stage. Noam Chomsky has suggested that the basics of grammar are innate, and that we come equipped to learn at least two alternative forms—word-order and inflected. This proposal initially met considerable skepticism, but subsequent research on language development in mixed cultures points strongly toward at least one innate "default" grammar.

When two or more cultures speaking distinctly different languages come to live and work together (as has happened many times when various groups have been imported to an area to work), the communication barrier must be bridged. Inevitably a pidgin evolves, incorporating elements of the various vocabularies, and built on a twisted and highly simplified version of each speaker's own grammar. Within each cultural group, people continue to speak their native tongue.

In the next generation, if children of the various linguistic groups mingle at the time they are acquiring language, something quite different happens. While all learn their parents' language, they spontaneously develop another system that they use with each other. It is this *creole*, which often has features not found in any of the formal parental languages, that will be learned and used by the children of these children.

Studies of various creoles in Africa, Asia, South America, and the Pacific Islands reveal that they have many features in common. Most obviously, they all use a word-order grammar similar to that of English. (This should not be surprising: English developed to permit communication among the early Britons of different tribes, and though today it is highly refined and distinguished by a large vocabulary drawn from many sources, it was formed as a creole.)

Child Language	*English Creoles*
Where I can put it?	Where I can put om? (Hawaii)
Daddy throw the nother rock.	Daddy t'row one neda rock'tone. (Jamaica)
I go full Angela bucket.	I go full Angela bucket. (Guyana)
Lookit a boy play ball.	Luku one boy a play ball. (Jamaica)
Nobody don't like me.	Nobody no like me. (Guyana)
I no like do that.	I no like do that. (Hawaii)
Johnny big more than me.	Johnny big more than me. (Jamaica)
Let Daddy get pen write it.	Make Daddy get pen write am. (Guyana)
I more better than Johnny.	I more better than Johnny. (Hawaii)

Source: D. Bickerton, Creole languages, *Scientific American* 249 (1), 116–122, 1983.

Relatively young creole languages generally have the same parts of speech, distinction of number, and patterns of conjugation. Three particles indicate whether the action expressed by a verb was successful, unsuccessful, or repeated. Double negatives are permitted, and questions are indicated by intonation rather than a change in word order.

Many of the grammatical errors made by young children (and illiterate adults) in non–creole-speaking cultures parallel these features of creole. Careful studies indicate that children *begin* with a creole grammar and learn from experience the modifications necessary to conform to the local dialect. In short, the rules of grammar are innate, a species-specific characteristic of humans.

In addition to neural connections for programmed grammar and sign-stimulus–based syllables, the brain is organized ab initio to decode and encode speech. The underlying anatomical specializations first came to light from systematic studies of head wounds. We now know that there are two regions crucial for language, Broca's area and Wernicke's area.

Decoding occurs in Wernicke's area, which is conveniently located between the auditory cortex (which feeds it speech sounds) and the angular gyrus, a region that converts written language (as displayed in the visual cortex adjacent to the gyrus) into an auditory analogue, which is then passed on to Wernicke's area. Destruction of the angular gyrus leaves vision and speech recognition unaffected, but destroys the ability to read; if the function of Wernicke's area itself is lost, language cannot be comprehended.

Encoding of thoughts into words begins in Wernicke's area, and information is fed to Broca's area, where it is given grammatical organization. From there the pathway continues to the adjacent motor cortex where the vocal apparatus is controlled. Damage to Broca's area results in great difficulty in expressing thoughts through language but no apparent loss in the ability to think and communicate in other ways, such as by overt actions or drawings.

In most people the vast majority of formal linguistic processing occurs on the left side of the brain; Broca's and Wernicke's areas are smaller on the right, and there seem to deal more with decoding and encoding emotional tone and making pictorial associations with words than with conventional language tasks. The right side also seems to be the site favored for recalling memorized material—poetry, songs, stock phrases, frequently delivered brief lectures. (For reasons that

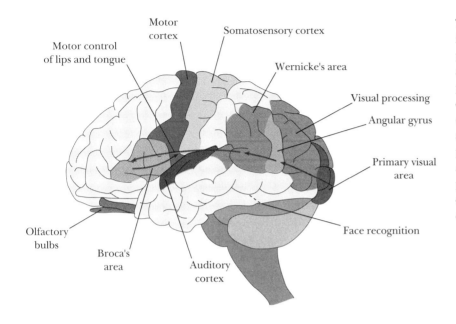

Motor control
of lips and tongue

Motor
cortex

Somatosensory cortex

Wernicke's area

Visual processing

Angular gyrus

Primary visual
area

Face recognition

Olfactory
bulbs

Broca's
area

Auditory
cortex

The human brain, like those of other animals, is highly modularized. Shown here is the pathway of information flow when we read aloud: the visual image of the written text is passed to the angular gyrus where it is converted into something like an auditory experience, which is then sent to Wernicke's area for decoding; from Wernicke's area the partially recoded signals are passed to Broca's area, where they are subjected to further processing and then used to direct the operation of regions of the motor cortex that control the organs of speech.

are not understood some people, including most who are left-handed, process language primarily on the right.)

Word storage also appears to be highly organized in ways that, because they are consistent from one individual to another, are probably innate. Strokes, which cut off the blood supply to a restricted area of the brain and kill a localized group of cells, often lead to the loss of groups of related words—flower names, for example. This pattern indicates that our vocabulary is stored in a way that probably makes access and searching easier. Indeed, given that bright youngsters with highly verbal parents or peers generally pick up something like 15,000 words between the ages of 6 and 8—about 20 words a day, the meanings of all of them inferred from context—some sort of preordained and optimized filing system seems essential.

In sum, then, we are safe in classifying human language as a species-specific cognitive ability. Every element of language, its acquisition, its use, and the means of storage of its words is innate; the sole exceptions are a particular language's vocabulary and grammatical idiosyncracies. Language, it seems, is not a supreme intellectual achievement but another remarkable product of natural selection. Nevertheless, though we cannot take credit for its invention, language permits our highly exact and extremely elaborate thinking, planning, and coördination; it probably evolved to serve just these functions.

SEXUAL SELECTION

In addition to providing us with a mode of expressing thoughts and ideas, the unseen hand of our behavioral inheritance is at work in a variety of ways that shape our thoughts themselves, and determine other aspects of our existence we have always attributed to free will. One of the most interesting of these is the way we choose mates.

Among the nonhuman animals a variety of strategies have evolved to effect adaptive mate choice. Beyond merely identifying a sexually mature and receptive member of the opposite sex of the appropriate species, many animals narrow down the field by using additional criteria to optimize their genetic investment. In polygamous species, in which one or both sexes mate several times with different individuals, these various stratagems can be roughly divided into two categories: *contests*, in which one sex—usually the males—competes either for some resource that the other sex is programmed to look for, or for the status that will allow undisputed access to partners, and *choices*, a system that permits one sex—nearly always the females—to choose a mate from among members of the other sex on the basis of something other than a resource—the loudness of a call, for instance, or the brightness of feathers.

Among monogamous species, both sexes tend to be selective, and each sex may compete for potential partners. Males typically advertise health and status, but they focus their efforts on obtaining and showing off any territory they control or their ability to obtain perishable resources like food; these resources would be available for the young, and thus enhance their chances of survival. Females tend to be choosier about potential mates and concentrate their displays on indicators of youth and health, strong correlates of reproductive potential. Because both sexes usually exert some degree of choice, the result is assortative mating: the "best" males pair with the "best" females (where "best" is specific to the species in question).

A substantial proportion of human literature is concerned with romance and sexual encounters, and no one who remembers his or her teenage and college years can deny that these topics occupy a significant percentage of the imaginative free time of young post-pubescent humans. Major sectors of the economy depend on our apparent desire to look our best (or better than our best) to members of the opposite sex. The mixture of thinking, planning, evaluating, talking, and overt behavior that goes into courtship provides an excellent opportunity to look at the role of these elements of our cognitive repertoire.

No one familiar with the tactics of sexual selection in nonhuman animals can fail to notice similar patterns in humans. Males are far more likely to compete for status and its trappings, demonstrate strength, and show off wealth or earning potential. Females, as the clothing and cosmetics industries testify, tend to concentrate on apparent youth and health.

These sex-specific emphases do not appear to be misplaced. Males and females on six continents from 37 different societies—ranging from tribal cultures to groups in developed countries—were asked to rank a variety of traits they might look for in a potential mate. The two consistent sex-specific differences were a female preference for males with resources and a male preference for attractive females—that is, men who can contribute materially to the welfare of offspring, and women who can bear healthy young.

These preferences lead to just the type of assortative mating that we see in other species. The correlation between male resources and female attractiveness in newly married couples, for instance, is 0.45; only the value for degree of education (0.6) is higher among the many factors that correlate. (More usual are values near 0.3, typical for weight, height, eye color, and other physical characteristics, indicating some selection, but not a strong correlation.) In short, individuals in our species make mate choices that are very like those observed in monogamous birds, a group with no literature of love. Unless we credit birds with the ability to perform sophisticated and conscious cost-benefit analyses of potential mates—analyses based on criteria that are still being worked out by human students of bird behavior—then we must wonder whether any overt reasoning is needed at all in human mate choice.

A cynic could argue plausibly that language and our extreme cognitive powers play no role in human mate choice whatsoever beyond justification of our choices and generally passing the time. But, as in birds, there are so many cases of clever individual strategies that it seems clear that reasoning (or, to be more specific, cunning) is fre-

Characteristic	Average Correlation between Spouses
Race	0.9
Age	0.8
Religion	0.8
Education	0.6
Female beauty/male earning capacity	0.5
Political views	0.5
Intelligence	0.4
Physical attractiveness	0.4
Height	0.3
Weight	0.3
Eye color	0.3
Socioeconomic status	0.3
Number of siblings	0.2
Ear-lobe shape	0.1

Source: J. L. Gould and C. G. Gould, *Sexual Selection* (New York: Scientific American Library, 1989).

quently involved. And in humans it is obvious that language plays a major role in courtship stratagems; birds, for instance, are denied the option of a tactic reported among undergraduates in a recent study—keeping potential suitors away from a girlfriend by spreading rumors that she carries a transmissible venereal disease.

A less extreme view is that language is merely another tool, like thinking and planning, that serves innately determined ends. Free will, therefore, is an illusion; language serves to justify the inevitable. Certainly it can be argued that our species overestimates the role of conscious choice in our behavior. In a classic demonstration, a psychologist set out a table with dozens of pairs of stockings and then offered a free pair to each of several women. Each woman examined one pair and then another, closely comparing the possible choices, and then selected one.

After each of the women had made a choice, the psychologist asked her why she had chosen that particular pair. Without hesitation each explained that her selection was the softest or sheerest or had the most flattering color. All the pairs, however, were identical; our highest cognitive faculty was being used for the automatic social exercise of self-justification. Could it be that language is primarily a social tool with far less cognitive use or potential than we normally assign it?

BRAIN, MIND, AND CREATIVITY

The modular brain regions dedicated to specific language functions are by no means the only ones so highly specialized. There is a specific area that matches names and faces, and lesions in that region leave affected individuals unable to identify photographs of family members, though the ability to recognize them by the sound of their voices is unimpaired. Damage to another structure, which sorts and stores incoming information, leaves a person unable to learn or remember anything new (except novel motor tasks), but still in full possession of memories.

Modern techniques allow researchers to observe mental processing as it occurs. Nerve cells use far more energy and oxygen when they are active than when they are at rest; thus, monitoring the pattern of energy use in neurons, or the rate of local blood flow in the brain, provides an accurate picture of the area where mental activity is concentrated from one moment to another. When we touch something with a finger, for instance, the part of the sensory cortex associated with that finger "lights up," and shortly thereafter other regions of the brain may become active if any response or analysis is required.

There is more brain activity when a task is more intellectual. When an individual looks at an object, for instance, the information reaching the visual cortex is relayed simultaneously to the lower temporal lobe (an association area), the parietal lobe, and a part of the frontal lobe (a decision-making region). The temporal lobe identifies the object while the parietal lobe identifies its spatial location; this information is fed back to association areas near the visual cortex.

When no clear identification can be supplied by the temporal lobe, the frontal lobe makes the kinds of probabilistic deductions that are the basis of the conceptual categorization we looked at in pigeons; this information too goes to the association areas. This modular organization is almost certainly prewired.

The modular organization of the brain is evident in these PET scans of the head of an individual manipulating words in four different ways.

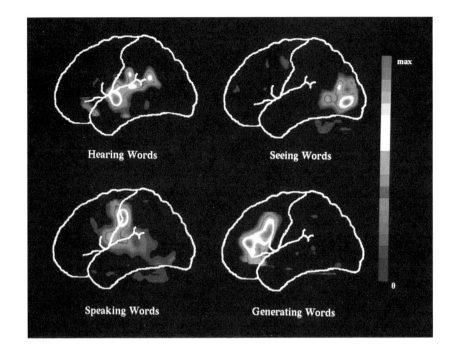

Work on patients who have had the connections between the two hemispheres of the brain severed (an operation that cures certain types of severe epilepsy) demonstrates that the associations generated on the left side are more often verbal (and can include such verbal connections as puns and rhymes); those produced on the right tend to be pictorial. Thus, just as with language, the two sides of the brain have different processing biases. Indeed, these hemispheric proclivities tend to separate logical processing from intuition and algebra from geometry. Stimuli appear to be processed in parallel according to separate strategies within and between the hemispheres, and the results are shared at the last moment.

The same technique reveals that when a person imagines an object, the pathways run in reverse: the association area sends out to the various lobes for information, and these cerebral consultants feed their results to the visual cortex. Thus the same area that acts as a television screen for the eyes appears to operate as a projector for the imagination. No wonder we can close our eyes and imagine objects and events; realistic dreams probably play themselves out in the same mental theatre. Associations are being made unconsciously and served up for our viewing pleasure.

What does this tell us about other animals? Modular organization is at least as evident in nonhuman creatures: birds have special areas for song production and recognition, and bats have regions that work in parallel to extract information from echoes and "picture" acoustic targets. Moreover, lateralization is often a feature of nonhuman brains. As in humans, species-specific vocalizations are generally processed on one side while other sounds are routed to the other hemisphere; primates identify abstract features better on one side and recognize learned objects better on the other. Again, selection seems to have favored two specialized minds working in parallel over a single more generalized structure.

Although real-time imaging of nonhuman brains is just beginning, it seems highly likely that the same general patterns will be observed as have been seen in our species. Given the limited resolution of current techniques, unfortunately only a few species have mental organs large enough to scan—and most of those cannot be used because they are aquatic. Certainly the same anatomical elements are present, and lesions of the pathways connecting these regions produce just the behavioral deficits we would expect.

The major difference between the human brain and those of other animals is the size of the association areas and information-processing lobes: the human cortex is almost entirely devoted to these "frill" areas; even a rodent brain, by comparison, has very little area left over after the basics of sensory processing and motor control are accommodated. Obviously, the area available for association and information processing provides a concrete limit to the capacity of a mind. Pigeons may be able to categorize, plan, and engage in a limited amount of reasoning, but they lack the degree of "excess" capacity found in primates that must make possible the much more complex plans and more extensive memory of our nearest relations.

Equally obviously, we know that creativity and innovation depend on our data base of information and our ability to make imaginative connections. Though many species seem able to make novel connections between memories (hence the phenomenon of latent learning), a species with more brain mass devoted to collecting data, sorting and connecting it, and visualizing the alternative results is more likely to

The sensory and motor areas occupy most of the brain of nearly all mammals; much of the remaining part of the cortex is devoted to making associations. Some primates have at least as much association space as sensory and motor regions combined; the highest known proportion of association area is found in humans.

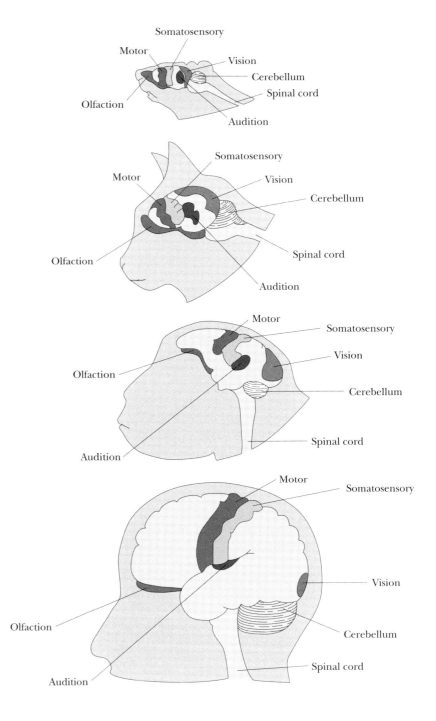

produce good ideas, optimal solutions, and striking innovations. Indeed, we all know that our minds are constantly exercising their connective potential at an unconscious level: many ideas seem to "pop into our heads," often when we have turned our conscious attention away from the problem to which the idea relates.

In the end, then, it seems that both the in-kind and in-degree arguments have part of the answer about human creativity and uniqueness. We have seen that no single isolated aspect of human cognitive ability is in fact unique. Animals of many species can engage, at least in certain contexts, in the kind of goal-oriented behavior that requires thinking and planning. Many species can categorize and classify to some degree; many seem to imagine objects or events. A few demonstrate an ability for formal reasoning.

At the same time, we have seen that much of human behavior is essentially automatic and unconscious. Our language is largely if not entirely an innate and species-specific adaptation; the choice of a mate, which fuels so much of human passion and creativity, relies on deeply ingrained criteria; culture itself is shaped by ancient guidelines. In short, nonhuman animals are smarter than is generally believed, and humans are not nearly as clever as we give ourselves credit for. We are part of an evolutionary continuum, unique only in the last few million years of our phylogenetic trajectory.

But difference of degree, if sufficiently great, *is* difference in kind, a difference brought about by the explosive growth of neural connections and the incredible potential for cultural transmission that the tool of language has provided. As selection worked to enlarge our brains, presumably to overcome our physiological shortcomings in meeting the tremendous challenges and opportunities of our niche, the result was a multiplier effect that has catapulted human behavioral potential far beyond that of any other species.

Given the gap that the accelerating enlargement of our brains and vocabulary has generated, it is no wonder we are tempted to treat humans as a special creation, somehow exempt from the constraints of our genetic inheritance. It is not surprising that many people consider nonhuman animals a lower form of life, ruled by instincts and mindless drives. But most likely it was evolutionary chance that put us where we are. We probably owe our species' present exalted status as much to luck—to the inelegant fact of having been in the right place at the right time, next to the developing plains in the Rift Valley of southeastern Africa—as to the preëxisting cognitive abilities of early humans. As the niche came into being, our ancestors were in position to appropriate it. They alone had the physical characteristics, the omnivorous lifestyle, and the social organization to make the riches of the savannah their own. When we look at other species, then, we should remember that there, but for natural selection, we might still be.

PROLOGUE

GRIFFIN, DONALD R. *The Question of Animal Awareness*. New York: Rockefeller University Press, 1976.
PFUNGST, OSKAR. *Clever Hans*. New York: Henry Holt, 1911; Holt, Rinehart & Winston, 1965.

CHAPTER 1: VARIETIES OF SENSORY EXPERIENCE

GOULD, JAMES L. *Ethology: Mechanisms and Evolution of Behavior*. New York: W. W. Norton, 1982.
HUBEL, DAVID H. *Eye, Brain, and Vision*. New York: Scientific American Library, 1988.
LYTHGOE, J. N. *The Ecology of Vision*. Oxford: Clarendon Press, 1979.
ROCK, IRVING. *Perception*. New York: Scientific American Library, 1984.
VON UEXKÜLL, JAKOB. A stroll through the world of animals and men. In *Instinctive Behavior*. Edited and translated by Claire H. Schiller. New York: International Universities Press, 1957.

CHAPTER 2: INNATE BEHAVIOR

AGOSTA, WILLIAM C. *Chemical Communication*. New York: Scientific American Library, 1992.
COLLIAS, NICHOLAS E., and ELSIE C. COLLIAS. *Nest Building and Bird Behavior*. Princeton: Princeton University Press, 1984.
FRISCH, KARL VON. *Animal Architecture*. New York: Harcourt Brace Jovanovich, 1974.
GOULD, JAMES L. *Ethology: Mechanisms and Evolution of Behavior*. New York: W. W. Norton, 1982.
HESS, ECKHARD H. *Imprinting*. New York: Van Nostrand Reinhold, 1973.
LORENZ, KONRAD Z. *Studies in Animal and Human Behaviour*. Vol. 1. Cambridge, Massachusetts: Harvard University Press, 1970.
SMITH, ANDREW W. Investigation of the mechanisms underlying nest construction in the mud wasp. *Animal Behaviour* 26, 232–240, 1978.
TINBERGEN, NIKO. *The Study of Instinct*. Oxford: Oxford University Press, 1951.

SELECTED

READINGS

CHAPTER 3: THE NATURE OF LEARNING

BRELAND, KELLER, and MARIAN BRELAND. The misbehavior of organisms. *American Psychologist* 16, 681–684, 1961. Reprinted as an appendix in James L. Gould, *Ethology: Mechanisms and Evolution of Behavior* (New York: W. W. Norton, 1982.)

GLEITMAN, HENRY. *Psychology.* New York: W. W. Norton, 1986.

GOULD, JAMES L., and CAROL G. GOULD. *The Honey Bee.* New York: Scientific American Library, 1988.

GOULD, JAMES L., and PETER MARLER. The instinct to learn. *Scientific American* 256 (1), 74–85, 1987.

HINDE, ROBERT A., and JOAN STEVENSON-HINDE, eds. *Constraints on Learning.* London: Academic Press, 1973.

MARLER, PETER, and H. S. TERRACE, eds. *The Biology of Learning.* Berlin: Springer-Verlag, 1984.

PAVLOV, IVAN P. *Conditioned Reflexes.* Oxford: Oxford University Press, 1927.

SCHWARTZ, BARRY. *Psychology of Learning and Behavior.* New York: W. W. Norton, 1984.

STADDON, J. E. R., and R. H. ETTINGER. *Learning.* New York: Harcourt Brace Jovanovich, 1989.

WATSON, JOHN B. *Behaviorism.* New York: W. W. Norton, 1930.

CHAPTER 4: INSIGHT OR INSTINCT?

BECKOFF, MARK, and D. JAMIESON (EDS.). *Readings in Animal Cognition.* Cambridge, MA: MIT Press, 1996.

COMROE, JULIUS H. *Retrospectroscope: Insight into Medical Discovery.* Menlo Park, California: Von Gehr Press, 1977.

GOULD, JAMES L., and PETER MARLER. The instinct to learn. *Scientific American* 256 (1), 74–85, 1987.

GRIFFIN, DONALD R. *Animal Thinking.* Cambridge, Massachusetts: Harvard University Press, 1984.

HINDE, ROBERT A., and J. FISHER. Further observations on the opening of milk bottles by birds. *British Birds* 44, 393–396, 1951.

HOAGE, R. J., and LARRY GOLDMAN, eds. *Animal Intelligence.* Washington, D.C.: Smithsonian Institution Press, 1986.

KAWAI, M. Newly acquired precultural behavior of the natural troop of Japanese monkeys on Koshima Islet. *Primates* 6, 1–30, 1956.

KÖHLER, WOLFGANG. *The Mentality of Apes*. New York: Harcourt Brace, 1927.

KREBS, JOHN R., and N. B. DAVIES. *An Introduction to Behavioural Ecology*. Oxford: Blackwell Scientific Publications, 1993.

RIOPELLE, A. J., ed. *Animal Problem Solving*. Baltimore: Penguin Books, 1967.

CHAPTER 5: INVERTEBRATE COGNITION: A CASE STUDY

FRISCH, KARL VON. *The Dance Language and Orientation of Bees*. Cambridge, Massachusetts: Harvard University Press, 1967.

———. *Animal Architecture*. New York: Harcourt Brace Jovanovich, 1974.

GIURFA, M., B. EICHMANN, and RANDOLF MENZEL. Symmetry perception in an insect. *Nature* 382, 203-210, 1996.

GOULD, JAMES L., and CAROL G. GOULD. *The Honey Bee*. New York: Scientific American Library, 1988.

LINDAUER, MARTIN. *Communication Among Social Bees*. Cambridge, Massachusetts: Harvard University Press, 1961.

MENZEL, RANDOLF, K. GEIGER, J. JOERGES, U. MÜLLER, and L. CHITTKA. Bees travel novel homeward routes by integrating separately acquired vector memories. *Animal Behaviour* 55, 139-152, 1998.

SEELEY, THOMAS D. *Honeybee Ecology*. Princeton: Princeton University Press, 1985.

CHAPTER 6: ANIMALS AS ARCHITECTS

FRISCH, KARL VON. *Animal Architecture*. New York: Harcourt Brace Jovanovich, 1974.

GILLIARD, E. T. *Birds of Paradise and Bowerbirds*. London: Weidenfeld and Nicolson, 1969.

GRIFFIN, DONALD R. *Animal Minds*. Chicago: University of Chicago Press, 1992.

RISTAU, CAROLYN A., ed. *Cognitive Ethology*. Hillsdale, N.J.: Erlbaum, 1991.

WILSON, EDWARD O. *The Insect Societies*. Cambridge, Massachusetts: Harvard University Press, 1971.

CHAPTER 7: HUNTING AND ESCAPING

GRIFFIN, DONALD R. *Animal Minds.* Chicago: University of Chicago Press, 1992.

HELEY, S. (ED.). *Spatial Representation in Animals.* Oxford: Oxford University Press, 1998.

HIGUCHI, HIROYOSHI. Cast master [bait-fishing in herons]. *Natural History* 96 (8), 40–43, 1987.

ISACK, H. A., and H.-U. REYER. Honeyguides and honey gatherers: interspecific communication in a symbiotic relationship. *Science* 243, 1343–1346, 1989.

MITCHELL, R. W., and N. S. THOMPSON, eds. *Deception: Perspectives on Human and Nonhuman Deceit.* Albany: SUNY Press, 1986.

PEPPERBERG, IRENE, R. BALDA, and ALAN C. KAMIL (EDS.). *Animal Cognition in Nature.* San Diego: Academic Press, 1998.

SHETTLEWORTH, SARAH J. Memory in food-hoarding birds. *Scientific American* 248 (3), 102–110, 1983.

RISTAU, CAROLYN A., ed. *Cognitive Ethology.* Hillsdale, N.J.: Erlbaum, 1991.

CHAPTER 8: SOCIAL AND PERSONAL KNOWLEDGE

BYRNE, R., and A. WHITTEN, eds. *Machiavellian Intelligence: Social Expertise and the Evolution of Intellect in Monkeys, Apes, and Humans.* Oxford: Oxford University Press, 1988.

CHENEY, DOROTHY L., and ROBERT M. SEYFARTH. *How Monkeys See the World: Inside the Mind of Another Species.* Chicago: University of Chicago Press, 1990.

COHEN, D. B. *Sleep and Dreaming.* New York: Pergamon, 1979.

DE WAAL, FRANS. *Peacemaking among Primates.* Cambridge, Massachusetts: Harvard University Press, 1989.

FAGEN, ROBERT. *Animal Play Behavior.* New York: Oxford University Press, 1981.

GOODALL, JANE. *The Chimpanzees of Gombe.* Cambridge, Massachusetts: Harvard University Press, 1986.

HEYES, C. M., and B. G. GALEF (EDS.). *Social Learning in Animals: the Roots of Culture.* San Diego: Academic Press, 1996.

MITCHELL, R. W., and N. S. THOMPSON, eds. *Deception: Perspectives on Human and Nonhuman Deceit.* Albany: SUNY Press, 1986.

SEYFARTH, ROBERT M., and DOROTHY L. CHENEY. Meaning and mind in monkeys. *Scientific American* 267 (6), 122–128, 1992.

CHAPTER 9: LOGIC AND LANGUAGE

GARDNER, R. A., B. T. GARDNER, and T. E. VAN DANTFORT, eds. *Teaching Sign Language to Chimpanzees.* Albany: SUNY Press, 1989.

PREMACK, ANN JAMES, and DAVID PREMACK. Teaching language to an ape. *Scientific American* 227 (4), 92–99, 1972.

PREMACK, DAVID, and ANN JAMES PREMACK. *The Mind of an Ape.* New York: W. W. Norton, 1983.

RISTAU, CAROLYN A., ed. *Cognitive Ethology.* Hillsdale, N.J.: Erlbaum, 1991.

ROITBLAT, HERBERT L. *Introduction to Comparative Cognition.* New York: W. H. Freeman, 1987.

SAVAGE-RUMBAUGH, E. SUE. *Ape Language.* New York: Columbia University Press, 1986.

SAVAGE-RUMBAUGH, E. SUE, and ROGER LEVIN. *Kanzi, the Ape at the Brink of the Human Mind.* New York: John Wiley, 1994.

TOMASELLO, M. and J. CALL. *Primate Cognition.* Oxford: Oxford University Press, 1997.

CHAPTER 10: HUMAN COGNITION

BICKERTON, DEREK. Creole languages. *Scientific American* 249 (1), 116–122, 1983.

BICKERTON, DEREK. *Language and Species.* Chicago: University of Chicago Press, 1980.

BOUCHARD, THOMAS J., DAVID T. LYKKEN, MATTHEW MCGUE, NANCY L. SEGAL, and AUKE TELLEGEN. The sources of human psychological differences: the Minnesota study of twins reared apart. *Science* 250, 223–228, 1990.

BOWER, T. G. R. *Development in Infancy.* New York: W. H. Freeman, 1982.

BUSS, DAVID M. Human mate selection. *American Scientist* 73, 47–51, 1985.

EIMAS, PETER. The perception of speech in early infancy. *Scientific American* 252 (1), 46–52, 1985.

GESCHWIND, NORMAN. Specializations in the human brain. *Scientific American* 241 (3), 180–199, 1979.

GOULD, JAMES L. *Ethology: Mechanisms and Evolution of Behavior.* New York: W. W. Norton, 1982.

GOULD, JAMES L., and CAROL G. GOULD. *Sexual Selection.* New York: Scientific American Library, 1989.

JENCKS, CHRISTOPHER. *Inequality.* New York: Basic Books, 1972.

LEE, RICHARD B. *The !Kung San.* Cambridge University Press, 1979.

MILLER, GEORGE A. *The Science of Words.* New York: Scientific American Library, 1991.

PINKER, STEVEN. *The Language Instinct.* New York: William Morrow, 1994.

PLOMIN, ROBERT. *Nature and Nurture.* Pacific Grove, California: Brooks/ Cole, 1990.

*Drawings by Dimitry Schidlovsky;
diagrams, charts, and graphs by
Hudson River Studio.*

FRONTISPIECE
Michael Nichols/Magnum

FACING PAGE 1
T. Bewick, *Select Fables of Aesop and Others* (Newcastle, 1784).

PAGE 2
K. Krall, *Denkende Tiere* (1912)

PAGE 4
J. L. Gould

PAGE 7
Art Wolfe

PAGE 8
W. H. Thorpe, *The Origins and Rise of Ethology* (London: Praeger Scientific, 1974). Photograph by Olga Linkelmann.

PAGE 11
Gerry Ellis Nature Photography

PAGE 12
TOP, John Downer/Planet Earth Pictures

BOTTOM, Thomas Eisner

PAGE 14
Art Wolfe

PAGE 16
G. Kanizsa, Subjective contours, *Scientific American* 234 (4), 48–52, 1976.

PAGE 18, INSET
Thomas Eisner

PAGE 19
Katy Payne

PAGE 20
Union Pictures

PAGE 21
Adapted from J. L. Gould, The case for magnetic sensitivity in birds and bees (such as it is), *American Scientist* 68, 256–267, 1980.

PAGE 23
Gerry Ellis Nature Photography

PAGE 25
Todd Fink/Daybreak Imagery

PAGE 26
TOP, Lary Shaffer

BOTTOM, Frans Lanting/ Minden Pictures

PAGE 27
G. P. Baerends and J. P. Kruijt, Stimulus selection, in R. A. Hinde and J. Stevenson-Hinde, eds., *Constraints on Learning:*

S O U R C E S

O F

I L L U S T R A T I O N S

Limitations and Predispositions (London and New York: Academic Press, 1973), 23–50.

PAGE 29
Drawn from a photograph by John Sparks, BBC Natural History Unit.

PAGE 30
J.-P. Ewert, *Neuroethology* (New York: Springer-Verlag, 1980).

PAGE 31
Thomas Eisner

PAGES 32, 33
K. Lorenz and N. Tinbergen, Taxis und Instinkhandlung in der Eirollbewegung, *Zeitschrift für vergleichende Physiologie* 21, 699–716, 1935.

PAGE 34
K. Lorenz, The evolution of behavior, *Scientific American* 199 (6), 67–78, 1958.

PAGE 36
J. A. Shuck Collection, Western History Collections, University of Oklahoma Library.

PAGE 37
Nina Leen, Life Magazine

PAGE 38
Gary Larson/Chronicle Features, San Francisco

PAGE 39
K. Lorenz, *King Solomon's Ring* (New York: Thomas Y. Crowell, 1952).

PAGES 40–42
A. P. Smith, Nest construction in the mud wasp *Paralastor, Animal Behavior* 26, 232–240, 1978.

PAGE 43
Art Wolfe

PAGE 45
H. Silvester/Black Star

PAGE 46
Sovfoto

PAGE 47
Johns Hopkins University

PAGE 48
K. S. Lashley, The mechanism of vision: I. A method for rapid analysis of pattern vision in the rat, *Journal of Genetic Psychology* 37, 453–460, 1930.

PAGE 50
Drawn from photographs by Robert W. Kelly.

PAGE 51
Ken Heyman/Black Star

PAGE 52
Yoav Levi/Phototake

PAGE 54
Stephen Dalton/NHPA

PAGE 58
Culver Pictures Inc

PAGE 59
H. M. Jenkins and B. R. Moore, The form of the autoshaped response with food or water reinforcers, *Journal of the Experimental Analysis of Behavior* 20, 163–181, 1973.

PAGE 61
Mansell Collection

PAGE 63
K. Lorenz, *King Solomon's Ring* (New York: Thomas Y. Crowell, 1952).

PAGE 66
Bancroft Library, University of California Berkeley. © Regents, University of California.

PAGE 69
Marco Capovilla

PAGE 71
Kenneth Lorenzen

PAGE 73
Richard Howard

PAGE 76
E. B. Newman and the Department of Psychology, Harvard University.

PAGES 78–80
W. Köhler, *The Mentality of Apes* (London: Routledge & Kegan Paul Ltd., 1925).

PAGE 82
L. C. Drickamer and S. H. Vessey, *Animal Behavior* (Boston: Willard Grant Press, 1982). Photo by M. Kawai, Kyoto University Primate Research Institute.

PAGE 83
K. & K. Amman/Planet Earth Pictures

PAGE 84
Edward Ross

PAGE 85
Tui de Roy/AUSCAPE International

PAGE 87
Christopher Morris/Black Star

PAGE 89
Kenneth Lorenzen

PAGE 90
K. von Frisch, *Erinnerungen eines Biologen* (Berlin: Springer-Verlag, 1957). Photograph by W. Ernst Böhm.

PAGE 91
TOP, John Free

BOTTOM, Kenneth Lorenzen

PAGE 95
Kenneth Lorenzen

PAGE 98
Alex Michelsen

PAGE 101
Kenneth Lorenzen

PAGE 103
Stephen Dalton/NHPA

PAGE 105
M. Lindauer, Schwarmbienen auf Wohnungssuche, *Zeitschrift für vergleichende Physiologie* (37), 263–324, 1955.

PAGE 109
LEFT, Kenneth Lorenzen

RIGHT, Scott Camazine and Sue Trainor

PAGES 110, 111
J. L. Gould

PAGE 115
H. H. J. Koch/Focus/Matrix

PAGE 116
Robin Smith/Tony Stone Images

PAGE 123
Anthony Brandenburg/Minden Pictures

PAGES 125, 129
Gerry Ellis Nature Photography

PAGE 131
C. K. Lorenz, The National Audubon Society Collection/Photo Researchers.

PAGE 133
Art Wolfe

PAGE 135
Carol Farneti/Planet Earth Pictures

PAGE 137
From a sketch by Carolyn Ristau

PAGE 138
Hellio & Van Ingen/NHPA

PAGE 141
Bernd Heinrich

PAGE 143
Robert F. Sisson/National Geographic Society

PAGE 144
R. P. Balda and R. J. Turek, Memory in birds, in H. L. Roitblat, T. G. Bever, and H. S. Terrace, eds., *Animal Cognition* (Hillsdale, N.J.: Erlbaum, 1984), 513–532.

PAGE 145
E. W. Menzel, Chimpanzee spatial memory organization, *Science* 182, 943–945, 1973.

PAGE 146
M. D. England/Ardea

PAGE 148
LEFT, Anthony Bannister/NHPA

RIGHT, Nigel Dennis/NHPA

PAGE 151
Gerry Ellis Nature Photography

PAGE 152
D. L. Cheney and R. M. Seyfarth, *How Monkeys See the World* (Chicago: University of Chicago Press, 1990), 105.

PAGE 154
R. M. Seyfarth and D. L. Cheney, Vocal development in vervet monkeys, *Animal Behavior* 34, 1640–1658, 1986.

PAGE 155
R. M. Seyfarth and D. L. Cheney, Do monkeys understand their relations?, in R. W. Byrne and A. Whiten, eds., *Machiavellian Intelligence: Social Expertise and the Evolution of Intellect in Monkeys, Apes, and Humans* (Oxford: Oxford University Press, 1988).

PAGE 156
F. M. B. de Waal, *Peacemaking among Primates* (Cambridge: Harvard University Press, 1989).

PAGE 157
G. G. Gallup, Mirror-image stimulation, *Psychological Bulletin* 70, 782–793, 1968.

PAGE 158
Donna Bierschwale, USL-New Iberia Research Center

PAGE 160
Frans B. M. de Waal

PAGE 161
D. L. Cheney and R. M. Seyfarth, *How Monkeys See the World* (Chicago: University of Chicago Press, 1990).

PAGE 163
F. B. M. de Waal, *Peacemaking among Primates* (Cambridge: Harvard University Press, 1989).

PAGE 165
Bob Torrez/Tony Stone Images

PAGE 166
Art Wolfe

PAGE 167
F. B. M. de Waal, *Peacemaking among Primates* (Cambridge: Harvard University Press, 1989).

PAGE 171
Michael Goldman

PAGES 172, 173
Richard Herrnstein

PAGE 177
Alan Levenson/Time Magazine

PAGE 179
I. M. Pepperberg, An interactive modeling technique for acquisition of communication skills: separation of "learning" and "requesting" in a Psittacine subject, *Applied Psycholinguistics* 9, 63, 1988.

PAGE 180
I. M. Pepperberg parrot experiment: Michael Goldman

PAGE 182
Alan Levenson/Time Magazine

PAGES 185, 189
A. J. Premack and D. Premack, Teaching language to an ape, *Scientific American* 227 (4), 92–99, 1972.

PAGE 187
Michael Nichols/Magnum

PAGE 193
Kari Rene Hall, Los Angeles Times

PAGE 195
R. Holloway, Brain, in I. Tattersall, E. Delson, and J. V. Convering, *Encyclopedia of Human Evolution and Prehistory* (New York: Garland, 1988), 98–105; data from H. Stephan et al., *Folia Primatology* 35, 1–29, 1981, and personal communication from H. Stephan.

PAGE 199
G. Wald, The receptors of human color vision, *Science* 145, 1007–1017, 1964; and M. H. Bornstein, W. Kessen, and S. Weiskopf, The categories of hue in infancy, *Science* 191, 201–202, 1976.

PAGE 204
W. Strange and J. J. Jenkins, Role of linguistic experience in the

perception of speech, in R. D. Walk and H. L. Pick, eds., *Perception and Experience* (New York: Plenum, 1978), 125–170.

PAGE 206
P. Ladefoged, *Elements of Acoustic Phonetics* (Chicago: University of Chicago Press, 1962).

PAGE 214
Marcus E. Raichle

Other books in the Scientific American Library Series